THE CHURCH
God's Agent for Change

THE CHURCH

God's Agent for Change

EDITOR
BRUCE J. NICHOLLS

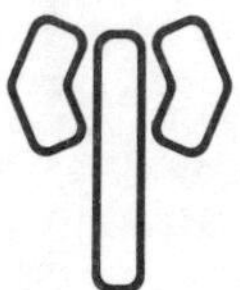

Published on behalf of the
World Evangelical Fellowship by
The Paternoster Press

AUSTRALIA:
Bookhouse Australia Ltd.,
P.O. Box 115, Flemington Markets, NSW 2129

SOUTH AFRICA:
Oxford University Press,
P.O. Box 1141, Cape Town

British Library Cataloguing in Publication Data

The church : God's agent for change.
1. Church and social problems
I. Nicholls, Bruce J.
261.1 HN31

ISBN 0-85364-444-6

Typeset by Photoprint, Torquay, Devon
and Printed in Great Britain for The Paternoster Press,
Paternoster House, 3 Mount Radford Crescent, Exeter, Devon
by A. Wheaton & Co. Ltd., Exeter

Contents

SECTION VII : **The Church Triumphs in Suffering**

SECTION VIII **God Renews his Church for Change**

Foreword

D. JOHN RICHARD

Chairman, WEF Commission on Church Renewal

In recent years several conferences have been held in various parts of the world to highlight the fact that it is by means of the Church that God's manifold wisdom should be made known (Eph. 3:10). Four such conferences which I attended were those in Lilongwe (Malawi); Bangalore (India); Seoul (Korea); and Wheaton (USA). These gatherings have in some small measure helped to recover the centrality of the local church in God's program.

The world is not what it ought to be. A deep and a lasting change is, therefore, necessary. And that is God's intent. No amount of external legislation can produce that inner transformation. The governments of the world know it. All those in authority know it. And parents know it, too.

The Church alone is God's agent to bring this change. More specifically, it is the local church. Through the preaching of Christ's gospel, the local church transfers people from the realm of darkness to that of light, from the realm of self-centredness to that of self-giving. The one and only business of the Church is to turn out new creations by the enabling power of the Spirit of Christ.

But a Church that is spiritually asleep is ill qualified to effect the change we have in mind. Therefore, we plead for Church renewal worldwide—that renewal which awakens the Church and thrusts it forward to scatter abroad the seed of change enclosed in the kernel of Christ's life-giving gospel.

Introduction:

I Will Build My Church

BRUCE J. NICHOLLS

The nature and mission of the Church has become a central issue for evangelicals engaged in the task of world evangelization and in the planting and nurturing of churches across new and old frontiers of resistance to the gospel. It is also central in the Church's understanding of and response to human need, and to the dynamics of the relationship between evangelism, social responsibility and human justice. The role of the local church in Christ's kingly reign on earth is being given renewed attention in both free and restricted situations. Disunity and fragmentation of churches, continuing paternalism of mission and development agencies, growing tensions between Church and para-church bodies all point to the need for a biblical and incarnate theology of the Church that will undergird the enormous amount of activity that has been generated by evangelicals in the four decades since World War II. Evangelicals are known to be strong on the praxis of the Church but are often weak on the doctrine of the nature and mission of the Church. The serious consideration of these issues can be delayed no longer.

The Wheaton '83 Conference on the Nature and Mission of the Church held at the Graham Center, Wheaton College, Illinois, USA from 20th June to 1st July 1983 was a small but truly international gathering of evangelicals. This conference of more than 350 participants from 60 countries—theologians and teachers, pastors and evangelists, missionaries and lay leaders—was convened by the World Evangelical Fellowship and sponsored by many churches and agencies worldwide. It was one conference but worked in three simultaneous consultations which dealt with the Church in its Local Setting; the Church in New Frontiers for Missions; and the Church in Response to Human Need. The materials have been collected and edited, in some cases very severely, to form the chapters of this book. They include selections of the plenary Bible studies, the four plenary papers, and selections of papers and case studies of the first consultation on the Church in its Local Setting. (The materials contributed from the consultations on the Church in New Frontiers for Mission and the Church in Response to Human Need have been published in separate volumes.) This volume is not a compendium of the Wheaton '83 document, but an interpreted selection of materials focusing on the theme "The Church: God's Agent for Change."

In response to Jesus' question to his disciples, "Who do you say that I am?", Peter confessed, "You are the Christ, the Son of the living God." This theological affirmation and personal commitment of Peter and those with him drew from our Lord one of His most climactic statements, "You are Peter, and on this rock I will build my church, and the gates of Hades will not overcome it" (Matt. 16:18). This profound statement of Jesus, set in the context of his coming kingdom, points to the Church as the Kingdom community of God's people who acknowledge Jesus Christ as King and Lord and whose lifestyle and testimony bear witness to His reign in their lives. To God's people are given the keys of the kingdom and the awesome authority to bind and to loose. The other side of this is suggested by Paul's words, "If our gospel is veiled it is veiled to those who are perishing" (II Cor. 4:3).

One Holy Universal and Apostolic Church

The Church is a gathering community with a sending mission to the world. Throughout its history, the Church has confessed its nature as one holy, catholic and apostolic Church whose foundations are the apostles and prophets and whose cornerstone is Jesus Christ. But the Church's nature is inseparable from her mission. As Christ's agent sent into the world to fulfil his mission of redemption and liberation, the Church ever points to His coming reign as judge and king. This hope gives joy and courage to all Christians who suffer for His name's sake especially in restrictive and repressive situations. To fulfil this mission, Christ gave to the Church the Holy Spirit to rebuke and convict the world of sin, to enlighten the believer, to impart His many gifts, to equip the Church for ministry and to empower the Church for witness and service in the world.

We rejoice that God is building his Church in remarkable ways throughout the world today, especially in Africa, Asia, Latin America, the Caribbean and in the South Pacific—as many of the case studies in this volume give witness. The story of the growth of the Church in China during the past 35 years is beyond human expectation and has profound lessons for our understanding of mission worldwide today. At the same time it raises important issues about the nature of the Church and its institutional structures, and also its relationship to political power.

The concept of the Church as the Kingdom community is unique in the world of religious faiths. The Church is a household of faith with many members. But it is more than a club with individual membership. It is the mystical body of Christ, a divinely created fellowship of those who are in Christ—a oneness that transcends sex, race and social distinctions. In some religions there is very little concept of the communion of saints. Every Hindu worshipping in the temple stands alone before his deity. It is significant that nearly every reformed movement in Hinduism (not to mention the rise of the modern eclectic guru movements) attempts in some form or other to build an approximation to the Church. On the other hand, Islam has a strong sense of equality in brotherhood, as can be seen in the mosque on any Friday. But the distinction between male and female is very marked. From this perspective it can be understood why the Christian concept of Church as a body or a Kingdom community is sometimes the envy of other religions. The manifesting of this unity in true worship and service becomes in itself a very powerful evangelistic witness and through it people are drawn to Christ. Thus authentic witness is a primary cause of the growth of the Church in village and urban situations in countries which are dominated by other religious faiths. Evangelicals have often ignored the effective witness of true congregational worship.

The tragedy of Christianity, as we are all painfully aware, is the fragmentation and disunity of the Church. Causes of this range from doctrinal apostasy to moral breakdown, and from personality cultism to cultural misunderstandings. The modern missionary movement has not only been used of God to reach the unreached and to build indigenous churches, but has brought with it its own historical, ecclesiastical and cultural traditions which have fragmented the emerging Church. In a strange way the missionary movement has been a major factor in the secularizing of the Church in developing countries. Some of this fragmentation is unavoidable and the consequence of the necessary contextualization of theology and practice. In other cases it is caused by "paternalism, insensitivity and abuse of power", to quote from the Wheaton '83 *Letter to the Churches*. Christian unity is not an optional luxury or the fruit of human diplomacy; it is the gift of God. The indestructibility of the Church's unity is grounded in the unity of the Triune God—Father, Son and Holy Spirit. Therefore Paul exhorts us to "strive to keep the unity of the Spirit through the bond of peace."

The unity of the Church is not unity without differentiation as in Judaism or in Islam. It is a unity in rich diversity; it is incarnate in the cultures of mankind and yet always transcending these creation-bound distinctions. This diversity is the manifold work of the Holy Spirit himself.

The distinction between the visible and invisible Church is helpful in some contexts but not in others. The Church is universal and cosmic and yet visible and local in a variety of assemblies, large and small. The Church is as visible as its members. As the European Reformers saw, it is gathered by God's Word and marked by Christ's ordinances. But it is equally true to say that the Church is the embodiment of Christ's mission to the world. Mission itself is part of the nature of the Church "as fire is to burning."

However, the visible Church is more than the local church or assembly. It embraces what are often described as para-church agencies for specialized ministries. The Church also includes national and regional church bodies and national and global denominations, interdenominational and ecumenical organizations.

A significant factor in describing the nature of the Church is the relationship of individuals and families as units of the Church's life. Eternal salvation is personal and individual and therefore the baptized believer is the basic unit of the Church. Yet at the same time individuals are part of families and the family continues to be the social unit of decision-making in many parts of the world. Marriage arrangements or changing one's religion are never private affairs; they involve the action of the whole family. Where the family is divided through an individual's decision to follow Christ, the task of ongoing evangelism is made more difficult. The extended family was the basic unit of the societies in which the New Testament Churches were planted. It also accounts for the rapidity of Church growth in many parts of Asia and Africa today—despite the outward appearance of modern secularity with its individualism and fragmentation of the family. When a pastor in India is asked the size of his congregation he invariably replies in terms of the number of families in his church. The family as the unit of the Church has important implications for our understanding of the nature and mission of the Church, of the role of sacraments, of evangelism and Church growth, of discipline and discipleship making and of the government of the Church.

Holiness belongs to the very nature of the Church. The Scriptures furnish many images and symbols of the Church's holiness. Paul's image of a bride adorned for her husband is one that appeals to every human heart. The search for a pure Church this side of Christ's return is always beyond our grasp. An overemphasis on purity can stultify Church growth as much as laxity in moral standards does. Yet one of the missing marks of the Church today is discipline in the moral and doctrinal lives of its members. Unfortunately, the exercise of discipline in our relativistic society only feeds the growth of sectarian and psuedo-spiritual movements. The need for counselling and pastoral care is greater than ever before.

The claim to be apostolic has often been misunderstood and misrepresented through Church history. We praise God that Christ's

Church is built upon the teachings of the apostles and prophets who received the Word of God and ministered it to us. Christ sends us into the world in obedience to his Great Commission and empowers us by the Holy Spirit.

The Church and the Kingdom of God in the World

One of the major issues discussed in the Wheaton Conference was the dynamics of the relationship between the Church and the Kingdom of God and the parameters of both in the world. We do not equate the Church with the Kingdom, as the older Catholics did, nor do we isolate one from the other as some evangelicals continue to do. We understand and affirm that "the Church is a Community of Christ's saving rule, made up of those who bear and confess the name of Christ" (*Letter to the Churches*). The Church is visible as the Kingdom community only insofar as it manifests Christ's reign over all its life and activity. The relationship is a dynamic one of judgement and saving grace.

The Church is God's special signpost in the world, ever pointing sincere pilgrims to the fulness of Christ's coming reign. Insofar as the Church is on the frontier of the Kingdom it is God's agent for change. Yet the Kingdom penetrates the world beyond the boundaries of the Church. The Holy Spirit as the agent of the kingdom goes ahead of the Church in penetrating the world of religious and secular faith and preparing men and women to receive the gospel when they hear it, and in restraining the institutions of human society from self-destruction. In this sense God can call Nebuchadnezzar "my servant" and likewise Chairman Mao of China. The two dimensions of Christ's reign in the heavens and on earth are held together by this eschatological hope that when Christ returns the Church and the Kingdom will be coterminous. Much of the recent debate on the relationship of evangelism to social responsibility, and the priority of one over the other, could have been harnessed for mission if we had had a clearer understanding of the relationship of the Church and the Kingdom in the world.

The Church and the Kingdom of God in the World

A true theology of liberation from suffering and oppression must be undergirded by a theology of redemption from sin and evil. Both need a theology of the Church that puts the new redeemed and liberated community at the centre of God's cosmic purpose as his appointed agent for proclamation, service and justice in the world. As Ronald Sider has argued, "Evangelism and social responsibility are equally important, genuinely distinct and inseparably related in the Church's life." Though Wheaton '83 comprised three consultations it was one conference committed to the discipleship of Him who announced, "I will build my Church and the gates of Hades will not overcome it."

The Church and Cultural Conditioning

This book seeks to weave together a mosaic of evangelical reflection on biblical truth and church experience in the service of Christ. The complexity of cultural conditioning and expression in some of the case studies discussed in this book is both bewildering and enriching. While we need to beware that we do not draw our theology from case studies, they are extremely important in the process of interpreting biblical truth for our generation. In the materials of this book it will be observed that there are three distinct but overlapping circles of cultural conditioning. These are the Hebrew (and to a lesser extent the Greek) cultures of the biblical word of God; the distinctive cultures into which the Church is being transplanted in pagan soil; and the cultural containment of those who communicate the gospel. We are confronted with a hermeneutical task never fully grasped by earlier generations of missionaries and church builders. The task of identifying ourselves with and yet distancing ourselves from both biblical culture and the culture of the hearers of the good news is an ongoing process. The modern social sciences have made a valuable contribution to this process, but caution is needed; for they are good servants but bad masters. The traditional grammatico-historic goal approach to hermeneutics continues to be fundamental to our task, but it is insufficient to lead us from exegesis to interpretation.

It is not easy to distinguish between abiding principles in Scripture and culturally conditioned practices found in local churches, as the contemporary debate, on the role of women in the Church, the rights concerning divorce and marriage, and the place of nuclear weapons in containing war, all too painfully show. Much of the fragmentation of the Church comes from missionaries and national leaders who fail to develop an adequate hermeneutic in relating text to context. The validity or otherwise of churches made up of homogeneous people's groups, the advocacy of one mode of baptism or another, the insistence on democratic forms of church government—all of these must be tested on sound hermeneutical principles. Many cross-cultural church planters have had great difficulty in separating biblical Christianity from their own brand of cultural Christianity. It is not difficult to recognise the cultural heritage of an ex-Anglican church in India, a Presbyterian church in South Korea or a Baptist church in the Philippines. Where the communicator is unable to distance himself from his own culture and indiscriminately identifies himself with the host culture, sectarianism results, and prophetism and authoritarianism arise in the Church. The emergence of the thousands of independent churches across Africa is an all too sad testimony to this failure. The boundary between faithful contextualization of the gospel and the destructive consequences of cultural and theological syncretism is never easy to discern. We are in desperate need of a divine wisdom that transcends our human understanding; and only the Spirit of God can give us this enlightenment, and the courage to be faithful to His Word.

The Renewal of the Church

The renewal of the Church is a central theme in this book. It is not enough for missionaries to cross the last frontiers of unreached people. The Church needs to be constantly renewed if it is to carry forward the ongoing task of evangelization. It is sometimes said in South Asia that for every ten Muslims who become Christians seven revert to their former faith, embittered against the Church that was unprepared and unable to receive them. Since independence in 1947 it is estimated that thousands and perhaps hundreds of thousands of converts in North India have reverted to their Hindu faith. The reasons are many, but one thing is clear. The Church that loses its missionary vision, whose leaders are not adequately prepared to shepherd the mass movement converts of an earlier generation, and the Church whose ethic is hardly distinguishable from that of the world, can never be God's agent for change. The sixteenth century Reformers spoke of the *ecclesia reformata semper reformanda*—the need of the reformed Church continually to be reformed. The renewal of the Church must be the renewal of the whole life of the Church to meet the total spiritual need of our whole society.

Renewal calls for an ongoing reformation of faith on the principles of *"sola scriptura"*—scripture alone. Unless the Church is built on this foundation it will not stand against the storms of secular humanism, religious fanaticism or crusading atheism. A Church that is continually being reformed must recover the centrality and authority of biblical preaching, the searching of the Scriptures in small study groups and the training of its members in biblical evangelism and pastoral care.

Renewal calls for revival and spiritual awakening in the Church. This is preeminently the work of the Holy Spirit. The revival in Wales in 1903 was repeated in the Punjab in North India with the formation of the Punjab Prayer and Praise Union and the Sialkot Convention in 1905. During the next ten years, as revival spread from church to church, the number of Christians doubled, a new generation of clergy and lay leaders came forward, and the mighty acts of the Holy Spirit were made plain to all. That was eighty years ago and the need for revival is urgent, especially in the Punjab, overwhelmed as it is by a wave of violence and disunity.

Renewal calls for a recovery of the ethics of the Kingdom as taught by our Lord and elaborated in the letters of the New Testament. I am grieved when Hindus indicate that they feel they have nothing to gain by becoming Christians. They point to the divorce rate in America, to the racist attitudes of the Christians in South Africa and to the greed and insensitivity of the Western business world. All too often Christians are criticised for their laziness, their moral laxity and their quarrelsome spirit. In some situations these accusations are true; in others they are not. Theological renewal and spiritual revival without change in ethical lifestyle is an open denial of the gospel. People turn a deaf ear to the gospel and evangelism fails. Christ began his ministry proclaiming, "The time has come; the Kingdom of God is near; repent and believe the Good News" (Mark 1:14). In Asia in particular the key to an authentic gospel is the visible transformation of the lives of Christian families. The quality of family life of Christians in China during the past thirty-five years has probably been the most important factor in the unbelievable growth of the Church in that land.

Renewal calls for an incessant renewal of the institutions of the Church. The New Testament Churches were marked by simplicity and flexibility. Function controlled structure. The institutional life of the Church developed to meet evident needs. This is seen in the blossoming of house meetings to supplement worship in the temple. The appointment of deacons and elders, the institutionalising of baptism and the Lord's Supper as ordinances of the Church, the systematic collection for the needs of the poor, were all part of the Church's life as a living organism. The same flexibility is needed today in both traditional churches and the younger churches in the emerging nations. The institutional life of the Church belongs to the nature of the Church, for the Church is both invisible and visible, personal and communal. It is a living organism.

"Ecclesia reformata semper reformanda."

SECTION I

Biblical Foundations for the Missionary Church

1

The Church in the Old Testament

WILSON CHOW

Introduction

Church renewal is the work of God, the result of the mighty acts of the Holy Spirit. It cannot be attained by mere programs, or induced by formulated spiritual exercises. "Nor by might nor by power, but by my Spirit, says the Lord Almighty." (Zechariah 4:6). Yet while we honour God's sovereignty in His renewing and refreshing of the Church, we do need to seek earnestly His blessings, to prepare ourselves with the right mind and attitude, to examine ourselves before the Lord. We should cry out to the Lord in the words of the prophet Habakkuk, "O Lord, revive thy work in the midst of the years, in the midst of the years make known; in wrath remember mercy" (Hab. 3:2; KJV). Let us seek the Lord with a spirit of expectancy—"Restore us again, O God our Saviour, and put away your displeasure toward us again, that your people may rejoice in you" (Psalm 85:4,6: NIV).

I do not believe church renewal will come so abruptly as to make any effort of preparation unnecessary. It begins with prayer. For us who are members of the Church of Jesus Christ and who have engaged in the work of the ministry for a good period of time, it is essential that we pause and re-think the nature and the mission of the Church. A true renewal of the Church must be based on a biblically sound self-understanding of her nature and mission.

The Old Testament Church as God's Redeemed Community

When we speak of the Church in the Old Testament, we refer to ancient Israel, which was chosen by God to be the object of His special love and instrument of His blessing. The theological significance of Israel as a people and a nation, her relationship to the Church in the New

Testament, and her role in redemptive history, continue to arouse different opinions and debate even among evangelical Christians. We do not want to address these problems here. But it is beyond dispute that Israel was God's chosen people in the Old Testament, and a type of the New Testament Church.

The passage on which we now focus our attention is Exodus 19:1–6:

> In the third month after the Israelites left Egypt—on the very day—they came to the Desert of Sinai. After they set out from Rephidim, they entered the Desert of Sinai, and Israel camped there in a desert in the front of the mountain. Then Moses went up to God, and the Lord called to him from the mountain and said, "This is what you are to say to the house of Jacob and what you are to tell the people of Israel: 'You yourselves have seen what I did to Egypt and how I carried you on eagles' wings and brought you to myself. Now if you obey me fully and keep my covenant, then out of all nations you will be my treasured possession. Although the whole earth is mine, you will be for me a kingdom of priests and a holy nation.' These are the words you are to speak to the Israelites." (NIV)

These events took place at Mount Sinai, where Yahweh God was about to make a covenant with Israel, on the basis of which Israel would become the people of God. This passage is so fundamental for the Old Testament and so rich in its meaning that we must use it as a starting point for an understanding of the Church in the Old Testament.

Out of Egypt

The Israelites had just left Egypt (verse 1); they had been delivered from oppression and slavery in the land of Pharaoh. The exodus is the Old Testament redemption. The people had experienced the power of God in His deliverance: "You yourselves have seen what I did to Egypt." The memory of the series of events that had brought them out from Egypt was still vivid in their minds: they had witnessed the ten plagues with which the Lord had struck the land of Egypt, culminating in the killing of the first-born of the Egyptians. They had seen how God divided the Red Sea before their eyes to enable them to go through the sea on dry ground. In this way, the Israelites experienced liberation from subjection to slavery and oppression, and gained their freedom as a people. From a biblical-theological perspective, we understand redemption here portrayed as a deliverance from a realm of sin and evil. It is deliverance from enslavement to an alien power, as well as rescue from inward, spiritual degradation and sin. Salvation comes from God. The Church as God's redeemed community comes into existence as a result of His saving acts. The exodus is a demonstration of God's sovereign grace and power.

Sinai Before Canaan

Israel departed from Egypt and headed towards Canaan, the promised land flowing with milk and honey, as their final destination. But first they came to Sinai. It was God's plan that Israel should meet Him at Sinai after the exodus. It was important that God should make a covenant with Israel whereby their status as God's people would be affirmed. Now in Exodus 19 we find Moses going up to the same mountain where, not so long ago, the Lord had called him to bring the people of Israel out from Egypt. Right then the Lord had given him this instruction: "When you have brought the people out of Egypt, you will worship God on this mountain" (Ex. 3:12). The arrival at Sinai was by divine appointment.

This became clear as the Israelites left Egypt. Scripture states that when Pharaoh let the people go, God did not lead them on the road through the Philistine country, though that was shorter. Instead, God led the people around by the desert road towards the Red Sea (Ex. 13: 17–18). God's guidance was unmistakable: in a pillar of cloud by day and a pillar of fire by night. The "wilderness experience" was significant for Israel. God's intention was to give protection to His people, that they might avoid the Egyptian garrisons located along the coast. "If they face war, they might change their minds and return to Egypt" (Ex. 13:17–18). The desert journey, with its concomitant lack of water and food, also provided occasions on which the Israelites' faith in Yahweh was tested. "Is the Lord among us or not?" they asked (Ex. 17:7). They had come to trust in God for His faithful provision. It was a valuable lesson that they learned in the wilderness. But most important of all, they were led to Sinai.

Thus the Israelites travelled to Sinai, their journey figuratively described as their having been carried on eagles' wings, which expresses both God's tender care and safe transport. Sinai stands for the fact that God had brought Israel to Himself, to become His people. It was not simply a deliverance from Egypt, but a bringing into the presence of God and becoming His people. Liberation alone does not constitute salvation, nor has a liberated people attained redemption on the basis of national freedom or independence. Sinai is significant in that it points to a unique relationship established between Yahweh and Israel in the form of a covenant. Yahweh was their God, honoured by the nation as her Lord, and in turn, Israel was accepted as God's people, in fulfilment of the promises that God made to the patriarch Abraham.

Three-Fold Identity

After this reminder of their recent experiences and God's divine purpose, Israel's privileged position and her proper function in the world is next set before the people (verses 5–6). She was given a three-fold identity in her relationship to God and to the world. Inherent in this identity were also responsibilities which she had to fulfil and which made relevant her existence in the world. The nature and the mission of God's people are inseparable; the Church's nature defines her mission and gives meaning to it, while her mission is an expression, an outgrowth from her nature.

a. *God's treasured possession*

Israel was called God's treasured possession. The word *segullah* means "special treasure, possession." In 1 Chronicles 29:3 it refers to a king's private treasure which he can use as he chooses; in Deuteronomy the usage is in the context of God's choice of Israel out of all the peoples on earth (7:6; 14:1,2), and with emphasis on Israel's observance of God's commands (26:16–18). Thus the word implies special value and special relationship as well as divine choice.

Israel was God's people, the Church is God's Church. The mark of divine possession is clear. Israel was to belong to God, whose choice of her made her of special value. God takes pleasure in the possession of His people. The psalmist praised the Lord for His goodness, "For the Lord has chosen Jacob to be His own, Israel to be His treasured possession" (Ps. 135:5). It is indeed a great privilege to be God's "precious and honoured" in His sight, and to be loved by Him (Isa. 43:4). Who we are is as important as what we do—if not indeed more important.

b. *A kingdom of priests*

This phrase does not occur elsewhere in the Old Testament. However, a similar idea is found in the parallelism in Isa. 61:6, "And you will be called priests of the Lord, you will be named ministers of our God." In the New Testament, this expression is used several times with reference to God's people (1 Pet. 2:5, 9; Rev. 1:6; 20:6).

The term "kingdom" recalls Ex. 15:18, where the Lord is exalted as king who will reign forever. Yahweh is Israel's king and He is about to provide them with laws for the theocratic state. But what is the meaning of "a kingdom of priests" (or "a kingdom in respect of priesthood")?

Here the mission of Israel is implied. God's "particularist" choice of Israel has a wider "universalist" purpose. There were priests in Israel who came before the Lord on behalf of the people in the service of the tabernacle and of the temple, including intercession, the offering of sacrifices, seeking God's will, and in the instruction of God's Law. But Israel as a nation also has a mediatorial role; she stands between Yahweh and the other nations. She should be a witness of Yahweh before other nations, and seek the Lord's blessings upon them on their behalf. Israel was God's people, but she must not be so isolated from other nations, so remote from them, as to make her presence among them immaterial or irrelevant. This missiological task was already given to Abraham when God called him from Ur and made a covenant with him. It was God's plan that all people on earth would be blessed through Abraham and his descendents (Gen. 12:3; 18:8; 22:18; 26:4; 28:14). This theme continued to be prominent in the patriarchal narratives. Along with the promise of offspring and the land of Cannaan, it was repeated to every patriarchal generation.

The calling of Abraham and the election of Israel among the nations was not an end in itself, but a means in the fulfilment of God's plan of salvation for the world. The people of God were called to worship God, to enjoy His presence, but were also sent to witness, to proclaim the Name of Yahweh, and to make known His mighty acts.

The people of God must look beyond themselves to the world around them. There is no room for detachment or self-interest. Instead, in order to be worthy of the noble status given to them by God as a kingdom of priests, the people of God must be involved and concerned with other people interceding for them in God's presence. In this way, the election of Israel was put in its proper perspective, and the divine purpose for the whole world declared in seed form, to be more fully unfolded later: "I will also make you a light for the Gentiles, that you may bring my salvation to the needs of the earth" (Isa. 49:6).

c. *A holy nation*

The word "holy" basically means "set apart, consecrated". The people of Israel were set apart from the other nations to belong to God, for the worship and service of Yahweh. At first the concept of holiness may not have had moral connotations. Then, because of the revealed nature of Yahweh, such holiness as descriptive of God took on a strong moral meaning, so that God's holiness became a compelling moral demand on His people.

As a holy nation, Israel was to be different from the other nations. Negatively, they must not do as the people did in Egypt, neither must they do as the people did in the land of Canaan. "Do not follow their practices" (Lev. 18:3). Positively, the Lord commanded the entire assembly of Israel, "Be holy because I, the Lord your God, am holy" (Lev. 19:1). "Consecrate yourselves and be holy, because I am the Lord your God. Keep my decrees and follow them. I am the Lord, who makes you holy" (Lev. 20:7–8).

The Church as God's holy people must stand against the tide of the day. Today we are facing a world very advanced in technology and yet, at the same time, so secular and permissive that this has direct bearing on the values of everyday life and ethics. To what extent has contemporary society influenced the Church? The Church must stand on guard against the tendency to secularization and compromise. God's people must be willing and ready to say "No" in issues that run contrary to biblical teaching or against our Christian conscience. Our activism must not betray our Christian principles; our relevance should not impair our identity as God's holy people. We may well remember the Apostle Paul's exhortation, "Do not conform any longer to the pattern of this world, but be transformed by the renewing of your mind" (Rom. 12:2). In his exposition of the Sermon on the Mount, John Stott uses the expression "Christian counter-culture" to indicate why and how "the followers of Jesus are to be different—different from both the nominal church and the secular world, different from both the religious and irreligious". This is the message that Israel was to bring to their generation through their life, witness and obedience to God's commandments. We must affirm a "Christian value-system, ethical standard, religious devotion, attitude to money, ambition, life-style and network of relationships—all of which are totally at variance with those of the non-Christian world. And this Christian counter-culture is the life of the kingdom of God, a fully human life indeed but lived out under the divine rule."

God's People Fore-Warned

When the people of Israel were about to enter the land of Canaan, God gave them clear instructions as to what they should be and do in this new environment (Deut. 8:1–18). The difficult years of desert wandering, with lack of water, food and safe shelter, would soon be over. The Lord had disciplined them, and they had learned through God's faithful provision the precious lesson that "man does not live on bread alone but on every word that comes from the mouth of the Lord" (Deut. 8:3). Now they were facing a good land which the Lord would give to them, "a land with streams and pools of water, with springs flowing in the valleys and hills; a land with wheat and barley, vines and fig trees, pomegranates, olive oil and honey; a land where bread will not be scarce and you will lack nothing; a land where the rocks are iron and you can dig copper out of the hills" (Deut. 1:9). How rich and full of resources was the land before them! What a promising life that was waiting for the Israelites!

As the Israelites were about to begin a new page in the history of their nation by possessing the land of Canaan, Moses, their leader, gave them solemn warnings and fatherly exhortations.

a. *Do not forget the Lord your God*

Three times in the text the Israelites were warned not to forget the Lord (verses 11, 14, 19). To 'forget' in this context does not mean an inability to recall what has happened. The past events certainly remained registered in the minds of the Israelites. What this warning pointed to was the tendency to *neglect or disregard*, so that the past experience of

God's deliverance and provision ceased to be part of a living memory of the reality of God. This speaks not so much of the mind as of the heart. A forgetting of Yahweh as Lord, a disregard of His goodness in the past, and an unawareness of His presence now will open the door for sins of various kinds.

It was because of this that Moses also repeatedly urged the Israelites to bear in their hearts what they had experienced of God's power and grace, and what lessons they had learned. "Know then in your heart," Moses reminded them, "that as a man disciplines his son, so the Lord your God disciplines you" (8:5). Or again, Moses charged the Israelites to "remember how the Lord your God led you all the way in the desert these forty years" (verse 2).

It is important that the people of God should carry on the remembrance of God in the form of worship, celebration and service. The Church of Jesus Christ must be a worshipping community, rendering to God praise, adoration and thanksgiving of which He alone is worthy. "When you have eaten and are satisfied, praise the Lord your God for the good land He has given you" (8:10).

b. *Do not become proud*

The Israelites might think that it was their power and the strength of their own hands that had produced wealth and prosperity. Then they might become victims of their pride. It is tragic that we sometimes find complacency, pride and even arrogance in Christians and churches which have become so successful that they think it is by their wisdom, program planning and strategy that they have achieved phenomenal results. It is true that we have wisdom and ability, but in the words of Moses, "Remember the Lord your God, for it is He who gives you the ability to produce wealth" (8:18).

c. *Do not follow and worship other gods*

Since their entry into Canaan after the conquest, the Israelites were always in danger of following other gods. They were attracted to pagan worship of various kinds, from pure idolatry, Baalism, to syncretistic religions. It is difficult to conceive how and to explain why a nation such as Israel, being God's covenant people with the divine ordinances that instructed them in religious matters, could still turn away from Yahweh to follow other gods. It has been suggested that idolatry and Baal-worship came from a pragmatic motive. In order that they might be blessed with a materially more wealthy and prosperous life comparable to that which the Canaanites had been enjoying, the Israelites followed the Canaanite religious way, supposing that a life of comfort and abundance was brought by the fertility cult. While we are not certain of the reasons for their apostasy, its effect on the nation was clear. It led to doom and destruction.

Idolatry may take different forms today in the life of the Christian and of the Church. When God is robbed of His Glory, when God is dethroned, when any person or any thing has taken the first place of God in terms of our worship and allegiance, other "gods" will creep in. Even in the secularized world of today, there is no religious vacuum. Let us guard ourselves against idols.

Yahweh's Case Against God's People

Israel's history has witnessed God's grace and protection, but Israel herself stood condemned by her unfaithfulness to the Lord and her failure to be His witness among the nations. Moses' warnings went unheeded. Towards the end of the period of the Judges, Israel asked for a king to rule over her. "Then we will be like all the other nations, with a king to lead us and to go out before us and fight our battles" (1 Samuel 8:20). They wanted to have a national hero. As time went on, Baalism prevailed, and only a man of such power and courage as Elijah was able to stand against the Baal prophets. Yet Yahweh's prophets were a minority. The Baal cult was the popular folk religion; the false prophets dominated the religious scene. How sad it was to see the true, historical, orthodox religious tradition of Israel become merely one of the religious options for the people of God.

In the book of Hosea, we read that Yahweh had a charge to bring against the Israelites. The indictments were as follows: "There is no faithfulness, no love, no acknowledgement of God in the land" (Hosea 4:1). Yahweh is portrayed as the marriage-Lord of Israel in Hosea, and the sin which Israel as a nation committed against Yahweh is described as a want of conformity to the ideal of marriage-affection and loyalty. The following chapters continue to elaborate the sinfulness of the people which included religious, moral, social and political sins. Their lack of the "knowledge of God" meant a disrespect for the law of God: the priests were guilty of ignoring God's law (4:6), and failed to instruct the people in the Word of God. Hosea also spoke of a spirit of prostitution which led them astray (4:12), a figurative description of the sin of serving other gods. They sacrificed to the Baals and burned incense to images (11:2). They were fed by the Lord, and when they were satisfied, they became proud and forgot Him (13:6). The description of their spiritual condition unfortunately fits almost perfectly the warning given by Moses centuries ago.

With religious apostasy, there were yet other evils: social injustice, oppression of the weak and the poor and immorality. At a time when Israel was enjoying a revival of material prosperity under Jereboam II, few would know that the end of the northern kingdom was fast approaching. The prophets called the people's attention to the judgement of God. "Woe to you who are complacent in Zion, and to you who feel secure on Mount Samaria! . . . You lie on beds inlaid with ivory and lounge on couches. You dine on choice lambs and fattened calves. You strum away on your harps like David and improvise on musical instruments. You drink wine by the bowlful and use the finest lotions, but you do not grieve over the ruin of Joseph. Therefore you will be among the first to go into exile; your feasting and lounging will end" (Amos 6:1–7).

The rebuke of Amos is timely and relevant to us today in the midst of an affluent society set in a world facing poverty and hunger. The Israelites were rebuked for their insensitivity to the needs of the common people and the crisis that the nation was facing. "But you do not grieve over the ruin of Joseph" stands as an accusation against their failure to identify with the people and to be concerned with the future destiny of the nation.

True spirituality is true knowledge of God with a just response to the cause of the needy and the afflicted. The prophets' criticism of social evil was based on the covenant which God had established with Israel. Israel's indifference and unfaithfulness to the covenant was shown in their trampling upon the poor and neglecting the needy. To the eighth century prophets, social injustices were most indicative of a falling away from the covenant God Yahweh. For this, Israel's doom was sure and her destruction at hand. There was a correlation between social injustice and Israel's experiences in history.

God's People Are Called To Repent And Return

Israel's history is a sad but a real story. It is sad because the people of God's Choice turned out to be unfaithful to Him, and went astray from following Him. It is real because Israel's failure and apostasy took place in time and space, and become warnings to the Church today. It is true that men's failures cannot frustrate God's purposes, but while God is pleased to use people to accomplish His will, only those who are right with God and whose lives yield obedience and holiness are worthy to be in His service. What happened to Israel reminds us of our human sinfulness and shortcomings. There is always the need to begin with God, to long for Church renewal at the most basic level of a right relationship with God.

The prophet Hosea exhorted Israel to return to God and offered a prayer of penitence as a way of approaching Him (Hosea 14:1–3). The basis for his prayer is the gracious and compassionate nature of God. He is there willing to forgive and to bless. He is there awaiting our return, like the father standing at the door to welcome his prodigal son. God's loving kindness invites us to return to Him, and assures us of His forgiveness. Hope for renewal lies not in us, but in God. At the same time, there must be an awareness of where and how one has gone wrong. Israel's own sin had become the stone of her stumbling. Now God's people must first return to God in repentance, and revive their exclusive loyalty to Yahweh. They were to declare their submission to him by a three-fold vow, whereby they denounced their pro-Assyrian politics, their trust in military power for deliverance, and their idolatry. They had to abandon earthly securities in order to place their trust in God alone.

And so it is for us. So it must be, if we are to focus on God Himself as our resource and power in our calling to be His church today.

Dr. Wilson Chow is Principal, China Graduate School of Theology, Hong Kong

2

The Church in Rome: Reflection on Romans 16

VALDIR STEUERNAGEL

Introduction

The Church in Rome—what Church is this? What do we know about it? Perhaps it will be necessary from the start to demythologize both our minds and our conditioning. We are not speaking of the Vatican City, of the crowning of Popes, of sumptuous garments, of Peter's "throne." Neither are we referring to the victorious arms of Constantine and the adoption of the Christian faith as the official religion. We are not alluding to any official church, recognized, applauded and even imposed. We are talking of the Church of the persecuted, of wandering people. We are thinking, above all, about slaves, women and poor people in Rome. Simple people made up the greatest part of this Church, planted as a sign of grace and of judgement in the centre of the vast Roman Empire.

I would like to invite you to look at chapter 16 of Paul's Epistle to the Romans. In it, a long list is made of twenty-nine names to which he makes special reference with a personal greeting. This is unusually long, considering that Paul had not been in Rome, although he repeatedly longed to go there (Rom. 15:22). Some of the names are known to us from other Bible references. The majority are new.

The end of the letter seems to me to be a "golden close." So much doctrine had been conveyed, so many theological concepts had been elucidated, that there could not now fail to be a personal touch. It is the special greeting to several of the brethren, the reminder of situations which they had gone through together which enriches the body of Christ. Among us Brazilians, we would say that the final "hug" could not be missing.

Some specific brethren get to know about other specific brethren, and a healthy interchange is established between the churches.

Paul must have had contact with several of these persons during his missionary journeys. Some of them had left Rome because of the decree which Claudius had made in 52 A.D., expelling the Jews from the city. After his death, some of them returned to Rome. Among them there were those who had become Christians through Paul, and even became his cooperators. Returning to Rome, they became pillars of the Church, then so new and so important.

A Message for Rome

The very existence of the church was making a statement to the city.

"Oh, Rome, you who are so beautiful and important. You who believe that your sovereigns are gods, and who think you are the centre of the world. You have grown and become great, and you arrogantly register your dominion in pomp, in war, in tyranny and in the control of religion.

"At first you did not notice, but soon you perceived in your midst the existence of a people whom you will not manage to keep under control—the people of that abominable Christ, the itinerant preacher from humble Galilee. This small flock of poor and insignificant persons who meet at daybreak or secretly in your catacombs, represents the fall of your arrogance, the fall of your 'political system', the destruction of your intention to control religion and thus to control men and the way they organize their life.

"Oh, Rome, you who are accustomed to deal with armies and peoples in rebellion. You who make law out of force and who make religion an instrument of political control—suddenly you will find yourself unarmed. Your instruments of war do not intimidate and your lions can't manage to deal with this 'elect race', with these 'mediocre and fanatical Christians' who so valiantly refuse to worship your gods.

"These, Rome, have discovered the living God. That is to say, the source of life itself. They are pledged to that God who is not made by human hands, and who has been concretely manifested in the person and work of Jesus Christ. This becomes the point of reference for every man in every place.

"The seriousness of this way is witnessed by Polycarp, at the hour of his death. 'Swear,' says his executioner, 'by the genius of Caesar, retract; shout:—down with the atheists!' Polycarp, very gravely, looking at the pagans who fill the ranks of descending places for spectators, signals to them and, sighing, exclaims: 'Down with the atheists.' The proconsul insists, 'Swear and I will let you go. Insult Christ.' Polycarp answers, 'I have served Christ for eighty-six years. Christ has never done me any harm. How should I blaspheme against my King and Saviour?'

"In actual fact, Rome, your days are numbered. The banner of faith, raised higher by the blood of the martyrs, will not be lowered by you; you will not manage to do it. It has arrived to stay, for it is the flame of that which is eternal."

To the Church in Rome

To this Church Paul writes his letter, leaving it a mature legacy of solid Christian doctrine. The Church is invited to go deep into the heart of grace and faith.

The contents of this letter were central not only for the Church in Rome. The letter has followed the history of the Church and, over and over again, in a new manner, it has been a lighthouse in the darkness. We need only mention the reformer Luther and his re-discovery of this letter, so fundamental for the trajectory of the faith. "He who through faith is righteous shall live" (Rom. 1:17) has been the touchstone which revealed how radical grace is in freeing us from slavery to the idea or practice of salvation by works or one's own merits. It is necessary to remember this fact this year when we commemorate the five hundredth birth anniversary of Luther.

But there is more than doctrine. Paul also opens up to his brethren in Rome the apostle's life and career, motivated by his concept of salvation. He is "under obligation both to Greeks and to barbarians" (Rom. 1:14) and therefore he wishes to go to Rome too, to give witness and for mutual encouragement (Rom. 1:9 ff.).

The dimension of the family also appears in the letter, as we have already seen. It is good to hear that Paul wants to go to Rome to impart "some spiritual gift," so that they may be "mutually encouraged" (Rom. 1:11–12) as he says. This already is a reality for a certain group of people, as chapter 16 shows us:

Phoebe, who has been a "helper" of Paul (v. 2);
Priscilla and Aquila, "who risked their necks" for his life (v. 4);
Andronicus and Junias, "my fellow prisoners" (v. 8);
Urbanus, "our fellow workers in Christ" (v. 9);
Stachys, "my beloved" (v. 9); and Rufus, "also his mother and mine" (v. 13).

An Invitation to the Church Today.

I invite you to rejoice with me because of the reality of the family of faith—also present among us here. We need doctrine concerning the nature of the Church. We need missions—that is obvious. But in order for both to become legitimate, and for us to be credible, it is necessary that the Church be the Body of Christ, the family of God through the bonds of love. I am speaking not only about the festive love of these solemn moments. I am speaking about fraternity in the daily living out of the Christian life there on the battlefield. I don't know where you live or whom you represent. But I know that we, in Brazil, need to listen to this message about the family, because we really live in a very individualistic manner; perhaps we are not the only ones.

Let us now look at one last point: the mobility and the flexibility of this Church. Aquila and Priscilla are the greatest and most eloquent examples of this reality. Sometimes they are here, sometimes there, but always at the service of their Lord and Master.

To speak about the nature of the Church, then, is to speak about men and women like Aquila and Priscilla, Julia and Nereus, and so many others who made up the family of the faith in Rome. Men and women who have discovered the right direction in life, edified in the Almighty and in His Son, guided by the Scriptures in the service of the Kingdom among the nations, following the way of obedience (vv. 25–27).

Chapter 16 of the letter of Paul to the Romans does not merely make an enumeration of names. In it, the Lord of the Church, to whom all glory belongs, is spoken of. It mentions the missionary task among the nations and the family of the faith: men and women who are walking in the kingdom and who have discovered that their citizenship is in heaven; for the feet of them who announce good news are blessed (Rom. 10:15b). The same chapter warns against those who are prophets of their own appetites, who guide people into the slavery of delusion, and not into the obedience which brings joy and wisdom. Paul is happy because the faithfulness and the righteousness of the brethren in Rome have been shown in obedience.

Obedience leads to worship of God the Father, to following the Son, to a life guided by the Spirit in the light of the Scriptures. Obedience makes us fully part of the family of faith and puts us on the road to missions, which is the journey of faith.

If there were more obedience, there would be more life.

Dr. Valdir Steuernagel is a Lutheran Pastor in South Brazil.

3

St. Paul's Church (India) and the Antioch Church: A Comparison

A Bible Study for small groups

THEODORE WILLIAMS

St. Paul's Church

St. Paul's Church was established in a town in India which had sprung up when a big steel plant was set up by the government. It was started by those who moved in from other places for employment in the industry. Later, people who were converted from other faiths joined the Church.

The members of St. Paul's Church are very regular in church attendance and in observing the practices and traditions of their denomination. But in their financial decisions, economic choices and business dealings, there is no Christian testimony. Greed, selfishness and dishonesty are evident and the non-Christians among whom they live see this. In fact, as far as their lifestyle is concerned, there is not much difference between them and the non-Christians. Their ethical decisions and their social and economic practices are influenced by culture and customs and are often determined by expediency. The Scriptures have little bearing on them. In connection with marriage and other social and family affairs, they observe many practices and customs which are not Christian and have been brought in from their non-Christian background. Consulting the horoscope and looking for auspicious days to arrange important functions is very common. Many of the members do not know what the Bible has to say on these matters.

The pastor is a good man. But due to his liberal theological training, he is not able to preach and teach the Word of God to his congregation. Among the members there is hardly anyone who can teach the Bible, and no time is set apart for Bible study in the Church programme. The Sunday School consists of a few children below the age of eleven.

The church can barely maintain the pastor and be financially self-supporting. Though the members have good incomes and are mostly upper-middle-class, they do not give to the church as they should. There is no missionary interest. They do not give to any cause outside their own church. There are numerous social needs in the town as it is a newly established industrial town, but St. Paul's Church has no answer to these problems. Apart from the Sunday morning service, which is well attended, there is hardly any activity in the church, and the building remains closed during the rest of the week.

Antioch Church (Read Acts 11:19–30, 13:1–3)

Antioch was the third largest city in the Roman Empire at that time. It was a centre of learning and commerce and was situated in a strategic location. The Church was established here by nameless pioneers from Cyprus and Cyrene who were scattered from Jerusalem through persecution. They must have been influenced by the teaching of Stephen and certainly had a vision for reaching the Gentiles with the Gospel. The Church in Antioch had Jews and Gentiles and people of varying social background in its membership.

The Church was rooted in the Scriptures and built up through the encouraging and instructive ministry of Barnabas and Saul. There were clear evidences of conversion and change in the lives of the members. The witness of their lives was noticed by the people of Antioch. Their discipleship was genuine and radiant.

When they heard of a famine that would come all over the Roman world, they were concerned about the Christians in Judaea because they were economically poor. They collected what they could from among themselves, each person giving as he was able, and sent it to the Church in Jerusalem through Barnabas and Saul. Thus they acknowledged and confessed their oneness with the Christians in Judaea in the Body of Christ. They also had a concern for those who had not heard the gospel of Jesus Christ in other parts of the world. As they fasted and prayed seeking to know the mind of the Lord, the Holy Spirit gave them a plan for involvement in world missions. They sent Barnabas and Saul as their first missionaries to those who had not heard the gospel.

Questions for the group to discuss

1. How do we deal with nominalism in the Church?
2. It is true that the Church must be rooted in the culture of the people, but how can we deal with the infiltration of false cultural practices and customs into the Church?
3. How can we sensitize the local Church to the physical and spiritual needs of others in the neighbourhood and in the world?

Rev. Dr. Theodore Williams is a Methodist minister in Bangalore, S. India. He is president of WEF *and Executive Secretary of the* WEF *Missions Commission.*

4

A Pastoral Perspective on the Nature of the Church

ROLANDO GUTIERREZ

Introduction

To speak of the Church of Jesus Christ in today's secular world is to encounter a variety of attitudes, ranging from hostility through indifference or tolerance to acceptance. Many nations in the West are going through a real social restructuring. Among non-Christian religions, we discover similar attitudes to the Church, sometimes intensified by harbored fanaticisms.

And in the Christian sphere, we find divisions stemming from historic or liturgical traditions; institutional or doctrinal suspicion; and isolation caused by lack of information or individual convenience. Our mission is seen as *a theme for debate* rather than *a work to do together*. The differing emphases of the many para-church agencies accentuate this disparity. What can we say of the Christian sphere where the consistent renewing of the mind is not shared equally, but each seeks his own advantage? What can we say, when the repititiousness of theological discourse underscores the stagnation of methodology?

It is against this secularly complex, religously confusing, and ecclesiastically unmarked background that we speak of the *nature of the Church*. We do so from three main viewpoints: its *nature*, its *mission*, and its *pastoral work*. The first two have been spoken of many times, but of the last very little has been said. I will try to conduct my analysis from a pastoral perspective.

I. The Nature of the Church

What constitutes the nature of the church? What are its fundamental characteristics?

From Identity to Witness in the World

In the gospel of Matthew, Jesus names the Church with a possessive pronoun that indicates plainly how He thinks of it: "My church" (Matthew 16:18). Later, the apostle Paul, using the image of a building, says that Christ is the foundation, ". . . and no one can lay any other foundation" (1 Corinthians 3:11). This same apostle, writing to the Corinthians with plainly pastoral intent, calls Christians to think of themselves in terms of a building as well as in terms of a body (1 Corinthians 3:10–17). Thus, the Church is as a holy edifice of the Lord's own body, which He "feeds and cares for" (Ephesians 5:29) with the presence and gifts of His grace (Ephesians 3:7).

Now, since *it is Christ who constitutes the church,* His pastoral characteristics—love, forgiveness, reconciliation, restoration, service, and exaltation—are inherent in its nature. As with Christ, the Church's love must be sacrificial (Ephesians 5:2); its forgiveness unlimited (Matthew 18:21–22); its reconciliation prompt (Matthew 6:22–26); its restoration with a spirit of meekness (Galatians 6:1); its service ready and generous (1 Timothy 6:17–18); its exaltation full of grace (Philippians 2:5–11). From its identity, the church is called to be a faithful witness of its nature in the world.

This establishes the Church as eminently pastoral. Its characteristics are decisive for the transforming mission that it carries out and the careful upbuilding through which it works to accomplish the sensitive ministry of evangelism. It is the identity of the church that sustains its missionary and pastoral work on equal terms, like the two rails of a track upon which its evangelistic message travels.

But in order to understand how Jesus Christ is the very identity of the church acting pastorally, it is necessary to notice the way in which this knowledge reaches man.

We are not talking of a rational knowledge only, but also of an understanding by faith, through which the grace of God is revealed in the Son as the Savior of the world (Ephesians 2:4–10). It is a revealed knowledge (Galatians 1:11–20) through means other than flesh and blood (Matthew 16–17; Galatians 1:16), similar to that which allows us to know that God has made "what is seen out of things which do not appear" (Hebrews 11:3). It is a revelation that is "by grace" (Ephesians 2:8) so that the glorification of the church might be due to the Master.

The Scriptures record the immortal words of Peter's answer to the Lord's question concerning Himself: "You are the Christ, the Son of the Living God" (Matthew 16:16). It is in the revelation of that knowledge that Peter bases his confession of faith. This is the confession that, through the centuries, has been the hallmark of all disciples who follow and serve Him. Indeed, each follower must not only believe in his heart that Jesus is the Son of God and that He rose from the dead by His power, but also confess Him publicly with his mouth (Romans 10:9).

Therefore, *identity in Jesus Christ,* and the *confession of faith* by virtue of the *revelation of His Spirit,* are fundamental elements of the nature of the church. No efforts, as noble or necessary as they might seem, can take the place of this *revelation*.

But to know Jesus Christ by faith is an ineffable blessing that cannot be expressed only in private. It is also necessary to confess Him *with our mouth*. Besides following Him, it is necessary to go to all the world proclaiming the gospel that He has come, incarnate, as the great mystery of godliness that was revealed in the flesh (1 Timothy 3:16). Concerning this mystery, the congregation of the redeemed is called to be the "pillar and foundation" that supports and spreads His truth (1 Timothy 1:9–11).

In this way Jesus Christ is the object of faith. Confession, as the manifestation of the "knowledge" that man receives by grace, points to *recognition of the Lordship* in which the proclamation of the gospel is sustained and takes on meaning (1 Corinthians 1:17): a Lordship based on sovereign power.

The acknowledgement of His Lordship involves an inescapable imperative to evangelize. Evangelization springs from the nature of the church from where its identity—the revelation of Christ, and the acknowledgement of His Lordship—unite and flow into the specific tasks of proclamation, teaching, discipling nations, trusting and waiting on Him.

From Transformation of Mind to Building Living Churches

To be transformed by the renewing of the mind is inherent to the Church. The apostle Paul points this out when he writes to the brethren in Rome (Rom. 12:1–2). There, Christians faced an unprecedented challenge: a powerful paganism legitimized as civilization by the customs of the empire.

But at last the Christian diaspora had come to Rome. Beginning at Jerusalem and traveling to Samaria, Antioch, and Asia Minor, it had now reached the very heart of Caesar's stronghold. Astrological determinisms fostered for centuries were confronted decisively, and philosophical streams that came from Greece to dwell amongst the principal Roman thinkers were debated (Acts 17:21–31). And the immoral practices at Rome—incest (1 Timothy 1:9–11; Galatians 5:19–21), homosexuality (1 Timothy 1:9–11; Galatians 5:19–21), drunkenness (Galatians 5:19–21), orgies (Galatians 5:19–21), kidnappings (1 Timothy 1:10)—were the result of a moral anarchy that ran throughout the territorial networks of the empire.

Even the economic system which sustained the empire was challenged by the gospel of love that called the masters to be brethren with their slaves (Philemon). The political hatreds that provoked rulers to unjust persecution of Christians for their faith, were rechanneled by intercession (1 Corinthians 15:9–10). Moral laxity in the home was handled with pastoral skill. Similarly, marital crises caused by the conversion of one spouse were treated carefully (1 Corinthians 7).

That is why we talk of a challenge without precedent. Transformation by the renewing of the mind affected personal habits, deeply rooted customs, the stability of the home, the economic support of the empire and the legal justifications for the political behaviour of its citizens. It was not a superficial mission, but rather one that affected mental, ideological, moral, economic, political and religious structures.

If there is a point at which the building of the church will be hard, it is where popular idols are followed by an entire people. Hard, because the popular beliefs are difficult to penetrate; hard because vested interests are affected which refuse to submit to the will of God. But the hardship must be accepted so that there may be testimony to the gospel of redemption. This was the case in the controversial city consecrated to Diana of the Ephesians. And today's world is no better off. Religious, ideological, economic and political idols are everywhere visible.

The blood of Jesus Christ is profoundly significant. In the specific case of Ephesus, as Paul taught, Jews and Gentiles would recognize it as their common birth certificate. Before they could face Diana (a religious, ideological, economic and political idol), they had first to confront each other in the light of the crucifixion. They had to knock down barriers and transcend racial and religious discrimination. They had to be one in the Lord and allow His upbuilding to affect their personal lives and family relationships. They had to realize that, as each of them submitted, the body of Christ would be built up. The *mission* starts with *submission.*

It is time to examine ourselves in depth and with boldness, in order to fulfill, in every local church, our responsibilities of discipleship, commitment and fellowship in which love, forgiveness, reconciliation, restoration, service and exaltation are lived out daily in concrete situations, not from afar, or by remote control via satellite.

If great buildings require the best possible care in their design, the calculation and meticulous construction of each part, then how much more so the building of God! We are its living stones—He wants to gather us in our local churches to train us in the great discipline of fellowship lived in His Name. The best way to serve the Lord is in an open fellowship. Since the time when the aspostles first showed their concern for cultivation of prayer and the ministry of the Word, in the earliest days of the church, it has been well understood that the *koinonia* required a *diakonia* of spiritually capable brethren; but *diakonia* also required *koinonia*, since this was its reason for being.

Pastoral work is arduous. It requires the cultivation of fellowship as an authentic sign of Christian service. We may well ask how we can be in the faith with those whose race, traditions, popular beliefs, economic and political systems differ from our own. Only the cross can unite us. That is why the ultimate identity of the church lies in the effects of the blood of Jesus.

II. The Missionary Nature Of The Church

We are *light* to illuminate; *salt* to season; *yeast* to leaven. In this lies the dignity of our discipleship and the value of our ministry. It is a matter of insisting on a costly discipleship that demands we put our hand to the plow without looking back. It is a matter of insisting on the importance of *regeneration*. Regeneration brings about the gospel's transformation of the mind, emotions, and will of men; their families; their social relationships; the relationships between nations; and someday even the regeneration of nature itself.

The Primacy of Worship

If the goal of the Church is to be the *praise of his glory*, care must be given to liturgical teaching. Community life has grown careless and so has worship in community. And as individuals we have grown careless both in our lifestyles and also in the worship we render to the Lord. Nevertheless, in both areas, communally and personally, we are called to worship.

Almost no-one today considers the worship that millions of Christian communities around the world offer to the Lord as their number one missionary activity. But it is there that men are taught to raise their souls exclaiming with Christ himself, "Praise the Lord, Maker of heaven and earth!" (Psalm 115:12–18; Revelation 19:5) There the secular world, other religions—yes, the entire world—receive the most profound witness of two or three gathered in His name.

It would be unjustifiable to think of the nature of the Church only in terms of its terrestrial dimension, and forget its heavenly mission. Or does anyone suppose that we will cease to worship the Lord in the eternal Marriage of the Lamb?

No, the fervent worship of a Christian community demonstrates the joyful longing with which it lives out its mission in the world.

The forms of worship can be different in each situation. Martyrs over the centuries have worshipped even before death! But we need to encourage worship as *an integral element* in the primary exercise of the church's mission. As the Princeton theologian, Otto Piper, has pointed out, the theme of the whole New Testament seems to revolve around the glorious song of Philippians 2, where the church proclaims: "Every

life with its implications of involving all believers in the work of ministry. Unfortunately, many professional Christians use their trips and activities as an excuse not to become involved with the responsibilities of their local churches. This pastoral work of the church must be exercised concretely, not just in theory. It should extend as far as the neighbors that surround every Christian family and with whom every Christian community relates. Why? Because there the prophetic and praying ministry combine with the preaching of the gospel.

III. The Pastoral Nature Of The Church

"Pastoral-fraternal" work has been exercised throughout the centuries in the Christian Church. In this work, each one is his brother's keeper, because he knows the common fatherhood of Him who is indeed in the prayer of Jesus.

The criterion of this work is the *upbuilding of the body of Christ*. Every word and action is ruled by this principle. It channels the godly influences of the Holy Spirit so that all the ligaments of the body may be strengthened (Ephesians 4:16; Colossians 2:19). Unity and mission are renewed in each as part of the whole.

It is difficult to maintain pastoral work in a numerically growing congregation. Typically, insufficient time is spent in discipling one by one those whom the Lord is adding to the church. We must be alert, because spiritual growth as well as growth in the capacity to give and give of oneself is essential for every Christian, so that the gospel may continue to spread throughout the world.

We must see to it that the influence of the Holy Spirit in the renewing of each church member grows into a real vision of the Kingdom and world-wide mission.

The People of God in Pastoral Counselling

In the complexity of today's world, pastoral counsel is needed to define problems and possible solutions. Thus, information is supplemented by analysis, and analysis in turn is supplemented by counsel as to how to use biblical knowledge with precision, in order to illuminate the chaos through which the world moves. Here, it counts to be the light of the world, lights of the kingdom which reveal the powers that try to hide in various human subterfuges.

Another task is that of the *identification* of problems, in order to attack them with the weapons of spiritual warfare, knowing what we are attacking. If God sends us among the 160 nations of the world, what role do we as Christians play among them, according to the possibilities which stir in each one of us? At times the pastoral burden seems so great that we are tempted to avoid it. Nevertheless the Lord sends us to the world.

For ease of understanding, we make a distinction between pastors as leaders, and lay people as church members. But in the New Testament, the *laos* of God is composed of all the redeemed. The pastorate is a guiding function, in keeping with the image of the flock; and the people are seen as a responsibility guided in the fear of God. Therefore when we speak of *laos* we must consider it as a whole, a totality, in the perspective of the Kingdom. Herein lies the great responsibility of the "fraternal pastorate" that the whole church is to exercise in the heart of the world.

As the people of God, the Church must prepare itself and grow in the knowledge of the will of God, in order to fulfill its ministry in every context. The church ought to exercise its pastoral influence by being a guide to love. Forgiveness, reconciliation, restoration, service, and exaltation. In this way it will affect economic relations, judicial determinations, political decisions, and ideological undercurrents. Every Christian is a child of the Kingdom in a world which requires the godly influence of the gospel.

The Pastoral Programs of the Church

The pastoral work of the Church guides and involves the people of God. Their responsibility is to clarify problems by identifying the current fields of struggle, and then to develop programs which influence these situations with the power of the Holy Spirit. The struggle demands tactics and strategies. But after we have designed them carefully, we must commend them to the Lord who has the final word.

No program works without adequately prepared people of proven loyalty. That is why the *training of leaders* is a first priority. They must be trained to define problems, identify battlegrounds, and bring the power of the Holy Spirit to bear, using each Christian and all available resources.

To fulfill God's purpose in the Church as well as in the world there are many para-church agencies. Thanks to their economic resources and organizational structure, they have opportunity to influence many fields. Their social, political, economic and ideological activities have affected evangelical missionary work in many countries.

Assistance from para-church agencies is welcome, if it is given in a spirit of brotherly respect and not from a presumptuous authoritarianism. The agencies are to be of aid, support, help, and encouragement, but they should not do business like powerful corporations. This ought to be so at every level: whether aiding in disaster relief, encouraging leadership, performing church work or youth work, or helping orphans or handicapped children.

Crises in the Pastoral Care of the Churches

The present crisis of the Church is in the exercise of its "pastoral-fraternal" work. The Church confronts a mass of confusing demands that make the identification of the real battlegrounds difficult for its leaders. It confronts an avalanche of powerfully supported propaganda that dislodges, neutralizes, or obscures its influence on its members. It confronts conflicting loyalties that tend to weaken its programs, or absorb leadership in local concerns; it confronts the difficulty of channeling the work of para-church agencies, so that they may be a support rather than an obstacle in the proclamation of the gospel. And, finally, it confronts the lack of true information about the world, history, man, and the very activities of the church itself.

The pastoral work of the Church requires that it clarify the meaning of the Christian faith, as it did in the first century; identify the crises of unity, mission and renewal that have occurred lately, and channel its resources to solve current problems.

We must adequately understand the needs of today so that as a Church we can serve in a variety of relevant ways. Whether it is at a personal or institutional level, we must exercise pastoral care, we must share as a congregation, and we must bear suffering as brethren. Then the reality of our faith will penetrate and transform the reality of the world.

Dr. Roland Gutierrez is pastor of a Baptist Church in Mexico City.

SECTION II

The Church as the Kingdom Community

5

The Church and the Kingdom of God: A Theological Reflection

PETER KUZMIČ

1. Introduction

The Kingdom of God and the Church of Jesus Christ are two key New Testament concepts, both crucial for the understanding of God's plan for humanity and central to the fulfilment of his redemptive purpose. While the Church cannot be identified with the Kingdom, for (as we shall show later) the latter is a larger and more comprehensive term, the two are nevertheless in close correlation and cannot be separated either. It may be significant to point out that the very saying of Jesus from which the theme *I Will Build My Church* is taken brings the Church and the Kingdom together. Peter's divinely revealed confession that Jesus is Messiah and God's Son provides the context in which Jesus for the first time reveals His intention to build "my Church" (*ekklēsia mou*) and promises the keys of the "Kingdom of Heaven" (*basileia ton ouranon*). This intention of Jesus is stated in connection with apostolic authority which is to be determinative for the spiritual destiny of mankind, as His plan "to build" is carried out on the basis of His work and their apostolic ministry.

The Church in Relation to the Kingdom

What exactly is the relationship between the Kingdom of God that Jesus preached and the Church He founded? It is of immense importance for us as we discuss the nature and the mission of the Church to understand the intentions of Jesus. I am somewhat concerned that in our evangelical and evangelistic activism we are tempted to put the cart before the horse. We must understand who we *are* before we can know what we are to *do*. It is imperative for us to examine both our conscious and our hidden assumptions in the full light of the divine plan and purpose, taking into account the totality of Scriptural teaching, so that our task may first of all be our obedient understanding of His task and that our mission may naturally proceed from the quality of our spiritual nature and being. *Acting* must be a natural outgrowth of *being*. The mission of God carried out in our world requires the people of God. The shining of the light in the world presupposes light, and the salty effect on the earth results from the quality of the salt.

We gratefully acknowledge the growth of the Church around the globe and joyfully celebrate the redeeming victories of Christ and His people in diverse contexts of our needy world. At the same time, we must face up to the fact that in many places the credibility of the Church is seriously undermined, that the Church is questioned, criticized, attacked, and here and there even brutally persecuted. The Church is seriously challenged in its mission and even in its very existence by the highly competitive and militant resurgence of Islam. It is criticized by the Marxists as offering an "opiate" to the people and thereby fostering the enslavement of the exploited masses who would otherwise work for the social and political liberation which they certainly deserve. Many in the Third World still see the Church as an export of Western civilization and culture and as an instrument of the powerful and superior. In the West, the working classes, the young and the intellectuals have (by and large) long been alienated from the churches, which tend to be predominantly either bourgeois or peasant-type, and the very make-up of a society supposedly built on Christian principles is undergoing a cultural and moral disintegration of unprecedented proportions.

The Church known to the world appears to have lost the keys to the Kingdom of God. As a result many, especially the young, seem to be saying, "Jesus Yes, Church No."

Was the Church a mistake? Or as Hans Küng phrased it, was it "a rather poor substitute for the Kingdom"?[1] Those who think so, because of the discrepancy they see between Jesus' life and proclamation and the empirical reality of most Christian communities, tend rather unfairly to cite the oft-quoted formula of A. Loisy: "Jesus proclaimed the Kingdom of God, and what came was the Church."[2]

Evangelicals rightly emphasize the authority and reliability of the Scriptures and the importance of the teaching of Jesus as recorded in them. This logically leads to searching the Scriptures and striving for faithful obedience to Jesus. Given such a commitment, it is clear that a proper understanding of the Church is possible only when the framework of Jesus' teaching on the Kingdom of God is its primary point of reference and central concern. For the Kingdom of God is "both the starting point and the goal of the Church."[3]

Speaking of the Kingdom as related to the Church means primarily to speak of the Reign of Christ exercised over and through the community called by His Name. That Reign of Christ in the present has, however, two most important points of reference. The first is a foundational one, the past Christ-event, encompassing the incarnation, the earthly life and ministry of Jesus and their culmination in His substitutionary death and victorious resurrection. The Kingdom came in the person of Jesus, and the Church is the result of that coming of the King.

The second point of reference is still in the future and will find its fulfilment in the return of Christ which will bring about the completion of the Kingdom and the absorption of the Church into it. What was *already* begun when Jesus inaugurated the Kingdom is *yet* to be fully realized when He comes in power and glory.

It is within this two-advent structure of salvation history that the Church exists "between the times." It has always to *look back* as it is built on the foundation laid by Christ and the apostles while it also *looks forward*, fully cognizant of the fact that while it "builds," it is *His* Church and He will come both to complete and to judge it (cf. 1 Cor. 3:10–15).

The Church has to learn to work because of what He has already done and wait for what He will yet do. As soon as it loses one of these perspectives it has become unfaithful. It must learn to live in the present tension produced by the overlapping of the old and the new age, knowing that although it works within the old it belongs to the new, and its work in the old is on the new's behalf.

The parameters of this christological understanding of salvation history, Scripturally based, provide the framework for a right understanding of the nature and mission of the Church as related to the central concern of Jesus—the Kingdom of God. They will therefore serve as the basic outline of this chapter. However, before we proceed to the main body of the chapter, let us briefly, and of necessity only partially, review the treatment of the topic in the post-apostolic history of the Church.

The Kingdom in Post-Apostolic History

In the first two centuries the Kingdom of God was largely interpreted either in eschatological and millenarian terms or in terms of the inner spirituality of individual believers. The Church was the present reality while the Kingdom was viewed as a hope belonging almost exclusively to the eschatological future, or as an individual's enjoyment of God's blessings. While the Christian Church, despite its advances, was still a minority suffering persecution at the hands of imperial powers, it strove to be the "pure church"[4] withdrawing from the world and awaiting the future coming of the Kingdom of God to vindicate its cause.[5]

The Constantinian reversal provided the religio-political context within which it became possible to think of the Church and the Kingdom in more closely correlated terms. The theologians of the Byzantine court developed the theology of the Christian *imperium* under the slogan "one God, one Logos, one Emperor, one Empire." The Kingdom of God came to be seen as the *Corpus Christianum,* ruled by the *regnum* and *sacerdotum.* The Church became a State Church, the servant of the interests of the Empire. Both the Eastern imperial theology and the Western episcopal theocracy reduced the Kingdom of God to the terrestrial realities of rule and power by Pope and Emperor. Although Augustines's thinking is more profound and more discerning, even he in his *De Civitate Dei* was tempted to identify the Kingdom of God with the Church. Not only the Church triumphant, but also the Church militant, became almost synonymous with the Kingdom. Augustine explicitly stated that "the Church even now is the Kingdom of Christ and the Kingdom of heaven."[6] The Medieval Church indiscriminately followed Augustine in identifying the visible ecclesiastical system with the Kingdom of God and in applying such views to sanction the unholy alliance of throne and altar. Such thinking and the subsequent alliance of Church and State led to tragic consequences, such as when serious attempts were made to create by force a "pure" Holy Christian Empire in which there was room for neither non-Christians nor Christian heretics. At worst the "holy" Crusades replaced the mission of the Church totally, and at best they were seen as equally important to the extension of the Kingdom of God.

The Reformers identified the Kingdom of God with the invisible Church. Ladd summarizes the view of the Reformers, although at some risk of over-simplification, by saying: "The Kingdom was to them the reign of God in the hearts of the redeemed and was therefore essentially a religious concept and primarily a present reality."[7] Yet it needs to be noticed that there is considerable divergence between the views of the Reformers with respect to the Kingdom. Zwingli's view is colored by his humanist conception of it. Luther varies, drawing heavily upon some aspects of Augustine's thinking, elaborating the christocentric emphasis of his own teaching, depending on the state for protection, and suiting his theological polemics to his own struggles against the more radical segments of the Reformation. Calvin has a well developed theology of the Kingdom of God, pointing to a christocracy characterised by (Geneva-style) Church control over the State.[8]

Christians following the Reformation tradition viewed the Church as it is defined in the Augsburg Confession: "the congregation of saints in which the Gospel is rightly taught and the Sacraments are rightly administered."[9] This definition of the Church as merely *congregatio sanctorum* (and *fidelium*) has rightly been criticized as partial and defective on two basic grounds.[10] First, it fails to relate the Church to its foundation in the Kingdom of God. Second, it leads to an ecclesiocentricity which forgets that the Church has a missionary function in the world. No wonder we find little emphasis on world mission in the period of Protestant orthodoxy. A full biblical ecclesiology knows no *congregatio* without mission.

The Modern Debate

The debate about the Kingdom of God over the last 150 years has been largely academic and in most cases somewhat divorced from the ecclesiological issues. Albrecht Ritschl (1822–1889) understood the Kingdom-concept in terms of the prevalent evolutionary understanding of history, and interpreted it as a present reality and force behind the progress which would find its full realization in this world. In the latter part of the nineteenth century Ritschl's thinking, presented within the framework of Neo-Kantian philosophy, was the most influential view. Skydsgaard summarized this period as follows:

> An immanent and spiritualistic conception of the Kingdom of God prevailed, which corresponded well with the optimistic view of man and of our world so typical of that period. Christianity was turned into a glorified *Kulturprotestantismus*, in many ways essentially a bourgeois phenomenon, which suited well the religious ideology of humanism.[11]

A revolution in New Testament studies at the turn of the century generated a strong reaction against this basically non-eschatological Ritschlian view of the Kingdom of God. Johannes Weiss,[12] Albert Schweitzer,[13] and others rediscovered the eschatological element of Jesus' teaching on the Kingdom of God. Their view (which later came to be known as "consistent eschatology") discounts the concept of an already present Kingdom in Jesus' teaching, claiming that He points only to an entirely future, apocalyptic reality which is to arrive by a cataclysmic inbreaking during Jesus' own life time.

C. H. Dodd,[14] the father of "realized eschatology", represents the opposing view to that of Weiss and Schweitzer, arguing that the apocalyptic elements in Jesus' teaching are to be taken as merely symbolic (the early Church having been mistaken in interpreting them literally), for the Kingdom of God is already a present fact with no future fulfilment. "The *eschaton* has moved from the future to the present, from the sphere of expectation into that of realized experience."[15]

The school of liberal Protestant exegesis that flourished until recently generally considered the Church to be a latter creation with no relation to the historical Jesus and His teaching on the Kingdom of God. Such a negative attitude toward the Church resulted from an unhistorical interpretation of the work and mission of Jesus Himself. (Catholic ecclesiology responded to such liberal challenges with the affirmation that "Jesus of Nazareth did found a clearly defined ecclesiastical organization and put Peter at its head as a kind of replacement for Jesus.")[16]

A number of serious exegetical and theological studies have attempted to recover the biblical balance and have synthesized the views of "thoroughgoing eschatologists" (like Weiss and Schweitzer) and the "realized eschatologists" (like Dodd and his followers).[17] We mention in passing especially the name of Oscar Cullmann,[18] who has been very influential in evangelical circles.

The recent renaissance of evangelical New Testament scholarship has much for which to be commended. The late George Eldon Ladd must be credited for bringing back to the evangelical agenda the topic of the Kingdom of God.[19] This has been unduly neglected in reaction to the one-sided approach to the topic typical of the "Social Gospel" movement and other liberal and secularized abuses of the theme.[20] Though there is still much confusion and lack of theological precision, evangelical thinkers are beginning to explore with great urgency the theme of the Kingdom of God and how it relates to both the Church and the world. Much study needs yet to be done in this area.

The most significant ecumenical treatment of the topic was the WCC sponsored conference, "Your Kingdom Come", held in May 1980 in Melbourne. The findings of that important gathering have been widely publicized. Evangelicals have discussed them extensively, and though evaluations vary, the Melbourne Conference has been criticized for its lack of biblical foundation, for one-sided (socio-political) thinking and activism, and for insufficient concern for the billions who yet need to hear the saving Gospel of the Kingdom of God.

2. The Church and the Community of the King: The Past Christ-event

The announcement of the nearness of the Kingdom of God, first by John the Baptist and then by James, sounds strange to our modern ears. We are not used to this monarchical concept or the manner of its introduction and are unsure of its meaning. It is obvious from the Gospel accounts, however, that the contemporaries of Jesus were acquainted with the concept and were not initially surprised or unclear as to its meaning. They had awaited the message and longed for the messenger for some time.

The Jewish Expectations of the Kingdom

Having suffered at the hands of foreign oppressors for several centuries the Jews of the intertestamental period clung to the Old Testament promises of the deliverance to come. They expected a Messiah who would bring about an apocalyptic reversal, defeating the forces of evil and restoring justice to the chosen people of God. They pictured a

Davidic King, a mighty conqueror over the enemies of Israel, a heavenly supernatural Son of Man who would come with "authority, glory and sovereign power" and whose "dominion will not pass away, and his kingdom never be destroyed" (Dan. 7:14). This idea of the coming Kingdom with its great reversal of evil and restoration of justice fired the imagination of the oppressed Jews and inspired their political hopes. They were looking for the Kingdom of God (cf. Lk 2:25,38; 23:51) and the time was ripe when John the Baptist appeared with his preparatory and prophetic message, "Repent, for the Kingdom of Heaven is near" (Matt. 3:2).

The same message was adopted and further elaborated by Jesus (Matt. 4:17) and, upon His commission, proclaimed by the apostles (Matt. 10:7). The Kingdom truly came in the very person of Jesus, who was the Son of Man of Daniel's vision. It was clear, however, that the popular expectations of the Jews were not met by what Jesus had to offer. He did perform miracles; and there were moments like the feeding of the five thousand when they were certain that He was the one for whom they were waiting; and so in their zealous impatience they even tried to make Him a King by force (John 6:15). Even His disciples were not immune to these false hopes, both before and after the resurrection (cf. Luke 24:21, Acts 1:6). But He did not come as a mighty king with glory and splendor, but rather as a man among men, in humility, poverty and weakness. His mission was different from their expectations. He was not to be their political liberator and king, nor was He to fulfil their nationalistic hopes and bring them material blessings.

Because of a special covenantal relationship, the Jews were expected to be the natural "sons of the Kingdom" (Matt. 8:12).[21] Jesus was mindful of this and the Kingdom was at first offered only "to the lost sheep of Israel" (Matt. 10:5–7). But they rejected it and He made it clear to their religious leaders that "the Kingdom of God will be taken away from you and given to a people who will produce its fruit" (Matt. 21:43). The blessings and privileges along with the responsibilities that earlier belonged to Israel were to be inherited by a new people of God, the Church of Jesus Christ.

The Kingdom of God and Eternal Life

The public ministry of Jesus begins with the proclamation that God's appointed time has come—"the Kingdom of God is near"—and the call to repentance and faith in this good news (Mark 1:15). In the first three Gospels the term "Kingdom" is used 121 times. Strictly speaking, *basileia* and the Aramaic *malkuth* should not be translated as "kingdom' but rather more exactly as "reign", "rule", "sovereignty" or "kingship". For it is not primarily a question of the *place* of God's rule but rather of

His reign itself. We shall use these terms interchangeably, always referring to the general reign of God, in particular as exercised by the Lord Jesus Christ over and through the Messianic community—His Church.

The idea of the Kingdom of God—this "master-thought" of Jesus, as it has been called—occupies a place of supreme importance in His teaching and mission. It is *the* theme; it is the Gospel, the Good News of forgiveness, joy and peace; it is the *summum bonum*, "the pearl of great value" (Matt. 12:45–56) for which everything is to be sacrificed; it is to be sought above everything else and it brings with it everything else (Matt. 6:33). Thus it is to be not only sought after but also prayed for. "Your Kingdom come" is a prayer that God may reign and His will be done on earth as it is in heaven.

The Kingdom focuses on the King, for it is His person and work that are the heart and center of the Gospel. With Him and in Him the new age of salvation has come and the gift of life and forgiveness is freely offered. The only conditions for entrance into this new realm of blessings are repentance (change of mind and lifestyle) and faith (personal trust) in the One who is King. Such receptivity to the redemptive activity of God's rule working among men in Christ brings new life with new values.

In the discourse following the encounter with the rich young ruler Jesus makes it clear that "the Kingdom of God" and "eternal life" are interchangeable terms.[22] John the Evangelist picks up the concept of the Kingdom under the theme of "life" or "life eternal", another thoroughly eschatological concept. Except for twice in the conversation with Nicodemus (John 3:3,5), he regularly replaces the Synoptic term "Kingdom of God" with "life" or "life eternal". It is beyond the scope of this paper to argue that there is no difference in meaning between the two forms, and that what we find here is a superb example of contextualization by one who skilfully and responsibly adapts Jewish eschatology for broader Christian use. We will give only one example by comparing

3:3,5– "unless a man is born again [from above], he cannot [*see*] *enter the Kingdom of God*" [*ou dunatoi eiselthein eis ten basileian tou theou*]	with	3:3,6– "whoever believes in the Son has *eternal life* [*zōen aiōnion*], but whoever rejects the Son will not see *life* [*zōen*]."

Both refer to the Age to Come which has broken into the present, offering its blessings to those who are receptive and bringing a judgment upon those who reject the free gift of life in the New Age. George Ladd has summarized the relation of *life* and *Kingdom* in the eschatological perspective of God's rule as follows:

> If Kingdom is the gift of life bestowed upon His people when He manifests His rule in eschatological glory, and if God's Kingdom is also God's rule invading history before the eschatological consummation, it follows that we may expect God's rule in the present to bring a preliminary blessing to His people.[23]

Jesus understood it as His mission to preach the Kingdom and the days of His ministry are characterized as the time in which "the good news of the Kingdom of God is being preached" (Luke 16:16). When shortly after His inaugural and programmatic sermon in Nazareth the people of Capernaum, impressed by His miracles, "tried to keep him from leaving them", he told them, "I must preach the good news of the Kingdom of God to other towns also, because that is why I was sent" (Luke 4:42–43).

In Jesus, then, we see the Kingdom manifested in two ways: in the Kingdom preaching-teaching and in the Kingdom's working miraculously (healings, exorcisms). The entrance of the New Age into the present Old Age is verbally announced and powerfully demonstrated by His person in acts of mercy defeating the powers of evil. The same pattern is evident as Jesus sends out His disciples with the twofold task of proclaiming the Kingdom and performing the signs that are characteristic of its arrival—healing the sick and casting out demons (see Luke 10:9, 11, 17). In obedience to His command, and empowered by His kingly authority, the disciples carried the message and demonstrated the power of the Kingdom in the same way that He did. And yet He reminds them that this is only an inauguration and that what is even more important is the full consummation of His rule in heaven where their "names are written" (Luke 10:20).

On one occasion within the controversy that arose from a victorious power-encounter, he explicitly announced that His victory over demons was the evidence that "the Kingdom of God has come to you" (Luke 12:20; Matt. 12:27). And to the question of the Pharisees as to "when the Kingdom of God would come", He replied, *"The Kingdom of God is among you"* (Luke 17:20–21).

The Church and the Keys of the Kingdom

"I Will Build My Church" (Matt. 16:18) is one of the only two cases in the Gospels where the word *ekklēsia* appears. It is no wonder that the authenticity of this saying of Jesus has been questioned by many who attempt to explain it away as a later ecclesiastical addition. There are, however, 114 occurrences of *ekklēsia* in the New Testament, mostly referring to Christian community, either universal or local. Does that mean that in the teaching of Jesus the "Kingdom" concept was central while the "Church" occupied only an insignificantly small place? Does it further suggest that in the apostolic age the Kingdom was relegated to a less important place and actually replaced by the Church as a sociologically identifiable body of believers? Did early Christians fail to comprehend Jesus' teaching about the Kingdom and so dilute it by substituting for it a more easily manageable human institution? Or did they invent the Church because of their embarrassment over the delay of the expected *parousia*?

Here it is important to note that, while the term *ekklēsia* is not often on Jesus' lips, the community of believers is implied throughout His message and is referred to in other forms. As F. A. Hort warned long ago, "This is one of the cases in which it is dangerous to measure teaching about things by the range of the names applied to things."[24] The very concept of a Messiah implies the Messianic community. The Great Commission's command to disciple and baptize clearly points to Jesus envisioning the continuation and growth of the *ekklēsia*. The technical term "The Twelve" may be taken simply to mean "disciples", and the whole concept of discipleship is certainly central to Jesus' teaching and to the conception of the Church. It is safe to conclude that "wherever we find disciples and discipleship in the Gospels, there we are dealing with what was a direct preparation for the founding of the *Ecclesia*."[25]

What is the relationship between the statement of Jesus "I will build my Church" and the following promise "I will give you the keys of the Kingdom of Heaven"? The very fact that Jesus speaks of the Church and the Kingdom in a logical sequence of thought must imply that the two are closely associated. Some will go so far in interpreting Matthew 16 as to claim a complete identification of the Church and the Kingdom. Others will point out that they are mentioned together because they are closely related as "two aspects of the same institution which Jesus will 'build'."[26] O. T. Allis states that "the expressions 'kingdom of heaven' and 'church' are in most respects at least equivalent, and that the two institutions are co-existent and largely co-extensive."[27] In further elaborating this thought, Allis then arrives at a debatable theological conclusion. He affirms: "The Kingdom and the Church are institutions which are both present in the world today; and they are so closely related, so nearly identical, that it is impossible to be in the one and not in the other."[28]

The question of the text can be properly settled only by looking at the context. The immediate context is Peter's confession of Jesus' Messiahship at Caesarea Philippi. The broader context, as provided by Matthew, is the preceding demand of the Pharisees and Sadducees (prompted by their expectations and doubts) that Jesus authenticate Himself by "showing them a sign from heaven" and Jesus' subsequent warning against them. The confession itself is the beginning of the disclosure of the "Messianic secret," namely that the true nature of Jesus' mission would lead him not to a national restoration of Israel and political crowning but rather to His own death in Jerusalem. From now on it is not the crowds that hear His message, but the select group of disciples who are instructed as to His purpose—an outcome so different from the popular expectations of Israel.

The keys of the Kingdom have something to do with the announcement of the Church. From now on the Kingdom is no longer active through Israel. A new people has been entrusted with the keys to the Kingdom. The Church is to take over the role of God's witness and redemptive agent in the world. The keys which are to open or close the doors leading to the enjoyment of the blessings of the New Age are now taken away from the leaders of the Jewish religion and entrusted into the hands of the apostles of Christ. The words "bind" and "loose" are actually rabbinical *termi technici* used to describe the rabbi's authority in doctrinal matters and simply mean "decide with authority". (It is beyond the intention of this chapter to provide a detailed exegesis of this passage or to speculate as to the further meaning of either of these terms—or for that matter of the term *petra* ["rock"]).[29]

Whatever our view, the Church is actually "built on the foundation of the apostles and prophets with Christ Jesus Himself as the leader and chief cornerstone" (Eph. 2:20). Peter, in confessing the Messiahship of Jesus, speaks as a representative of the apostles who became the foundation on which the church in its initial stages was to be erected. The intention of Jesus was certainly not—as traditional Catholicism interpreted it—to determine ecclesiastical power structures, "but rather to indicate the connection between the Church and the Kingdom and the conditions under which the one might be identified with the other."[30] In addition, the promise of the keys to Peter meant that in "calling Jesus Lord by the Holy Ghost, was the ideal of the Kingdom realized."[31]

Our interpretation of the meaning of the text is aided and clarified by comparing it to Luke 11:52 where we find a somewhat similar context in Jesus' condemnation of the Pharisees and Scribes. Because "you have taken away the key to knowledge, you yourselves have not entered, and you have hindered those who were entering."[32] The Jews had the keys of knowledge that leads to the Reign of God (cf. Rom. 3:2, "They have been entrusted with the very words of God"), but now they have rejected the King Himself. Therefore the Church becomes "a chosen people, a royal priesthood, a holy nation, a people belonging to God" (1 Pet. 2:9).

The Mid-Point of the Old and New Ages

As we have already pointed out, the Jewish expectations of a Messiah who was to be a political liberator, apocalyptic Son of Man and Davidic King were not met by Jesus. His final journey to Jerusalem ended not on David's throne, but on a scandalous cross. All four evangelists record the inscription of the title on the cross, *ho basileus tōn Ioudaiōn,* "the King of the Jews". When questioned by Pilate He made it clear, however, that His "Kingdom is not of this world" (John 18:36). The Jews chose Caesar (John 19:12, 15) and had the spiritual King crucified. His death, however, was divinely purposed so as to establish the basis of a *new covenant* for a new people of God, who by His merit, by His grace, and by their subsequent response of faith, would experience the forgiveness of sins and enter the "[eternal] life" or blessings of the Kingdom. The redeemed people are now "purchased people", the way to life leads through His death, and He has the full right on the basis of the price paid to call this new people "my Church".

The Church is an eschatological community because it is a christological reality. The central point in God's redemptive activity is the cross of Jesus Christ accompanied by His victorious resurrection. It is the mid-point of salvation history in which previous anticipations find their fulfilment and which is decisively determinative for the end-point of human history.

The "Gospel of the Kingdom" is inseparable from the "word of the cross" (*logos tou staurou*), for it is the message of the cross that brings salvation. For Paul, it is the cross that represents both the power (*dynamis*) and wisdom (*sophia*) of God (1 Cor. 1:18–24).

It is at the cross that we see Jesus as "our High Priest" (cf. Hebrews). All the aspects of His threefold office of Prophet, Priest and King are foundational for the Kingdom of God as it finds its expression in the community of believers who are called by His name. He is not only the Prophet proclaiming the Kingdom. He is the King Himself. He is not only the Priest who administers "once forever" and intercedes "unceasingly". He is also the Head of His Church and the Ruler of the universe.

We shall do well to listen to the admonition of Comenius, who well understood the need for the "total Christ" to be present among His followers. In his "Bequest of the Unity of Brethren", he says:

> Christ must find among you not only a pulpit for His prophetic office; not only an altar for His office as priest and bishop; but likewise a throne and a sceptre for His kingly office.[33]

The unique Christ-event of the cross and resurrection mark the beginning of the New Age and the beginning of the end of the Old Age. The disobedience of the first Adam brought the sentence of death upon humanity; the obedience unto death on the cross of the second Adam brings about the defeat of the powers of death and makes Him the Head of a new humanity, gathered in His Church.

Now the early Church expresses its faith in Christ the King and pledges its allegiance to Him in that short yet powerful confession,

"Jesus is *Lord*." The early christological hymn brings Christ's pre-existence, incarnation, crucifixion, resurrection, and the final consummation together as a short history of God's redemptive activity and rule recognized in the acknowledgement of his Lordship:

> Who, being in very nature God, did not consider equality with God something to be grasped, but made himself nothing, taking the very nature of a servant, being made in human likeness. And being found in appearance as a man, he humbled himself and became obedient to death, even death on a cross! Therefore God exalted him to the highest place and gave him the name that is above every name, that at the name of Jesus every knee should bow. (Phil. 2:6–10, NIV)

The King is thus at the same time the Suffering Servant (*cf.* the four "Servant Songs" of Isaiah) who gives His life functioning as the Priest and the supreme sacrifice, and He who, defeating the powers of death, being the "firstfruit" and guarantee of the life to come, becomes the Lord. Thus He, the risen Lord, in the context of the Great Commission declares, "All authority in heaven and on earth has been given to me" (Matt. 23:18). His ascension ended the short period of the post-resurrection appearances and placed Him in the royal position "at the right hand of God" (Col. 3:1).

The theme of the Kingdom of God, although used less frequently than in the Synoptic Gospels, is not totally absent from the apostolic proclamation.[34] The term *basileia* appears eight times in Acts and fourteen times in the Pauline writings, and the context reveals that the concept of Kingdom is of major importance in the preaching of Paul, and essentially synonymous with its use by Jesus. It is clear, however, that Paul took the original messianic language of the Kingdom of God as used by Jesus, with which the Jews were familiar, and translated and expressed it with a "dynamic equivalent", with which his new audience of the wider mission field was acquainted. We have seen that John more or less replaced the form "Kingdom of God" with "eternal life", retaining a continuity of meaning. Paul finds the best expression in a term that was widely used in a number of convergent areas: the Septuagint Greek Old Testament in which Yahweh is *Lord*, Roman politics marked by Caesar's claim to be the sole *Lord*, the heathen temple and the slave market. The baptismal confession that "Jesus (Christ) is Lord"[35] becomes the equivalent of the acknowledgment of Christ's Kingship and the point of entrance into the Kingdom of God.

K. L. Schmidt summarizes this aspect of the proclamation of the early Church as follows:

> We can see why the aposotolic and the post-apostolic Church of the NT did not speak much of the *basileia tou theou* explicitly, but always emphasized it implicitly by its reference to the *kurios Iesous Kristos*. It is not true that it now substituted the Church (*ekklesia*) for the Kingdom as preached by Jesus of Nazareth. On the contrary, faith in the Kingdom of God persists in the post-Easter experience of Christ.'[36]

The apostle Paul brings the whole spectrum of different aspects of the Lordship of Christ into focus and relates it to the Church as he prays for the Ephesians "that the God of our *Lord* Jesus Christ" may give them the "Spirit of wisdom and revelation" so that they might know Him better and have enlightened hearts to "know the hope, the riches and his incomparably great power." "That power is like the working of his mighty strength, which he exerted in Christ when he raised him from the dead and seated him at his right hand in the heavenly realms, far above all rule and authority, power and dominion, and every title that can be given, not only in the present age but also in the one to come. And God placed all things under his feet and appointed him to be head over everything for the Church which is his body, the fullness of him who fills everything in every way" (Eph. 1:19–23).

The Church as the Community of the Spirit

The resurrection of Jesus was the key event ushering the powers of the Age to Come into the present age by transforming the finality of the death of Jesus into a triumph over it. It was a significant event that marked off the disciples of Jesus as the community who believed in the Risen Lord. The Risen One has, however, announced another "end-time" event to follow shortly—the outpouring of the Spirit, promised for the "last days" (Acts 2:17). However we interpret the "Johannine Pentecost" (John 20:22), it is clear that John emphasizes a theological continuum between the cross, resurrection, ascension and the outpouring of the Spirit. The Spirit is to "replace" Jesus as the "other Paraclete" (John 14:16) and is given as a guarantee of the efficacious continuity of Christ's work in the community of His believers.

The representative group of 120 disciples was gathered in Jerusalem in direct obedience to the command of the risen Lord and bound together by their common belief in Him. The fulfillment of His promise was the experience of the mighty, visible and audible manifestation of the divine power as "all of them were filled with the Holy Spirit" (Acts 2:4). The Pentecost-event was crucial for the launching and constitution of the Christian Church, the new eschatological community bound together by their loyalty to the risen Lord and the common experience of the Spirit. The beginning of the Age of the Spirit is coterminous and coextensive with the Age of the Church, the Community of the Spirit. Like the resurrection of Jesus, Pentecost was seen by early Christians "as the precursor of the end" and as "the beginning of a whole new epoch of salvation-history."[37] The early Christian community itself tasted the power of the age to come, and it is not impossible that the outpouring of the Holy Spirit and the beginning of the Church was at first seen by them as a fulfilment of Jesus' words about the coming of the Kingdom of God. It is this Kingdom that is now predominantly manifested in and through the Church as the community of the Spirit.

The power of the Spirit was to make the new community a witnessing, missionary-oriented movement (*cf.* Acts 1:8). The Book of Acts shows that a church is essentially a community of the Spirit, experiencing at its very inception a last-day-like harvest and taking the Gospel to the ends of the world. This mission of the Church is not something that is carefully planned and executed according to a preconceived strategy of the apostolic leadership of the Jerusalem church. It is a spontaneous Spirit-driven and Spirit-controlled movement proceeding from the nature of the Spirit-filled community. The mission of the early church energized by the Holy Spirit universalizes the mission of Jesus, using the "keys of the kingdom" to open the gates of divine promise to the people of the new covenant from all nations and races.

3. The Church Participates in the Kingdom: The Present Reign of Christ

The Church is Not the Kingdom

In the previous chapter we have shown that the Church is the result of the coming of the King, the Lord Jesus, who is its founder. The Kingdom of God which Jesus announced and brought is of central importance for a right understanding of the Church and is its most dominant point of reference within God's redemptive economy. "The dogma of the Kingdom ought to be the main dogma of the Church, and the main dogma for every individual member of it."[38] Or, as W. Pannenberg puts it, "The doctrine of the church begins not with the Church but with the Kingdom of God."[39] The Church owes its existence to the Kingdom of God and "both conceptions belong closely together, so that it is hardly possible to reach a clear understanding of the nature of the Church without relating it to the basic New Testament conception of the Kingdom of God."[40]

A. M. Fairbairn states:

> The Kingdom is the immanent Church and the Church is the explicated Kingdom, and nothing alien to either can be in the other . . . The Church is the kingdom come into living souls and the society they constitute." And further: "The Kingdom is the Church viewed from above; the Church is the Kingdom seen from below.[41]

But while it is true that the biblical Church has to be defined in terms of its relationship to the rule of Christ, it is nonetheless impossible to identify the two as Fairbairn does. The Kingdom is a broader and more comprehensive concept and cannot be contained by the Church; nor has the Church any right to claim the Kingdom as its present possession.

However inseparable their relationship may be, the Church is not the Kingdom of God. The regenerate Church in which Christ is acknowledged as Lord and the life and power of the Holy Spirit are operative is at its ultimate, only the nearest approximation and the most authentic communal expression of the Kingdom of God in history.

The apostles were sent, like Jesus Himself, to preach the Gospel of the Kingdom. Several times the Book of Acts summarizes their proclamation with this term. The content of their proclamation of the Kingdom of God is usually identified with the *saving name of Jesus,* but never with the Church. In Samaria "they believed Philip as he preached the good news of the Kingdom of God and the name of Jesus Christ" (Acts 8:12). In the synagogue at Ephesus we find Paul "arguing persuasively about the Kingdom of God" (19:8). At the very end of the book Luke gives two summaries of Paul's ministry in Rome as he ministered to Jewish leaders: He "explained and declared to them the Kingdom of God and tried to convince them about Jesus . . ." (28:23), and in the final verses, "For two whole years Paul . . . welcomed all who came to see him. Boldly and without hindrance he preached the Kingdom of God and taught about the Lord Jesus Christ" (28:30–31).

Here we see how the proclaimer and bringer of the Kingdom in the early Church became the subject of proclamation. The early Church did not preach itself; it preached the Gospel of the Kingdom, that is, the good news about Jesus Christ. In none of these nor in other passages is it possible to substitute "Church" for "Kingdom"!

The attempt to identify the Church with the Kingdom is not only unbiblical, but also highly dangerous. The history of the church provides ample evidence for this, from the Constantinian era to the present. It teaches us that whenever and wherever the Church equates itself with the Kingdom of God, it will be tempted to grasp, hold and abuse earthly power. In this connection we do well to listen to W. Pannenberg's "prophetic" insight:

> The theological identification of the Church with the Kingdom of Christ has all too often served the purposes of ecclesiastical officials who are not attuned to the Kingdom of God. Many Christians, especially Church leaders, like to think they are in possession of the truth, or at least that they possess the ultimate criterion of the truth. Because they feel themselves to be so indispensably related to the very Kingdom of Christ, they fail to recognize the provisional character of all ecclesiastical organizations. They are unable to stand humbly before the coming Kingdom of God that is going to bring about the final future of the world. They are blinded to the ways in which even now, proleptically, the future manifests itself in the world (and not just in the Church, nor even always through the Church). Precisely because the Church mistakes herself for the present form of the Kingdom,

God's rule has often had to manifest itself in the secular world outside, and frequently against, the Church.[42]

The Church is the *result* of the preaching of the Kingdom of God, the fellowship of those who have experienced the power and tasted the blessings of the Kingdom. The Kingdom is its beginning, its foundation, but the Kingdom of God also remains its goal. For the Church is "the fellowship of aspirants of the Kingdom of God", as Hans Küng said, adding that "belonging to the Church is no guarantee, in this era of temptation, of belonging to the final Kingdom of God."[43] The Church is "an *anticipatory sign* of the definitive reign of God . . . The meaning of the Church does not reside in itself in what it is, but in what it is moving towards.[44]

The Cost of Entering Into the Kingdom

Biblical history is the story of God's redemptive acts directed toward the creation of a new humanity, a people who rightfully belong to Him and authentically represent Him among the nations. It is that people who recognize God as their King and constitute His royal priesthood on the earth. In the Old Testament they are called the *kehal Yahweh,* the "community [assembly] of God." The corresponding Greek term denotes the New Testament people of God as *ekklēsia tou theou* "the Church of God".

This community, addressed as "the people of God", the "Body of Christ", etc., is always a visible and identifiable company of believers on this earth. It is unfortunate and misleading that the words "Kingdom" and "Church" are nowadays frequently used as if they were autonomous entities. These concepts cannot stand on their own and if we are to understand the true nature and mission of the believing community we call "the Church", we must carefully adhere to the use of this terminology in the Scriptures. When we speak of the "Kingdom of God", the emphasis is on *God,* on His kingly power and reign, on His redeeming acts and sovereign authority. The operative word in the phrase "the Kingdom of God" is *theou.*[45] The phrase "is telling something about *God*" (the fact that he reigns), not describing something about *God* (the fact that he reigns), not describing something called 'the kingdom' . . . Reduction in modern usage to merely 'the Kingdom' is therefore questionable not only because it departs in fact from biblical usage, but primarily because it betrays a basic misunderstanding which takes 'the Kingdom of God' as a description not of God in His sovereignty, but of an identifiable 'thing'."[46]

We run a similar risk of emptying or reducing its biblical content when we speak of "the Church" without properly emphasizing that it is "the Church of God" (or "Christ"). Here the operative word is *theou* or *Christou.* The Church can rightfully be called so only if and when it recognizes the Lordship of Christ and submits to it. It is "the body of Christ" consciously living under His Headship. This new community of redeemed and forgiven people is "the elect" (*eklektoi*), called and chosen by God to be "the saints" (*hagioi*). Their origin, their very nature and their whole character are derived from the One to whom they belong, God Himself. Their character is an expression of God's character, for their life flows from the life God gives; and their mission is an extension of the mission of God's Son.

The proclamation of the good news of the arrival of the Kingdom of God in the person of Jesus of Nazareth demands a response of repentance and faith (Mark 1:15). Such a response results in the new life which God bestows. It means "being saved" or "born again", to use the most common evangelical parlance of our day. It demands a radical decision, a change of mind (*metanoia*), a transfer from the kingdom of darkness into the kingdom of the light of God's Son (Col. 1:13). Such a response to the message of the King and the subsequent change of life entailed means *entering the Kingdom of God*. This entry into the realm of the blessings of God's Kingdom is a gift; it comes at God's initiative and depends on His grace which is freely available to the sinful and undeserving. However, it is not so cheap as some evangelistic propaganda of Western evangelicalism superficially seems to suggest.

Jesus does not minimize the cost and the difficulties of entering into the Kingdom of God. It is true that the response to His message is made on an individual basis and in terms of personal acceptance. Its result, however, is not just the salvation of that individual's soul for heaven or a present sweet communion with Jesus expressed in almost private terms. Becoming a Christian, entering into the Kingdom of God, is a prospect open only to those who are willing to deny themselves and their own interests in order to acknowledge God's sovereign rule over the totality of their lives and relationships. It may entail giving up family (*cf.* Matt. 10:34–37) and wealth, as clearly demonstrated by the story of the rich young ruler (Mark 10:24ff.). These demands of the King Jesus can hardly be understood by believers who live in societies where Christian faith is culturally acceptable and respectable. It is in such contexts that the message of the Kingdom of God with all its demands is seldom heard, often diluted and frequently denied by those who claim to "know Jesus". In the proclamation the *demands* are usually replaced by promises, as if the two were not inseparably and conditionally related. "But seek first his kingdom and his righteousness, and all these things will be given to you as well" (Matt. 6:33).

Those followers of Jesus who live under totalitarian political regimes, or amongst militant Muslims, or wherever they are a faithful minority, know that belonging to Jesus the King, living under His Lordship, exacts a price. They know, as the early church knew, that serving Jesus means indifference towards the treasures and values of this world, abandoning all anxiety for trustful confidence in the heavenly Father, the King who rules even in the midst of adverse circumstances. The Church of Jesus Christ today needs to be reminded that persecution is a biblical sign of belonging to the Kingdom of God. "In fact, everyone who wants to live a godly life in Christ Jesus will be persecuted" (2 Tim. 3:12).[47] Faithful witness to Christ today does not in every case necessarily result in suffering, but H. Berkhof rightfully reminds us that suffering

> could well be a significant criterion for judging the genuineness of our words and deeds. Words that do not cost anything and deeds that are meant to make us popular have nothing to do with the apostolary firstfruit character of the people of God.[48]

The Church of Jesus Christ fulfills its mission in a fallen and antagonistic world, living in a tension produced by the overlapping of two ages, between the "already" and "not yet fully" of the Kingdom of God. Along with the present-day experience of the Church globally, this leads us to a realistic assessment of our situation. "In the world in which we live, in which every successful act of cooperation or reconciliation can be matched by cruelty and persecution on a very large scale, it is becoming very doubtful whether Christianity can register any worthwhile advance in the near future without suffering."[49] This statement was made fifteen years ago and its truthfulness has been already proven in the meantime, while we are and shall increasingly become witnesses to its relevance in our own days and in days to come.

Entering the Kingdom of God means joining the believing community, for "the spirit of the kingdom is love, and impels to fellowship."[50] Belonging to Jesus Christ means being part of that organic and authentic community which is the closest expression of the Kingdom of God on earth. It means being a member of *His* Church, built by Him and ruled by Him. It is in this new community of disciples of Jesus that the presence of God is experienced, His sovereignty acknowledged, His rule obeyed and His will carried out.

The Church is that community which God gathers by the Holy Spirit to be His own people and to be sent into the world to announce and live out the message of the King, who is the Lord Jesus. It is the company of men and women who by the very nature of their special calling are distinctively people of God, grounded in the redemptive purposes of God and sustained by His presence and power. The nature and mission of the Church are determined by this special relationship between God and His people, Christ and the Church.

The Church as the Servant of the King

In the incarnation, the King Jesus, very God, humbled Himself by "taking the very nature [form] of a servant (*doulos*)" (Phil. 2:7).

Speaking of the new kind of relationship between those who belong to His Kingdom, He emphasizes his own example which they are to follow, for He "did not come to be served, but to serve (*diakonesai*)" (Matt. 20:28; par Mark 10:45). At the Last Supper He washes the disciples' feet to challenge them to servanthood (John 13:15) and warns them not to be like "the kings of the Gentiles"; rather their leaders should be servants, even as "I am among you as one who serves." Jesus is saying this in fellowship around the table which is itself one of the signs of the arrival of the Kingdom and a pointer to its ultimate fulfilment in the *eschaton* "at my table in my kingdom." The crucial line in this discourse is "I confer on you a kingdom, just as my Father has conferred one on me" (Luke 22:29).[51]

The ministry of Jesus was marked by the threefold service of preaching, teaching and demonstrating the Good News of the Kingdom of God. He performed the signs pointing to its arrival in His own person, culminating in the ultimate act of service when he gave "his life as a ransom for many" (Mark 10:45). His exemplary ministry and the sacrifice of His life became a summons to service for all of His followers. John draws the conclusion from the sacrifice of Jesus that "we ought to lay down our lives for the brethren" (1 John 3:16).

The Church is not the Kingdom, neither can it claim a monopoly on the Kingdom of God. It will approximate the Kingdom and enjoy its blessings only in proportion to its submission to the King, as His servant. The contemporary evangelical movement, with its emphasis on individualism, its striving for measurable success, and its spirit of worldly competition in both the expansion of its programs at home and its missionary endeavors abroad, stands in grave danger of being permeated by the spirit and values of this world. To me, an outsider and relative newcomer to our global evangelical fellowship, and to many of my brethren, some of the Western-sponsored missionary and evangelistic enterprises come cross as self-serving organizations baptized with a Christian name, rather than an expression of the servant spirit of the Kingdom of God. May the Lord of the Church grant that I am wrong and forgive me if I speak unfairly.

The fact remains, however, that the true nature and mission of the Church are marked by humble service, and a recognition that we can claim no ownership of the things and people that belong to God alone. *He* is the King. We are to be His humble servants, always ready to obey His command and to do His will. Whatever exists outside this attitude has no right to be called the Church of Jesus Christ for it is out of tune with the Kingdom of God. The Kingdom demands commitment and obedience in service, following the model of the Servant-King. The nature and mission of the Church can be rightly understood, lived and practiced only in right relation to its founder and head, Jesus Christ, and in accordance with His central message about the Kingdom of God.

Only the church that is deeply rooted in—and wholly faithful to—the divine purposes disclosed in Christ will be sustained by the power of His Spirit, and effectively able to reach out in service and mission to the needy world.

The servant is known not only by his service humbly rendered to others, but also by his attitude of simple unquestioning trust and receptivity. Jesus elaborates this attitude in the Sermon on the Mount, and in His teaching that it is impossible to "receive the kingdom of God" or to "enter it" unless we are like little children (Mark 10:13–16). What a shock to find out that a great many evangelicals who adhere to the verbal inspiration of Scripture, and verbally acknowledge the Lordship of Christ, by some unbelievable exegetical gymnastics and the imposition of a foreign interpretive scheme upon the biblical record, have relegated a large part of the ethical teaching of Jesus to a future eschatological form of the Kingdom of God. May the Lord Jesus forgive us for lording it over His Word in such an unfaithful way, for perverting the holy intentions He has for His followers, and for disobedient evasion of the most central, demanding and challenging part of His teaching.

The Call to Repentance

When we seriously consider the intentions of Jesus and examine the visible expressions of the Christian faith in light of the biblical revelation, we may at times be tempted to despair over the empirical Church. We realize that "not even in the regenerate Church is the reign of God perfectly manifest."[52] At such a point we humbly recognize that although the Church must be defined in terms of its relationship to the Kingdom of God in its "already" of Jesus' life and message, the Kingdom is "not yet" its present possession. The Church is not yet *in patria*, but is still *in via;* it is "already", but is still on the way and has "not yet" arrived at its final destiny and completion. In pointing out this difference, Skydsgaard warns:

> She is the *ecclesia viatorum,* always exposed to the temptation of Antichrist to apostasy and emancipation. The moment the Church forgets that, when she establishes herself as the highest authority in the world, she ceases to be the Church of Jesus Christ and becomes renegade.[53]

We evangelicals would automatically assume such a statement to apply to the Roman Catholic Church and to some more or less liberal Protestant Church bodies. It is true that one of the gravest errors the medieval Catholic Church committed (with the help of Augustine) was to identify itself with the Kingdom of God. Thus the reign of Christ was perverted into the reign of the Church; christocracy became ecclesiocracy. The distinction between the two was blurred, to say the least.

Some modern-day ecumenical endeavors run the same risk as they rush to identify their own programs with the program of the Kingdom of God.

But are we evangelicals innocent in this area? Are we humble enough to recognize that despite our rich Reformation heritage and Scriptural orthodoxy, and in spite of our present-day successes in missions, evangelism and Church growth, we still need to say to our Master: "We are unworthy servants, we have only done our duty" (Luke 17:10)? Have we? Do we recognize that our distinction between the visible and the invisible Church is hardly a biblical one and that we frequently use it only as a cover for our sins and disobedience to the Lord of the Church? Does reality affirm that we believe in the *ecclesia semper reformanda*, or have we become so fossilized in our structures, so immobile in the ways in which we "serve the Lord", so dogmatic in some of our doctrinal formulations, that even the Lord Jesus Himself is unable to evoke the response and reform He desires from us? Is our understanding of the Church and its ministry so static that even the dynamic reign of the Kingdom of God is prevented from breaking in anew with a spirit of renewal and revival? Are not the evangelical churches along with all the others tempted to boast like the Laodicean church that we are rich, that we have acquired wealth and need nothing, when in reality such a declaration itself betrays the sad fact that we are "wretched, pitiful, poor, blind and naked" churches (Rev. 3:17), who feel self-satisfied and self-sufficient only because we have lost the touch of the Lord and the sense of His kingly presence? The Church (or mission or other Christian agency) that begins to glory and boast in its own achievements, while it stops repenting for its shortcomings and crying for the sins of the needy world, shows signs of backsliding which—unless there is repentance—will cause it to be rejected by the King Jesus. We may ponder Pascal's description of the Church: "*Bel état de l'Église quand elle n'est plus soutenue que de Dieu.*" (The Church is in good condition when it is supported by God alone.)[54]

Unless the first public command of the King Jesus—"Repent ye"—resounds again clearly, unmistakably and unapologetically as part of the Good News about the Kingdom of God, and unless we humbly take the servant role in submission to the King Jesus, many of our evangelical churches are in danger of ending up on the road that leads away from the Kingdom.

The first of Luther's 95 Wittenberg Theses, and thus the first public word of Reformation, was: "Our Lord and Master Jesus Christ desires that the whole life of the faithful should be a life of repentance." Visser't Hooft comments in this regard:

> But the tragedy of the Reformation churches is that this explosive truth, which was destined to give birth to a constantly reformed Church in daily renewed communication with Christ, was considered as an achievement and

> a ground for glorying. These churches of dynamic repentance became churches of arrested repentance. They dug themselves in, instead of remaining on the move. They fought battles for sterile victories.[55]

The rapid expansion of evangelical churches, their striving for numerical strength and respectability in the wider Christian and secular world, makes them easily susceptible to the same spiritual sicknesses and decay. We too are in danger of becoming secular and self-sufficient, lacking in the love, faith and courage by which the people of the King of Kings are known. We too are prone to think up "profound reasons for a profitable compromise with paganism." Our Church also needs to be "reminded how little it can count on itself and how easily it falls from reformation into deformation."[56]

Let us beware of the subtle temptation to mistake the Church for Christ. The Church of Jesus Christ is only that to the degree in which the people called by His name are faithful to him and live under his Kingship. *Ubi Christus, ibi ecclesia!*

The Church Open to the Power of the Holy Spirit

"For the Kingdom of God is not a matter of talk but of power" (1 Cor. 4:20). The Kingdom of God is a dynamic concept. Jesus not only preached the Gospel of the Kingdom but also demonstrated its power and His kingly compassion through the miracles He performed. His miracles signalled His sovereign authority which neither illness, demons nor death were able to withstand. He sent the apostles to preach the Kingdom of God and gave them power to heal the sick and cast out demons (Matt. 10:1, 7–8). It is clear that in the New Testament Church the Christ-given commission to preach the Good News of the Kingdom of God is linked with the equipping power of the Holy Spirit to overcome the forces of evil. The apostles did not regard preaching and healing as disparate tasks. To them the gift of the Spirit was not just a sign of the coming of the new age, but also the present manifestation of the power of the Kingdom. The Holy Spirit was the very life of the Church, not replacing but rather centralizing and always exalting Christ—which is the Spirit's primary mission. Christ rules where the Spirit moves, for the coming of the Kingdom in the convicting, cleansing and enabling power of the Holy Spirit is the beginning of the end of everything that opposes the rule of God.

In the theological thinking of the past, Christology has usually been considered the basis for ecclesiology. The connection of the two was often seen in ontological terms, which has not infrequently led to a very static view of the Church. Such a view was further fostered by institutionalization of the Church whose sole concerns were its own doctrine, order of worship and self-serving organizational structures. The powerlessness and sterility of such churches became evident as soon as they lost the support of worldly powers and had to stand on their own. Such negative developments, along with the more positive recent pentecostal-charismatic renewal, led to an increasing recognition that the doctrine of the Church must also be founded on pneumatology. The pneumatological aspect of the Church brings into focus the dynamics and power of the Kingdom of God, especially when the Spirit's role in energizing the believing community for its mission in the world is acknowledged. It is now increasingly and rightly recognized that in the Church the charismatic must have priority over the purely institutional.[57] Fossilized institutionalism, lifeless sacramentalism and narrowminded legalism can all be signs of the absence of the Spirit of Christ. Such churches are without power and without joy. "For the Kingdom of God is not a matter of eating and drinking, but of righteousness, peace and joy in the Holy Spirit" (Rom. 14:17).

When the Spirit of God is given freedom to move, the Church moves away from the unbiblical dichotomy between clergy and laity and a process of "democratization" takes place, leading to the discovery of the gifts of the Spirit by the members of the congregation and to the ministry of the whole body of Christ. To churches that give no freedom to the Spirit of God to work, the following description often applies: "The spiritual gifts of the laity have atrophied, while the responsibilities of ministers and administrators have hypertrophied."[58] Such congregations are impoverished with respect to two of the basic components of a biblical church—the *priesthood of all believers* and the true sense of Christian *fellowship*. Both their mission and their nature are incapacitated. Their assembling turns out to be the private show of the pastor for his private audience and often the result is that instead of mutual care for the well-being of each and all, growing into a fellowship of the Spirit, they have "degenerated until they consist of unrelated individuals who attend Church services for private reasons."[59] The Christian Church which takes the Kingship of Christ seriously will be a Church continually filled, renewed and controlled by the Holy Spirit. Otherwise it will easily become "the prey of secular social forces . . . influenced by the inexorable laws of sociology rather than by the creative force of the Holy Spirit."[60]

Lesslie Newbigin thirty years ago argued for a three-cornered understanding of the Church, which in addition to emphasis on right teaching, *i.e.* apostolic witness (the emphasis beloved of Protestantism) and true order, *i.e.* continuation of the apostolate (as stressed in Catholicism), must also include the Pentecostal emphasis on the role of the life-giving Spirit of God. He illustrates his criticism of the distortion and deficiency of the first two views by contrasting Scriptural and church-traditional criteria and practice.

> The apostle asked the converts of Apollos one question: 'Did you receive the Holy Spirit when you believed?' and got a plain answer. His modern

> successors are more inclined to ask either 'Did you believe exactly what we teach?' or 'Were the hands that were laid on you our hands?' and—if the answer is satisfactory—to assure the converts that they have received the Holy Spirit even if they don't know it. There is a world of difference between the two attitudes.

The beginning of the Pentecostal movement in the West, and its rapid spread and phenomenal growth in the countries of the Third World, also witness unmistakably to the fact that the Holy Spirit is not synonymous with the bourgeois spirit for which much of the Christian establishment seemed to have mistaken Him in their monopolizing approach to the Kingdom of God. "The spirit (like wind) moves (blows) wherever he (it) pleases" (John 3:8). The underdogs of any society, the poor and the oppressed, the working class and the despised and uneducated peasantry are nowadays recipients of the saving grace of Christ and participants in the powerful manifestations of the Holy Spirit's working. This truly is the sign of the Kingdom, for our Lord Himself was anointed by the Spirit "to preach *good news to the poor* . . . sent to proclaim *freedom for the prisoners* and *recovery of sight to the blind*, to *release the oppressed* . . ." (Luke 4:18). If our mission is to be modelled after the mission of Jesus, as we evangelicals have rightly emphasized (especially since Lausanne), then we must be consistent and face up to the challenge of the supernatural aspects of Jesus' and the apostles' ministry and the role of "signs and wonders" in the mission of the Church. Spiritualizing such passages as the above inaugural statement of Jesus, so as to suggest, for example, that Jesus "was talking about healing blinded hearts in captivity to sin," does no justice to the plain meaning of the text. Countless numbers of examples could be cited of hermeneutical abuses and unbelievable exegetical misconstructions, all obvious twistings of the Scriptural text in order to avoid the clear challenge of the full Gospel and justify the powerlessness of much of the contemporary Christian Church. The sad fact is that many evangelicals who swear their allegiance to an authoritative and inerrant Bible often were (and are) guilty of the most gross abuses of Scripture in this respect.

We are to beware of all sensationalism, superficial charismatic triumphalism and selfish searching for miracles. We are to be critical whenever and wherever miracles are sought after without the obedient acknowledgement of the Lordship of Christ and His sovereignty. We are also to distrust those who speak more about the gifts than the Giver. At the same time, however, we must face the totality of the biblical teaching on the mission of the Church, including the role of the supernatural in the spreading of the Gospel (especially in frontier and pioneering situations), and acknowledge the importance of the full range of the gifts of the Spirit for the proper understanding and healthy functioning of the Church.

Evangelicals still have to realize that "preaching the Word" alone is not enough. Many evangelical churches are known for excellent biblical preaching and yet they are impotent in evangelism. My experience in the Pentecostal movement, where preaching has regrettably often been poor in both content and form, has nonetheless convinced me that the presence of the Spirit is, as Wolfhart Pannenberg would say, "much more suggestive and inspiring than dozens of sermons delivered by inhibited preachers."[62] Donald Gee, one of the better known Pentecostal pioneers and Bible teachers, known for his balance and ability to express it, aphoristically pointed the way: "The Word alone will make you dry up, the Spirit alone will make you blow up, the Word and the Spirit together will make you grow up."[63]

"Without the *pneuma* there is no *soma*."[64] Let us, however, humbly recognize that the Holy Spirit is not our possession and can be neither controlled nor confined by the Church. He is never called "the Spirit of the Church" and no Church body (not even pentecostal or charismatic!) has any right to boast that it "has the Spirit." He is nobody's property! Let us confess that the whole Church needs a new infusion of the Holy Spirit in order to be renewed in its nature and empowered for the endtime harvest in its mission both at home and abroad. Let us humbly recognize that the Church of Jesus Christ is dependent on the Holy Spirit for its very life and that He is the chief and powerful executor of Christian mission.

We sum up discussion of this section with the relevant admonition of David Watson:

> There is no guaranteed bestowal of the Spirit at baptism, confirmation or ordination . . . The Spirit will not be tied to the church, nor to any ecclesiastical office within the church . . . The church which tries to tie the Spirit to its institutionalized forms, to its traditional patterns, or to its doctrinal statements, will quickly find itself moribund and powerless. True spiritual life and freedom will come only insofar as the church submits to the Spirit, listens to the Spirit and obeys the Spirit. At every stage we must learn to hear what the Spirit is saying to the churches, even if that word is sometimes a word of rebuke, or a warning of judgement. God gives the Spirit to those who obey him.[65]

4. The Church will Inherit the Kingdom: The Future Coming of Christ

The Church looks back to its beginnings in the first coming of Christ and forward to its completion at His second coming. While it enjoys the blessings of the "already" of the Kingdom of God it is also aware that the kingly rule of Jesus is "not yet" fully actualized. This recognition makes the Church both humble and hopeful, grateful and longing.

While it believes that the Kingdom has in Christ already arrived in history, it faithfully works on behalf of its greater realization within history and expectantly prays, "Thy Kingdom come", waiting for its full consummation at the end of history.

The Kingdom of God is from above; it is supernatural and cannot be produced by human effort nor realized without God. As David Bosch in his comparison of Melbourne and Pattaya stated: "Unless our salvation is grounded in the yesterday of God's normative revelation in Christ crucified and risen, and unless it stretches out towards the tomorrow of our ultimate salvation, we are engaged in the futile effort of building God's Kingdom with our own hands."[66]

Evangelicals are known for upholding the doctrine of the Return of Christ and for their emphasis on eschatology. Unfortunately, however, the knowledge and experience of this author with evangelical "eschatologizing' is a very negative one. It seems to me that evangelicals have almost universally traded the Kingdom of God for divisive millenarian debates and idle speculations about end-time chronology and related world events. In some Western countries, especially in the USA, "end time" teaching is a growing type of industry and a flourishing business. Sensational eschatology with its speculative guesswork, often popularized in the form of science fiction and made relevant by dubious yet dogmatic references to the political and economic events of our very day, seems to serve for millions of naive Bible-believing Christians as a religious substitute for astrology. Worse yet, much of this apocalypticism leads to "eschatological paralysis", passive withdrawal from the world and fatalistic despair, rather than to Christian hope that engenders ethical action and responsible involvement, which should be the result of a truly biblical eschatology.[67] Such perversion of Scriptural teaching is a theological heresy with far-reaching implications. This preoccupation with apocalypticism ends in attempts to de-eschatologize history and de-historicize eschatology, importing an unbiblical dualism into supposedly biblical teaching and thereby divorcing eschatology from ethics. Carl Henry is right in his criticism of dispensational theology which in its extreme forms

> evaporates the present-day relevance of much of the ethics of Jesus. Eschatology is invoked to postpone the significance of the Sermon on the Mount and other segments of New Testament moral teaching to a later Kingdom age. Dispensationalism erects a cleavage in biblical ethics in the interest of debatable eschatological theory. Dispensationalism holds that Christ's Kingdom has been postponed until the end of the Church age, and that Kingdom-ethics will become dramatically relevant again only in the future. New Testament theology will not sustain this radical repudiation of any present form of the Kingdom of heaven.[68]

We must remind ourselves that with Jesus Christ the eschatological future has already invaded our historical present. It is true that we are anticipating the coming of the Kingdom of God in its fullness, but it is also true that we are already participating in its blessings and have experienced the power of the *eschaton*. The First Coming of Jesus and His resurrection constitute the decisive event of redemptive history. The center of gravity of Christian faith lies not in the events that come at the end of history, but in the events that have already taken place within history. The end-point has been predetermined by the mid-point. The future tense is predicated on the past perfect tense of what God has already done in Christ. The Risen Lord, commissioning His disciples, has stated: "All authority in heaven and on earth has been given to me" (Matt. 28:8).

The blessed hope of the return of our Lord makes demands on our living in the present. We realize that God's perfect eschatological Kingdom is a radical critique of the present state of things in the world as well as in the Church. Christian hope cannot be reconciled to any acceptance of the status quo; it constantly challenges things as they are and calls for renewal, fervent prayer, active anticipation and faithful obedience. In short, Christian hope leads to Christian practice. We know that although we shall not bring about the completion of the Kingdom, our work is not futile for it is done on behalf of the King and in preparation for His final arrival. When our vision is focused upon the blessed return of our Lord with its assurance of His triumph, we are given new strength to carry on even amidst difficult circumstances.

The Church of Jesus Christ knows that it is not at home yet, it is still on the journey towards the eternal city and therefore has to be careful not to make itself too comfortable in any society, nor to identify itself with any worldly kingdom(s), but must always look ahead knowing that His day is close. The Church is the sign of the End, an indicator of what is yet to come, announcing to the world the final triumph of Christ the King. The One who came preaching the Kingdom of God and calling men to be His followers, His Church, will come again to bring the Kingdom to its full consummation and His Church to its completion. Then the Church will inherit the Kingdom, be fully absorbed by it, and the cosmic significance of the Kingdom of God will be fully realized, as he will be "all in all".

Until then the Church is to be faithful in fulfilling the mission of the Kingdom of God, for Jesus has said: "And this gospel of the Kingdom will be preached in the whole world as a testimony to all nations; and then the end will come" (Matt. 21:14). May we, the faithful servants of the King, be able truly to respond: "Come, Lord Jesus!"

5. Conclusion: The Kingdom Challenges The Church

The Kingdom of God continually challenges the Church. The Church is the people of the Kingdom. The Kingdom is its starting point and its goal. The Kingdom is at work in and through it while it remains above and beyond it. The Kingdom is the promise to the Church and the judgement over it. The Church is the servant of the Kingdom, the messenger and witness of its truth and power and the place where its blessings are already enjoyed. Wherever the biblical vision of the Kingdom of God is lost or diluted the Church is ill and weak; wherever it is kept in focus the Church is healthy and vigorous. Though they cannot be equated, the Church and the Kingdom are inseparably related.

The Kingdom of God is a call and challenge to the Church to repent and believe the King. We are to repent for our evangelical reductionism which has long ignored the most central concern of Jesus' life, teaching and works and developed ways of thinking and practice that fail to reflect and express His Kingship and Lordship in the life and ministry of our congregations. We are to re-examine our ecclesiology in the light of the biblical teaching on the Kingdom of God and the purposes He has for us, "a chosen people, a royal priesthood, a holy nation, a people belonging to God . . ." (1 Pet. 2:9). We are to repent; for often we have been tempted, and at times we have succumbed to the temptations, to serve other kings and kingdoms; for not seeking first His Kingdom and righteousness and failing to believe that if we do so, the King Jesus will meet all our needs (Matt. 6:33); for running our churches, missionary societies and other agencies as if they were human institutions; for allowing large-scale intrusions of secular thinking and worldly methods of operation into Christian work; for letting liberals and heretics set our agenda and thus developing a reactionary rather than a fully biblical theology and practice; for wasting energy and other resources in endless in-house fighting about secondary theological matters while ignoring the most crucial and demanding aspects of the teaching of our Lord; for triumphantly boasting in our orthodoxy, spirituality and measurable success while failing to acknowledge our total dependence on Christ the King; for our divisions, denominationalism and lack of concern for true Christian unity, ignoring the fact that there is only "one body and one Spirit . . . one hope . . . one Lord, one faith, one baptism" (Eph. 4:4–5), only one King and only one Kingdom; for privatizing the Lord Jesus and selfishly linking Him to the Church alone, failing to recognize that He is the Sovereign of the universe, that His Kingdom has a cosmic dimension, and His goal is to be "all in all."

In a report about the Melbourne Conference "Your Kingdom Come", Jerald Gort distinguishes three dimensions of the theme:[69]

1. the indicative: we confess that the Kingdom has already come;
2. the subjunctive: we pray for its coming in fullness;
3. the imperative: we are called to make it come.

Melbourne lost the delicate balance between three "moods" by emphasizing the third and tending to ignore the first two. We evangelicals are tempted toward just the reverse. Let us resist this temptation by committing ourselves both to fervent prayer that the King(dom) may come, and to active involvement on behalf of its coming; to obedient living and service under the Kingship of Christ by the enabling power of the Holy Spirit. Let us acknowledge His sovereignty, obey His rule and carry out His will. May the motto of Wheaton College be the motto for all followers of Jesus: "For Christ and His Kingdom"—*Christo et regno eius*!

Footnotes

1. D.J. Harrington, *God's People in Christ*, p. 28.
2. Alfred Loisy, *L'Évangile et l'Église* (Paris, 1902), p. III.
3. René Padilla, "The Kingdom of God and the Church," *Theological Fraternity Bulletin*, No. 1 and 2 (1976), p. 1.
4. The extreme case was the Donatists' attempts to create a perfectionist ecclesiology; see Augustine's polemic against their views.
5. There are striking similarities in doctrinal emphasis and behavioral patterns between the Jewish apocalypticists (see "The Jewish Hopes and Expectations" section of this chapter, pp. 9–10), certain segments of the Early Church and the modern apocalyptic sects. Parts of the evangelical movement of our day come dangerously close to the last named group.
6. Augustine, *The City of God*, XX, 9.
7. George Eldon Ladd, *Crucial Questions about the Kingdom of God* (Grand Rapids: Eerdmans, 1952), p. 25. The Reformers are followed by some contemporary evangelical reformed scholars such as G. Vos and O. T. Allis.
8. For more extensive and reliable discussions of Reformers' views see: Thomas F. Torrance, *Kingdom and the Church: A Study in the Theology of the Reformation* (Edinburgh and London: Oliver and Boyd, 1956); T. F. Torrance, "The Eschatology of Reformation," *Scottish Journal of Theology Occasional Papers*, No. 2, pp. 36–62; and Heinrich Quistorp, *Calvin's Doctrine of the Last Things* (London: Lutterworth Press, 1955).
9. *Augsburg Confession*, VII.
10. For more recent criticisms see W. Pannenberg, *Theology and the Kingdom of God* (Philadelphia: Westminster Press, 1969), pp. 75–76; Carl Braaten, *The Future of God* (New York: Harper and Row, 1969), pp. 112–116.
11. K. E. Skydsgaard, "Kingdom of God and the Church," *Scottish Journal of Theology*, IV, 4 (1959), p. 386.
12. J. Weiss, *Die Predigt Jesu vom Reich Gottes* (Gottingen: Vandenhoeck und Ruprecht, 1892; 2nd ed. 1900; ET 1971).
13. A. Schweitzer, *The Quest of the Historical Jesus* (1st. ET ed. London, 1910, many subsequent editions).
14. See especially his *The Parables of the Kingdom* (London: Nisbet, 1935). Dodd acknowledges his indebtedness to Rudolf Otto, *The Kingdom of God and the Son of Man* (ET, London: Lutterworth, 1943).
15. Dodd, *op. cit.*, p. 50.
16. Harrington, *op. cit.*, p. 27

17. See G. E. Ladd, *op. cit.*, pp. 35–39; *Jesus and the Kingdom: the Eschatology of Biblical Realism* (Waco: Word, 1964), pp. 23–38.

18. See especially Cullmann's *Christ and Time* (Philadelphia: Westminster Press, 1950) and *Salvation in History* (New York: Harper and Row; London: SCM, 1967). Of great relevance to the topic of this paper is also Cullmann's study "The Kingship of Christ and the Church in the New Testament," published in *The Early Church* (London: SCM, 1956).

19. See G. E. Ladd, *Crucial Questions About the Kingdom of God* (Grand Rapids: Eerdmans, 1952); *Jesus and the Kingdom: The Eschatology of Biblical Realism* (Waco: Word, 1964). Since 1974 the revised edition of the same work has been issued by the same publisher as *The Presence of the Future*; and there are popular expositions of the theme in *The Gospel of the Kingdom: Scriptural Studies in the Kingdom of God* (London: Paternoster, 1959) and *A Theology of the New Testament* (Grand Rapids: Eerdmans, 1974), especially pp. 45–134. Another significant evangelical treatment of the theme is Herman Ridderbos, *The Coming of the Kingdom* (Philadelphia: Presbyterian and Reformed, 1962).

20. For some historical descriptions of the evangelical reactions see the following: George M. Marsden, *Fundamentalism and American Culture* (New York: Oxford University Press, 1980); E. R. Sandeen, *The Roots of Fundamentalism* (Chicago: University of Chicago Press, 1970); Donald W. Dayton, *Discovering an Evangelical Heritage* (New York: Harper and Row, 1976); David O. Moberg, *The Great Reversal: Evangelism Versus Social Concern* (Philadelphia and New York: Lippincott, 1972); Timothy P. Weber, *Living in the Shadow of the Second Coming* (New York and Oxford: Oxford University Press, 1979).

21. The NIV translates inexactly *huioi tēs basileias* as "the subjects of the Kingdom".

22. Compare Mk. 10:23–24 and 30.

23. G. E. Ladd, *Jesus and the Kingdom*, pp. 201–202.

24. Fenton J. A. Hort, *The Christian Ecclesia* (London: MacMillan and Co., 1898), p.18.

25. *ibid.*, pp. 19–20.

26. Oswald T. Allis, *Prophecy and the Church* (Philadelphia: Presbyterian and Reformed, 1945), p.82.

27. *ibid.*, p.83.

28. *ibid.*, p.84.

29. See the Commentaries on Matthew; the extensive discussion in Oscar Cullmann, *Petrus: Junger, Apostel, Martyrer* (Munich and Hamburg: Sibenstern, 1967), available also in ET; P. Hoffmann, "De Petrus-Primat im matthäus-evangelium" in J. Gnilka, ed., *Neues Testament und Kirche: Für Rudolf Schnackenburg* (Herder, 1974), pp. 94–114; R. E. Brown, K. L. Donfried, J. Reumann, *Peter in the New Testament: A Collaborative Assessment by Protestant and Roman Catholic Scholars* (London: G. Chapman, 1974).

30. A. B. Bruce, *The Kingdom of God* (Edinburgh: T. and T. Clark, 1890), p. 264.

31. *ibid.*

32. G. E. Ladd comments: "The key of knowledge which should open the door of the Kingdom of God had been entrusted to the leaders of the Jewish people. This key was the correct understanding and interpretation of the Old Testament which should have led the Jews to recognize in our Lord's person and ministry the presence of the Kingdom of God and the fulfilment of the Old Testament promises . . . However, the scribes had taken away the key of knowledge; they so interpreted the Scriptures that they pointed away from Christ rather than to Him as the One who had come to fulfil the prophets. Thus they refused to enter into the realm of Kingdom blessings which Jesus brought, and they hindered those who wanted to enter." (*The Gospel of the Kingdom*, p. 193).
33. John Amos Comenius, *The Bequest of the Unity of Brethren* (English edition: Chicago, 1940).
34. See Acts 17:7, 19:8, 20:25, 28:23, 31; Rom. 14:17; 1 Cor. 4:20, etc.
35. See Rom. 10:9; 1 Cor. 12:3; 2 Cor. 4:5; Phil. 2:11; Acts 16:31, etc.
36. K. L. Schmidt, *"Basileia"*, *Theological Dictionary of the New Testament*, ed. G. Kittel (Grand Rapids: Eerdmans, 1964), I, p. 589.
37. See J. D. G. Dunn, "Pentecost", *New International Dictionary of the New Testament*, ed. C. Brown (Exeter: Paternoster, 1976), II, pp. 783–788.
38. Clutton Brook, *What is the Kingdom of Heaven?*, p. 126, cited by L. Berkhof, *The Kingdom of God* (Grand Rapids: Eerdmans, 1951), p. 10.
39. Pannenberg, *op. cit.*, p. 78.
40. Skydsgaard, *op. cit.*, p. 385.
41. A. M. Fairbairn, *Christ in Modern Theology*, 1893, pp. 528ff., cited in *Expository Times*, XLVII (May, 1936), p. 370.
42. Pannenberg, *op. cit.*, p. 78.
43. Hans Küng, *The Church* (New York: Sheed and Ward, 1967), pp. 95–96.
44. *ibid.*, p. 96.
45. See K. L. Schmidt, *op. cit.*, pp. 581ff; L. Newbigin, *The Household of God* (London: SCM, 1953), p. 28.
46. R. T. France, "The Church and the Kingdom of God: some hermeneutical issues" (an unpublished paper, read at the WEF's Theological Commission study unit, "Faith and Church", Cambridge, 1982).
47. See also 1 Pet. 2:20–21, 4:12–17; Matt. 5:10–12, 10:17–23, 24:9; Mark 13:9–13; Luke 21:12–17.
48. H. Berkhof, *Christian Faith* (Grand Rapids: Eerdmans, 1979), p. 419.
49. C. S. Duthie, *Outline of Christian Belief* (Nashville: Abingdon, 1968), p.87.
50. A. B. Bruce, *op. cit.*, p. 60.
51. Note carefully the whole discourse, especially vv. 24–30 and the fact that the following admonition is to Peter.
52. Carl F. Henry, "Evangelism and Social Action," *Crux*, XVI, 3 (Sept. 1980), p. 27.
53. Skydsgaard, *op. cit.*, pp. 392–393.
54. Quoted by W. A. Visser't Hooft, *The Kingship of Christ: An Interpretation of Recent European Theology* (London: SCM, 1948), p. 70.
55. *ibid.*
56. *ibid.*, p. 71.
57. See, for example, Howard A. Snyder, *The Community of the King* (Downers Grove: IVP, 1977).

58. Richard F. Lovelace, *Dynamics of Spiritual Life* (Downers Grove: IVP, 1979), p. 171.
59. Visser't Hooft, *op. cit.*, p. 76.
60. *ibid.*
61. Lesslie Newbigin, *The Household of God* (London: SCM, 1953), p. 104.
62. Pannenberg, *Theology and the Kingdom of God*, p. 90.
63. Donald Gee (source unknown to this author).
64. Padilla, *op. cit.*, p. 7.
65. David Watson, *I Believe in the Church* (Grand Rapids: Eerdmans, 1978), pp. 166–167.
66. David J. Bosch, "Melbourne and Pattaya: The Left Foot and the Right Foot of the Church?" (a paper available to this author only in its unpublished form), p. 7.
67. For a more extensive treatment of the future aspect of the Kingdom of God and how it relates to the present Christian responsibility see my CRESR paper, "Eschatology and Social Responsibility: An Evaluation of Evangelical Views and Attitudes," in B. Nicholls, ed., *In Word and Deed* (Exeter: Paternoster Press, 1985), pp. 135–164.
68. Carl F. Henry, *Christian Personal Ethics* (Grand Rapids: Eerdmans, 1957), p. 551).
69. Gort's report ("Your Kingdom Come", Amsterdam: Free University, Nov. 1980) was, unfortunately, not available to this author. Gort's conclusions and added observations are borrowed from David Bosch, *art. cit.*, p.5.

Dr. Peter Kuzmič is Director of Biblijsko Teoloski Institut Zagreb, Yugoslavia, and pastor of a Pentecostal church.

SECTION III

The Nature and Mission of the Church in the Local Setting

6

The Identity of the Local Church: Biblical Principles

LUIS BUSH

Introduction

Various contemporary writers contend that the crucial issue facing us today is the nature of the Church. Francisco Lacueva, a Roman Catholic priest who has become an active evangelical theologian in Spain, writes in his systematic theology that while the vital issue in the sixteenth century was justification by faith alone, today the vital issue is the very nature of the Church itself. He quotes O. Dibelius as saying, "We are in the century of the church."[1] Furthermore, J. Robert Nelson, a spokesman for theological liberalism, said: "The recovery and elaboration of the doctrine of the nature of the church is one of the chief aspects of Protestant Theology in this century."[2]

The importance of considering the identity of the local church is underscored by the value of the local church as seen in Scripture. Paul motivated the elders of the church at Ephesus to care for the church by reminding them that the "Church of God" was purchased with the very blood of Jesus Christ (Acts 20:28). Christ gave Himself for the Church (Ephesus 5:25).

In my own experience, pastoring an urban church in conflict-ridden El Salvador for the past five years, the importance of the nature and the role of the local church in a lost and needy world has been confirmed many times over.

The Etymology of the Term *"Ekklēsia"*

Ekklēsia comes from the word *ek* which means "out" and the verb *kaleō* which means "to call". Consequently, the word *ekklēsia* means "the called out ones." Although the usage of the term in classical and New Testament Greek changed, as we will see, the concept of the church as "the called out ones" matches the other terms used to denote the members of the church. In almost all of Paul's greetings in the epistles to the churches, he describes the Church as the saints in Jesus Christ by calling of God (Rom. 1:7, 1 Cor. 1:2, Eph. 1:1, Phil. 1:1, Col. 1:2, Rom. 16:15, 2 Cor. 13:12). The saints are those who are set aside by God for His use. They are those who have professed faith in Christ Jesus (1 Cor. 1:2). In the epistle to the Ephesians, in which the doctrine of the church is most clearly expounded, Paul refers to the members of the church at Ephesus as those who have been chosen in Christ (Eph. 1:4). Therefore, from the etymology of the word *ekklēsia* as supported by the term "saints," the church consists of those who have been called out of the world by God and separated as a distinct fellowship of those who profess faith in Christ.

The Greek term *ekklēsia* is always used to translate some form of the Hebrew word *gahal* which the lexicon defines as "an assembly, congregation, or convocation" (Gen. 49:6, Prov. 5:15, Num. 22:4, Jer. 31:8, Deut. 5:19, Mic. 2:5, Ezra. 10:2). On the basis of the Septuagint usage, as in classical Greek, *ekklēsia* means "an assembly."

In some cases the meaning of "assembly" can be attributed to *ekklēsia* in the New Testament. This literal use of the word can be observed in Acts 7:38, where it refers to the physical gathering or assembly of the Jewish people in the wilderness. In Acts 19:32, 39, 41, it refers to an assembly of Greeks called out in response to Paul's preaching. Sometimes the authors of the New Testament employ the term in a collective sense as in Acts 9:31: "So the Church throughout all Judea and Galilee and Samaria enjoyed peace . . ." The spiritual unity of the church is in view here, and not the physical unity. By far the most frequent use of the term in the New Testament refers to the local church as a Christian assembly that enjoys both physical and spiritual unity (1 Cor. 1:2, Gal. 1:2, Phil. 1:1). Of the 140 occurrences of *ekklēsia* in the New Testament, some ninety times it refers to the local church. The study of the word *ekklēsia* presents the church as an assembly of professing believers in Christ.

The Local Church as a Living Organism

Various metaphors present the truth concerning the universal church, such as the shepherd and the sheep (John 10), the vine and the branches (John 15), the cornerstone and the stones of the building (1 Peter 2), the High Priest and the kingdom of priests (1 Peter 2), the Bridegroom and the Bride (Eph. 5), and the Head and the Body (1 Cor. 12). Some of these metaphors can be applied to the local church as an expression of the universal church. Paul applies the figure of the building when he writes: "Do you not know that you are a temple of God . . ." (1 Cor. 3:16). As such, the local church lives, being indwelt by the very spirit of God. When Paul addressed the Ephesian elders he said: "Be on guard for yourselves and for all the flock among which the Holy Spirit has made you overseers, to shepherd the church of God . . ." (Acts 20:28). Again the imagery of sheep suggests that which lives. The most frequently used metaphor for the church is the Body of Christ (Rom. 12:15; 1 Cor. 10:16–17, 12:12–27; Eph. 1:23, 2:16, 4:21, 12, 16, 5:23, 30; Col. 1:18, 24, 2:19, 3:15). Paul applies this figure to the local church at Corinth: "Now you are Christ's body, and individually members of it" (1 Cor. 12:27). The metaphor emphasizes the fact that the Church is a living organism. Christ, as the Head of the body, has the pre-eminent place, as he guides, sustains, and directs the body. The body, a living organism, receives sustaining life from the Head. Thus, as a visible expression of the universal Church, especially in the figure of the Body of Christ, the local church is a living organism expressing the abundant life of God.

The Local Church as an Organized Community

While the church as organism has spiritual life, in which each member functions doing the work of the ministry to build up the body of Christ (Eph. 4:12), the New Testament also reveals an organized church structure, with spiritual leaders to equip the members (Eph. 4:12–15).

The apostle Paul left Titus in Crete for a specific reason, to "set in order what remains, and to appoint elders in every city" (Titus 1:5). Titus was left to organize the churches. Paul himself set the example when he "appointed elders for them in every church" on the return from his first missionary journey (Acts 14:23).

While there are various forms of Church government, three Scriptural principles are vital with regard to the organisation of the local church. First, there should be a plurality of leadership in each church (Titus 1:5, 7; Acts 20:17; James 5:14; Acts 11:30, 14:23, 15:2, 20:17; 1 Tim. 5:17; 1 Peter 5:1). Secondly, the leaders *must* be mature men of godly character with united families (1 Tim. 3:1–7; Titus 1:6–9). A third important principle relates to the autonomy of the local church. The local church has authority over its life and members (1 Cor. 5:13, 6:1–5, 11:23; Acts 6:1–6). This being so, each local church depends directly on the leadership of Christ and the indwelling of the Holy Spirit rather than on a council of church leaders.

The Local Church as a Worshipping Community

The early Christians present a model for worship in Acts 2:41–47. The activities involved in worship are mentioned. They observed the ordinances of baptism (Acts 2:21) and the Lord's Supper (Acts 2:42). They persevered in the Word of God (2:42). They devoted themselves to prayer (2:42). Surely they must have sung (Eph. 5:19, Col. 3:16). But perhaps more important than the activities of worship was the atmosphere of worship in the early Church. God was clearly present among his people producing a sense of awe (2:23). Miracles and wonders were taking place (2:43). The brethren came in direct contact with God in worship. "Everyone kept feeling . . ." (2:43); the heart was engaged. Gladness and sincerity of heart pervaded the church (2:46). The mind also joined in a unified chorus of praise and worship (2:46). The spirit was lifted in praise to God (2:47). The whole person and the entire Church joined together with one mind to worship God.

Unquestionably, before ministering to the world we should minister to God. There is no higher priority. The great world missionary enterprise began as one local church ministered to the Lord (Acts 13:2).

The Local Church as a Sharing Community

In recent decades the church renewal movement has sparked interest in the quality of church life. The importance of "one-to-another" can be clearly supported from Scripture.

In his book *The Measure of a Church*, Gene Getz suggested that the key biblical standard for the maturity of a church is love.[3] Certainly it best summarizes the mutual commitment in the local church. Believers are to unite together as spiritual brothers and sisters, related through Christ, to refresh each other (Rom. 15:32), speak the truth to each other (Col. 3:9), bear with one another (Col. 3:13), forgive one another (Col. 3:13), admonish one another (Col. 3:16), stimulate one another to good works (Heb. 10:24), and pray for one another (Rom. 15:30). But above all things each believer should put on love (Col. 3:14) and pursue love (2 Tim. 2:22). "Above all, keep fervent in your love for one another, because love covers a multitude of sins," said Peter (1 Peter 4:8). But the responsibility to love goes beyond just a superficial love to all the church family.

Though Christ loved all the world he committed himself in deeper fellowship to an inner circle. In his ministry, Christ, whose example we should follow (1 Peter 2:21), divided his time between the multitudes and his twelve disciples. The discipleship of a few was the method used by the Lord. Also, that was the word he used in the Great Commission when He said, "Make disciples" (Mt. 28:19). The importance of discipleship is further observed in the number of occurrences of the word in the New Testament. It can be found 238 times. Although the term "disciples" does not appear in the epistles, we are called to follow Christ's example (1 Cor. 11:1, 1 Thess. 1:6, 1 John 2:6, 1 Peter 2:21). The early church also practiced discipleship, meeting both in the temple and in small groups in houses (Acts 2:46, 5:42). The apostle Paul used the strategy of discipleship, taking a team with him on his missionary journeys and constantly ministering both publicly (Acts 19:19, 20:20) and privately (Acts 19:1, 9; 20:20b). Paul's last recorded epistle contains his principles of discipleship (2 Tim. 1) and the final charge to Timothy was to "entrust to faithful men who will be able to teach others" what he had learned from Paul (2 Tim. 2:22).

The Church as a Witnessing Community

From a beginning of 120 believers (Acts 1:5) 3,000 were added on the day of Pentecost (2:41). The number grew to 5,000 (14:4), excluding women and children, after which multitudes of both sexes were added to their number (5:14). The disciples grew rapidly (6:7) and following the persecution in Jerusalem, Samaria received the Word of God (8:14). All in Lydda and Sharon turned to the Lord (9:34) and many in Joppa (9:42) and a large number in Antioch believed in the Lord (11:21). In Antioch of Pisidia many believed "and the Word of the Lord was being spread through the whole region" (13:48–49). Many in Derbe were made disciples (14:21) and then we read of the churches increasing in number daily (16:5). In Thessalonica, a great multitude believed (17:4), as in Berea (17:12), Corinth (18:10), and Rome (28:24).

The Lord of the Church had commissioned his followers to be witnesses (Acts 1:8) and they had been just that, the result being church growth. First Peter in Acts 1–10, and then Paul in Acts 11–28, testified wherever they went in their many travels and thereby demonstrated to us how to be effective witnesses.

Each local church as a community of witnesses should seek to grow numerically whether through planning, biological growth or growth as a result of crises. In 1980, in a year of severe national crisis, many of the churches of El Salvador grew as much as 30% in one year.

On the basis of Acts 1:8 and the record of the history of the primitive church, the witness should reach right across the world. Every local church, regardless of size or geographical location, should have a world view and assume responsibility for its own Jerusalem, Judea and Samaria, through to the uttermost parts of the world.

The church at Antioch presents a model for witness. The positive spiritual life of the Church is reproduced in the world. One of the principles of reproduction is that reproduction is after its own kind; as in creation in which "God made the beasts of the earth after their kind . . ." (Gen. 1:25), so in the new creation, "That which is born of the flesh is flesh and that which is born of the Spirit is Spirit" (John 3:6). That is the reason why the outreach to the world comes after the upreach to God and the inreach to the brethren. Quality takes precedence over quantity. A local church in which the brethren criticize each other, are not concerned with one another, and do not love one another has very little to offer a lost world. In the church of Antioch there was genuine worship, mutual edification, and fellowship to share with the lost world (Acts 13:1–3). In Paul's pastoral letter to Titus, regarding the churches in Crete, he communicates the same principle. After setting in order (Titus 1:5) the internal affairs of the church (Titus 1–2), the local church should reach out to the world, reproducing itself (Titus 3).

The reproduction of the life of the church involves the planting of new healthy churches nearby, encouraging existing churches, developing social concern, and participating in a strong world mission thrust.

The local church is God's method for carrying out His work on earth. The essential elements of it could be described as follows: the local church is an assembly of professing baptized believers in Christ, and an organised fellowship which is autonomous in nature, committed to worshipping God; to mutual edification; and to evangelizing the world.

Footnotes

1. Francisco Lacueva, *La Iglesia, Cuerpo De Cristo*, (Barcelona: Clie, 1973), p. 13.
2. Earl D. Radmacher, *What The Church Is All About*, (Chicago: Moody Press, 1972), p. 11.
3. Gene A. Getz, *The Measure Of A Church*, (Glendale: Regal Books, 1975), p. 22.

Rev. Luis Bush is pastor of Iglesia Nazaret Church, San Salvador, El Salvador, Central America.

7

A Personal Reflection

SAMUEL ODUNAIKE

Every individual engaged in a para-church group should find his roots within a local church, no matter how small or relatively insignificant in size or influence that church is in relation to the "para-church" with which he is connected. As I said to the Association of Evangelicals of Africa and Madagascar in 1981, "If the local church is a divinely instituted means of grace for believers then I find no warrant for any believer of whatever standing to constitute himself into a supra-church outside the local church."

I wish to assert that I have no reason whatsoever to vary this position for the Church of Jesus Christ, world-wide. I see the local church as

—a "home" for the family of God.

—a "school" for the training, education and development of the children of God.

—a "workshop" for the equipment and practice of those that are being trained.

—a "restaurant" for the refreshment and rehabilitation of the weary and needy.

—a "hospital" for the care of the spiritually infirm.

—an "army camp" for mobilisation of workers for a continuous and massive onslaught on the seats of Satan in the hearts and lives of men—be they principalities, powers or anything that exalts itself against the name of God and of His Christ.

—an "orchestra" for chanting the praise, worship and adoration of Him who loved and washed us with His blood, who lives and was dead but now is alive for evermore and has promised His own that "Because I live, ye shall live also" Rev. 1:18; John 14:19).

Since the outpouring of the Holy Spirit world-wide at the beginning of this century, one of the gifts that has been highly exalted in the Church perhaps above most others has been that of the evangelist. We have also seen the rapid growth and development of large denominations which in themselves are the by-product of the growth and multiplication of local churches. I think that within this phenomenon the role of the pastor and the local church has been relatively submerged. The pastor has become something of a tool in the hands of powerful bureaucrats and manipulators rather than the significant instrument of change that God meant him to be. If you think I am being too hard on administrators, please be patient with me, for I am one myself. I am currently in my third term as General Supervisor of my denomination, and each term lasts five years. If you think the demands I have staked on pastors and the local church are too high, please understand that I am in my third year as Pastor of the Headquarters Church of our denomination—a local church whose Sunday morning worshippers currently average over 2,000.

What is the proper identity of the local church? It is not necessarily to be known by its high towers, stained glass, pipe organs, or high-toned music. It should not be known as an elitist gathering of the rich, the mighty and the noble; nor *exclusively* as a haven for the poor, destitute and down-trodden of the earth. The local church should not be a museum for the collection and display of trophies that made history in past generations, but a *theatre* of action where Jesus saves and demonstrates the translation of men from the kingdom of Satan to that of God's dear Son.

Dr. Odunaike, a businessman, is the General Supervisor of the Foursquare Gospel Church in Nigeria. He is also President of the Association of Evangelicals of Africa and Madagascar (AEAM).

8

Training Disciples for Mission

RENE DAIDANSO MA DJONGWE

Introduction

When the Lord Jesus Christ came into the world, he had a clear understanding of his mission, a vision and a precise goal: he came *to seek and to save* (Luke 19:10). This is why we see him in the Gospels going from place to place proclaiming the good news of the Kingdom of God. Always and until the end faithful in fulfilling this mission, he then passed it to his apostles and to all his disciples. The supreme command which Jesus gave to his disciples was to evangelize the whole world. After the Master had ascended to heaven, and after the coming of the Holy Spirit, the apostles applied themselves to fulfilling this mission with zeal and faithfulness, in the midst of tribulations, and for some, at the cost of their lives.

Today the task is our responsibility, we who know Jesus Christ and have found in Him our Savior, our Lord and Master.

In the times of the apostles "the Lord added daily to the Church such as should be saved" (Acts 2:47). He continues to do it even today. He said, "I will build my church." This statement concerns essentially two areas: the recruiting of the members and the edifying of the Church, that is, its quantitative and qualitative growth. It is a whole program of evangelization and teaching that is expressed in the Lord's command when he said: "As you go (*poreuthentes*) make disciples (*mathēteusate*) of all nations, baptizing (*baptizontes*) in the name of the Father, of the Son and of the Holy Ghost, teaching them (*didaskontes*) to observe all I have commanded you" (Matthew 28:19,20).

This is the reason why I intend to discuss evangelization and teaching as essential elements in the program of discipleship.

1. Evangelization

What is Evangelization?

The Bible in its entirety emphasizes the importance of evangelization. The word "gospel" (*evangelion*) and the expressions "to proclaim the gospel" (*evangelizomai*) and "to preach" (*kērysso*) occur frequently in the New Testament texts. The ministry of the evangelist is recognized as such, though the word seems to have lost some of its meaning.

Today, especially in Africa, the word has become a title rather than a ministry. Worse than that, the word is even being used to designate someone who is an assistant to a pastor but who has not yet been ordained as a minister. The question is now, are we ready to give back to the spiritual gifts and ministries the place which they should have in the local church?

The mission of the Church is to evangelize the whole of mankind. And this is founded on our Lord's command to his disciples. All of the first five books of the New Testament speak of that (Matthew 28:15–20; Mark 16:15–16; Luke 24:45–47; John 20:21–23; Acts 1:8). The Lord's command is clear: 'Go ye . . .". Many a church needs to hear this today and obey it. For some churches are becoming more and more inactive when it comes to the matter of evangelization. The Lord said to go where people had never heard about him—go throughout the world.

The Lord's command is to go and proclaim the good news and "make disciples". A disciple is a student, someone who follows the teaching of an instructor. Therefore in the gospels it is someone who is following Jesus. We are equipped to carry out the message. Jesus gave us His own power (Matthew 28:18) which is above the devil's power. We do not therefore go with our own authority, nor with our own competency, nor with our own wisdom and knowledge. We go in the power and the authority of the Lord Jesus. In addition, Jesus gives us the guarantee of His presence. The one who gives power is also present. Finally Jesus gives us the power of the Holy Spirit (Acts 1:8) so that we might be witnesses.

The apostolic message was essentially christocentric. The apostles firmly declared the identity of Jesus Christ and his redemptive work on the cross. We find a summary of this message in I Corinthians 15:1–4. This presentation of Christ is often followed by a call to repentance (Acts 2:37,38).

The mobilization of the whole Church

When we read the book of Acts we discover that what has contributed to the rapid growth of the gospel has been the involvement of everybody in the salvation of many. As commanded by their master, the apostles started the ministry in Jerusalem (Acts 2 and 3). Within a short period of time they had filled the city with their teaching (Acts 5:28) and very rapidly they evangelized Judea (Acts 8:1,4) and Samaria (8:5).

The personal testimony of each Christian is either lived or spoken or both at the same time only to the extent that each individual Christian really assumes his responsibilities at the local church level as a witness to Jesus Christ wherever God has placed him. To keep a city clean every single inhabitant must clean the immediate area facing his door. This same principle is also true in evangelism, that is, to evangelize a city or a region, each individual Christian must consider himself as a witness to Christ and be willing to engage himself in evangelizing those around him. For the early Christians the fact of becoming a disciple was not an end in itself but rather the beginning of a whole process of growth and commitment to God's work.

God has granted certain special gifts to some people for the proclamation of the gospel of salvation in Jesus Christ. Thus, Philip the evangelist (Acts 21:8) went from place to place, village to village to evangelize (Acts 8:5, 26, 40). The evangelist is a person given to the Church for the perfecting of the saints, for the work of evangelism. The evangelist is not only the one who evangelizes, but also the one who trains other people to do evangelism: "He gave . . . some as evangelists . . . for the perfecting of the saints, for the work of service to the building of the body of Christ" (Eph. 4:11–12).

According to the Lord's commandment, evangelism must be carried to the uttermost part of the earth (Acts 1:8). Saul of Tarsus (who then became Paul) went across the boundaries of Judaism and of Judea to bring the gospel to other people and countries (Acts 13). In the book of Acts we see that private testimony, the ministry of foreign evangelism and that of local evangelism, were functioning simultaneously. Which of the three is neglected in our church today? We are anxious to reestablish the balance.

The Ministry of the Holy Spirit

According to the Bible, evangelism is a ministry performed under the guidance of the Holy Spirit by men and women endued with His power. Jesus said, "You shall receive power, after that the Holy Spirit has come upon you; and you shall be witnesses unto me both in Jerusalem, and in all Judea, and in Samaria, and unto the uttermost part of the earth" (Acts 1:8). No one can be a witness unto God if the Spirit of God is not in him and the power of the Spirit of God does not rest upon him.

The perfect organization of our evangelistic meetings, the perfection of our methods, the abundance of our channels—these things do not confer efficiency. As far as evangelism is concerned the best method and the best channel has been and will always be the Holy Spirit.

If the Holy Spirit does not intervene in a man's heart no lasting results can be expected. It is therefore the work of the Holy Spirit to convince of sin and to bring man to repentance.

We may conclude, then, by saying that the mission of the Church is built on God Himself, the God Who sent and Who comes to us through Jesus Christ. This mission is expressed in the great commission, "Go ye into all the world and preach the good news to every creature." Jesus said, "As my father has sent me into the world, even so have I also sent you." The Church of Jesus Christ cannot but be a "sent people" to evangelize. To evangelize is to be a witness of Jesus Christ in one's own private life both in words and in acts, as was Paul (Acts 21:17–36).

To evangelize is to proclaim the good news and to make it heard, for "faith comes by hearing and hearing by the Word of God" (Rom. 10:17). To evangelize is to present Jesus Christ so that men will come to trust Him and will come to a knowledge of their sin in order to receive forgiveness and salvation through faith in Him (Rom. 10:9). To evangelize is to lead men to conversion, to take in the new converts so as to keep them in an atmosphere of intense fellowship with Christ and to engage them in the process of spiritual growth.

2. Teaching

We see the importance of teaching in the fact that our Lord has included it in His great commission. "Make," he said, "disciples of all nations, and *teach them to observe* all things whatsoever I have commanded you" (Matt. 28:19–20).

The practice of teaching

In this immediate context Christ was addressing the apostles. However, in general this commandment is addressed to all those who are responsible to teach and equip the saints for the work of the ministry (Eph. 4:11,12).

Teaching is needed to strengthen new converts. All newborn babes need some care, affection, food and exercise, so that they can develop in a balanced way. It is the same with newborn spiritual babies. Thus, the challenge of the Apostle Peter, "As newborn babes, desire the sincere milk of the word, that you may grow thereby" (1 Peter 2:2). The ultimate goal of teaching is to help the disciple go from the baby state to the full age of mature manhood (Heb. 5:12–14), "till we all come in the unity of the faith, and of the knowledge of the Son of God unto a perfect man, unto the measure of the stature of the fulness of Christ" (Eph. 4:13).

Disciples who are taught and trained may "approve things that are excellent", distinguishing the essential from the peripheral. They may be sincere and blameless. They will be filled with the fruits (Phil. 1:9–11). They will have their senses exercised to discern both good and evil (Heb. 5:14).

If we want our Christians to bear a witness as disciples of Jesus Christ, we need to go back to the practice of the early Christians who "continued steadfastly in the apostles' doctrine." For it is only the Word of God which gives wisdom and understanding (Ps. 119:130, 131).

The integration of a disciple

It is true that we cannot recreate exactly the experience of the first disciples in the book of Acts, where we find them in a communal life environment. However, we should strive to rediscover the family atmosphere which should exist in our local churches, in which members care for each other in a spirit of fraternal communion.

The image of the Church as a body is an excellent concept. Thus, the body is not made up of a unique member, but of many members joined together. It is important for each member to recognize his place in the body. The study of I Cor. 12 and other related texts will bring to light the fact that the body is one unit, indivisible but diverse.

The members of the body exist in solidarity with each other (I Cor. 12:26, Rom. 12:15). The members of the body need each other (I Cor. 12:24). The members of the body, through their functions, complement each other (I Cor. 12:18, 22).

A disciple needs to be instructed regarding his responsibility in the body of Christ, and regarding commitment to the service of Christ. Since each disciple receives from God a particular gift, he must be invited to use this gift in service to the other members of the body (I Peter 4:10–11), in such a way that the name of God may be glorified through his life, his actions and his testimony.

A Christian should be distinguished for the level of his commitment and the degree in which he is engaged in the service of God and his fellow men. The Word of God plays a great role in this kind of commitment.

When we know the Word, we cannot remain like children, "tossed to and fro and carried about with every wind of doctrine, by the sleight of men, and cunning craftiness, whereby they lie in wait to deceive"; but speaking the truth in love, we may "grow up into Him in all things, which is the head, even Christ" (Eph. 4:14,15).

The teaching program

A complete and well balanced program should be organized. The purpose of this program should be to ingrain in the disciple Jesus' character. Such teaching, and a steady contact with the Word, will allow him to acquire a sound doctrinal knowledge and lead him to a responsible commitment. Therefore, taking also into account his own personal needs, the plan for such a study program may include:

Personal meditation which will allow the disciple to develop a constant personal contact with God. It will allow him also to develop personal discipline in his own life. His prayer life also must be strengthened. It should help him to conquer temptations in his life through the study and the application of the Word of God to concrete circumstances. Counselling is also needed.

Doctrinal instruction will allow systematic teaching of Bible doctrines. It will train him to defend his faith and to give advice to other disciples. Because of the neglect of this, the theological and Biblical foundation of many of our churches is less than desirable.

Through such teaching, we can expect that the disciple will learn to *assume responsibilities* in the Christian community. He should now be ready to engage himself in telling his own testimony, to participate in evangelism and any other Christian service required by the church.

3. Conclusion

A disciple is in many ways the image of his master. In other words, a disciple reflects the knowledge and the life of his master. Thus, if we want disciples who will be faithful and well grounded in the things of God, we must start by giving them instructors who are faithful and well grounded. When we use the expression "making disciples", we mean more than bringing somebody to conversion. In fact, when a person is converted, in that very day he begins his walk on the road towards sanctification. The new convert progresses like a child from the maternal crib to the time when he takes his place as a grown-up member of the family which is the Church. A disciple is one who from the very day of his conversion has been directed on to the road toward a mature Christian life. The result depends a lot on the kind of person that the evangelist transfers to the pastor and the way in which the transfer is made.

It is necessary to encourage Christians to become evangelists. It is also necessary to provide adequate preparation for them, so that they may be able to teach the new converts in such a way that when they are transferred to the pastor, they are already disciples, ready to be fed as mature Christians. The pastor also must be adequately prepared to continue the feeding.

May the words that Paul addressed to Timothy become ours: "Preach the Word in all circumstances, favorable or unfavorable.

Perform the work of an evangelist, perform well your ministry; and the things that thou hast heard of me among many witnesses, the same commit thou to faithful men, who shall be able to teach others also."

Rev. Rene Daidanso ma Djongwe of Chad is now Associate Executive Secretary, Association of Evangelicals of Africa and Madagascar, Nairobi, Kenya.

9

The First Baptist Church, São Paulo, Brazil

A Case Study

IRLAND P. DE AZEVEDO

Introduction

The First Baptist Church of São Paulo is located in the heart of one of the five largest cities in the world. It is the church from which has irradiated Baptist influence throughout the whole state of São Paulo in 83 years of effective ministry.

It is a church which has demonstrated its missionary conscience in seeking not only to reach the center of the city, but to help churches in the interior. The FBC is helping to restore the fortunes of some of those churches in the interior that have difficulties due to the flow of their members to the big cities. In spite of the enormous inflation of the Brazilian economy, the church invests about 50% of her monthly income in evangelization and missions.

Baptist work in Brazil began in October 1892 with the organization of the First Baptist Church in the city of Salvador, Bahia. Its beginnings were quite modest—only 5 members, of which two couples were Southern Baptist missionaries. (The fifth member was a Brazilian, a former Catholic priest.) The vision of this small group was such that by 1899, when the FBC of São Paulo was founded, there were Baptist churches in Salvador and Maceio in the north-east and in Niteroi, Campos and Rio de Janeiro in the central south. These were important cities, and this enabled the later expansion of the Gospel in the surrounding areas.

The FBC of São Paulo, ever since her organization in 1899, has participated in the cooperative activities and in the missionary promotion of the Brazilian Baptist Convention. Today, 100 years after the founding of that first Baptist Church in Brazil, in the most Roman Catholic city of the country, there are about 4000 Baptist churches scattered throughout all the states of Brazil. And the FBC of São Paulo has played an important role in this church growth.

The Baptists followed a different policy from that which governed Presbyterian and Methodist work in Brazil. These latter churches preferred to begin their church planting in smaller interior cities where they soon had rapid growth. The Baptists began in the capital city itself and within a few years had reached out to plant daughter churches in the cities of the interior.

The FBC of São Paulo: Its Development

The FBC of São Paulo has been conscious of its tremendous responsibility to reach a great city which is characterized by intense economic and industrial activity. Approximately 13 million people live in Greater São Paulo. Some 70% of her population are descendants of immigrants, principally Italians, Portuguese, Spaniards, Germans, Arabs, Lebanese and Japanese.

In her 8 decades of existence the FBC of São Paulo has made great progress. She has organized 26 churches herself and through these determined the growth of 537 Baptist churches in the state of São Paulo with a total of almost 100,000 members.

The author of this case study (Pastor Irland) began his ministry at FBC on January 2, 1971. As he contemplated the city from the top of its highest skyscraper, his eyes filled with tears and he begged God to grant him to penetrate the concrete jungle and reach the millions of inabitants of the great city.

Pastor Irland began his ministry by mobilizing the church, training the laymen and imparting to them the challenge of São Paulo, as well as indicating the need to seek new methods to reach both the city-dweller and the inhabitant of the interior of the state.

In 1971 less than 5% of the budget was applied to evangelism and missions. But from 1973 the church began to increase its budget for evangelism and missions. It was so blessed that in these last three years more than 50% of the receipts has been applied in these two areas.

The FBC has been constructing a religious education plant over these last few years, using only monies designated for construction. (No tithe monies were so applied since we understand that the temples of which the Bible speaks were built with free will offerings. The tithes are used to underwrite the expenses of the worship services, the ministry and missions.)

Having developed its philosophy of work, the church began to accomplish her program of action through 5-year tasks within the resources (human and financial) that were available. The program of the first 5-year plan (1971–1975) left a few projects incomplete due to lack of resources. The second (1976–1980) saw its goals reached—among them, 7 daughter churches established, minister of music and assistant minister hired, and mission work expanded. We are now in our third 5-year plan (1981–1985). Of the annual receipts of tithes and offerings almost half was applied to evangelism and missions.

The church supported 11 mission points. Two of these are in the Capital, 8 in the interior and one in the state of Bahia (1,220 miles away). There is a program of evangelism, follow-up and religious education in these mission points which has as its objective their organization into churches during the next 3 years.

FBC has a daily 5 minute radio program on 13 stations. The program seeks to take the Gospel in a candid way to both the individual and his family and offers the listener a Bible study correspondence course. It encourages listeners to visit churches near their homes, helping in this way the smaller churches both in the interior and in São Paulo.

In 1982 the members of FBC passed out nearly a million pieces of literature (Bible portions, tracts, letters of consolation, and copies of telephone messages, as well as New Testaments and Bibles). This literature carries stamped in it the address and the hours of the worship service as well as the telephone numbers of the telephone ministry.

The church has five telephones in São Paulo and two in the interior. These register 2500 daily calls to hear a two or three minute message which, along with the plan of salvation, gives the hours of the services and the address of the church. These messages also offer Bible courses and opportunities for counselling. Many people have been saved from despair and suicide, many families from disintegration. The telephone ministry has opened many homes to our evangelists that otherwise would be inaccessible. This is particularly true of condominiums, which do not permit strangers to enter without invitation.

There are 500,000 abandoned or needy children in São Paulo. Every Saturday a group of dedicated teachers work with these children, giving them the Word of God, teaching them hymns and choruses. Hundreds of them are doing Bible correspondence courses and have made decisions for Christ. It is the desire of the church that they will return to the world rehabilitated and saved and that they will build their families according to the norms of the Word of God.

The church has also developed a work of visitation and evangelization in 2 hospitals and hopes to expand this to others in São Paulo. The work at Saint Mark's Hospital is the most touching since it treats those who are terminally ill. Every Wednesday a group of believers speak of the love and peace of Christ to as many as possible in this hospital. The leader of this work decided not to work on Wednesdays so that he could dedicate this day totally to his mission.

In São Paulo more than 250 people die every day. The funeral parlors are always full of people. Because of this situation the FBC has created an assistance program directed toward families that have lost loved ones. This program is conducted in the funeral parlors themselves.

A team which has been properly prepared draws near to the family and discovers the name as well as other information about the one who died. They give the family a letter of consolation, and with the permission of the family, distribute appropriate literature to all those present. Sometimes the team is asked to hold a funeral service for the family and friends. Many afterwards have expressed their gratitude to the church for its comforting presence, remarking how much the latter had helped them.

Just like the pioneer missionaries of modern missions, the FBC seeks to preach the Good News of redemption in the public squares (plazas). Every Sunday there is a service in the square located right in front of the church. Thousands of people through the years have heard the Word. Hundreds have become members of this church, or of others in São Paulo or across Brazil.

The FBC in São Paulo: Retrospect and Prospects

Looking back over the eight decades of the life of this church in the centre of São Paulo presents us with a multi-faceted vision. What positive or negative aspects should be underlined?

As we look back we can see that the pioneers had great perception of the future and anticipated the dimensions of the City when they planted FBC in the urban center of São Paulo. From there the witness to the Gospel spread with great rapidity.

Over the decades, however, FBC forgot those who lived near the church building. By the beginning of the 70s only 5–6% of her members lived in the center of São Paulo. After much diligent effort in the last 12 years, this percentage has been raised to 25–30%. Though located in an urban centre that is more business than residential, the church has been able also to show a constant growth in membership.

The church has also responded promptly to the missionary challenges of her present pastor, raising her financial participation in evangelism and missions from 5% to almost 50% of her normal income.

Through the years it has become clear how fragile have been the educational structures of the church in terms of conserving and developing the fruit of her evangelistic endeavors. As a result she has baptized less than 30% of those who have made decisions in her worship services and evangelistic campaigns. It has also been noted that some of our daughter churches which receive financial aid during the first 5 years of their existence have not progressed as much as we expected. Lastly, there is a large number of inactive believers who do not perceive the opportunities which are set before them, nor do they take up the challenge of this great city.

The present 5-year plan (1981–1985) indicates the FBC has adopted a bold program to multiply churches. She has set herself to organize *10 new churches in each 5 year period*. At the same time she is encouraging her daughter churches and the mission points which she sustains financially to organize two new centers per year.

A more effective program is being developed that will enable the church to reach those who live in the neighborhood of the Temple (within a radius of one kilometer). And the church plans to augment its outreach by airing programs on the radio. She hopes to be on 100 radio stations by 1985 and to double this number in the next 5 year plan (1986–1990). The church plans to use both TV and the secular press as a means of expressing her witness. We have hired a very capable and experienced minister of music to provide first-rate music for TV and radio.

The telephone outreach is being intensified so that we can reach more needy people, those that need sympathy and spiritual help. The religious education program is being overhauled with a view to providing every member, old or new, with opportunities to grow in the knowledge of the Word of God and in the Christian life.

The assistance which FBC gives to small churches both in São Paulo and in other parts of Brazil will continue to be given. This help is both financial and in human resources. Furthermore, starting in 1984, the church will offer an annual apprenticeship to 12 seminary students, preferably to those in their last academic year. The program is being developed with the view to giving the students effective training in every area of the Church's mission.

Lastly, the FBC trusts that until the Lord comes she will continue to be both a stimulus and a model of responsibility and faithfulness in her mission to the world: in adoration, in religious education, in edification of the saints, in the proclamation of the Gospel, in service to those in need.

Rev. Irland P. de Azevedo is senior pastor of the First Baptist Church, São Paulo, Brazil.

10

The Chung Hyeon Presbyterian Church, Seoul, South Korea

A Case Study

CHANG-IN KIM

Introduction

On June 25, 1950, the Korean War broke out—the most terrible conflict in all our history. In a short time the southern part of Korea was conquered by the Communist troops of North Korea. Only Pusan, a port town in the southernmost part of Korea, was not overrun. Some Christians who had moved south to avoid the communist persecution and other Christians who came down because of the war met together. When the war was over, many of them came back to Seoul to rebuild churches. It was at that time that 18 persons established Chung Hyeon Church and I was installed as its pastor on September 6, 1953.

Chung Hyeon Church was built in a place surrounded by several markets. As a result, middle class merchants played a most active role in our church.

Some Secrets of the Growth of the Chung Hyeon Church

Trust in the Presence of God

In 1907, there was a religious revival movement in the Korean churches which reminded us of the working of the Holy Spirit in the days of the early Church. At first Chung Hyeon Church consisted of the Christians who had experienced this, and they set a good tradition in our church. Chung Hyeon Church has always emphasized the work of the Holy Spirit. One of its main watchwords has been "Godliness in the presence of God the Father". This attitude reflects clearly in our worship. We have tried our best to see that every service returns all the glory to God. Our church people were taught to root out idolatry and keep the Lord's Day holy.

During the worship service I emphasize not only tithes and hearty thank-offerings, but also a solemn and committed attitude of devotion before our Father.

As the apostle Peter says in I Peter 5:3, pastors should be "examples to the flock", exemplary Christians in every respect, and that has been my motto for my pastoral life at Chung Hyeon Church.

Every time I received a vision from the Lord, I did not hesitate to carry it out although there was no help and much opposition from others. When we sent missionaries overseas, many people criticized us, saying it was premature to attempt it. And when we organized the Mission Foundation for North Korea, we were told it was an impossible and empty dream. When we purchased a plot of land to build our new church fifteen years ago, it was a field of little value. At that time nobody thought it right to buy, but now it is a valuable piece of land.

Since my childhood, I have suffered from tuberculosis. My pastoral duties often made me fall ill from overwork and caused me to cough up blood. However, I have tried not to excuse myself from preaching the sermons on Sundays because of illness.

Harnessing the Homogeneous Principle

An important characteristic of Koreans is that they are a homogeneous race. Our people have always lived in the same cultural *milieu* of language, history and customs. This characteristic has enabled the remarkable growth of Korean churches and contributed much to the speedy propagation of the Gospel.

In the early times, as we noted above, Chung Hyeon Church consisted of Christians who had suffered from persecution for their faith. They had been persecuted severely under the Japanese occupation. Moreover, religious persecution in North Korea made them come south over the border in very larger numbers. The homogeneous characteristic of the common experience of these refugees made our church grow numerically.

There were several market places around our church. Those church members who had come south from North Korea mostly carried on trade in these markets. Christian merchants preached the Gospel to their fellow workmen. Their common occupation brought them into close contact with one another, and provided an easy way to lead them to Christ. This was one of the secrets of Chung Hyeon church growth.

We nurtured our church members by strengthening this homogeneity. For example, Chung Hyeon Church appointed pastors for every department of our Sunday School. In 1967, we published our own Bible Teaching Text Books for all groups in our Sunday Schools. At that time even the General Assembly of our denomination was not prepared to undertake this work.

As I am convinced that Bible teaching is vital for the church and its growth, we are operating an "All-church-member" Bible Class at the Chung Hyeon Bible Institute, which is divided into a pastors class, an elders class, a class for ordained deacons, and a church employee class.

The Primacy of Evangelism

In the early missionary days, Korean churches were diligent to preach the gospel to the people. At first the objects of this evangelization were the people who lived around our Church, and then we took on the wider aim of evangelizing our nation, including fishing and farming villages and the military.

From 1960, our church took a direct hand in evangelizing rural and country churches. For the first time a Young People's Mission was delegated the responsibility for rural churches. They preached the gospel while they worked with the farmers and fishermen.

On June 19, 1966, our Church organized a Policemen's Mission to evangelize all the policemen in our nation. And the military is a golden place for fishing for souls. We trained the soldiers in our own Church to work among them.

One day I had the opportunity to baptize 2,000 soldiers at one time.

A Prison Mission was organized for criminals, and we found that some of them would become church members if a good opportunity was given to them after they were released.

The Importance of Sunday School for All Ages

The history of growth of our Church can be seen reflected in the fortunes of our Sunday School. I realized early in my ministry that our God regards this as being very important.

There are 16 departments in our Sunday school, classified by the age, type of occupation, and so on, of our church members. We organized a Teachers Training Department for our Sunday Schools in 1971 and now people who want to be Sunday School teachers have to undergo our training schemes.

For the first time in our country, we pioneered an Infant Department, a Newlyweds Department, and a Department for the Aged. These departments contributed greatly to the growth of our church through their special programs.

Home Visitation Through Cell Groups

Chung Hyeon Church had much concern for home visitation in its early days. We divided and expanded our cells continuously. The cell system is very productive in Korea because Korean people have good community spirit.

The Korean church was convinced of the importance of home visitation in its early days, and so pastors gave much effort to it. When Chung Hyeon Church was established, our church assigned many evangelists for home visitation and strengthened the cell system as church members increased continuously.

In 1955 Chung Hyeon Church was composed of 16 cells and at present in 1983 it has 631 cells. At present one cell usually consists of 5 families. Through this cell system and home visitation, we extend our fellowship. Our church members, especially cell leaders, have much concern about matters of personal importance such as weddings, healing ministry, birthdays and funerals. As a consequence, we have seen some of the unbelievers who attended these ceremonies being moved deeply and becoming Christians.

Our church especially takes care of old people aged over 70, and I have personally visited these people in order to comfort and encourage them to have heavenly hope.

Focus on World Missions

I became convinced that the more concern we have about overseas missions, the more we can accelerate the growth of our church. Therefore, we organized the Overseas Missions Association on November 24, 1968, to make our first step toward world evangelization. Three years later, on September 9, 1971, Chung Hyeon Church sent Rev. Su Man Soo to Indonesia as our first missionary.

In fifteen years of missions, we have sent 17 missionaries to 12 countries, and at present 12 missionaries minister in 12 regions. Some of them ministered to Korean residents abroad at first, and then to the nationals of their region after establishing a Korean Church.

A concern for world missions is one of the most important elements in church growth worldwide.

Rev. Chang-In Kim is Senior Minister of the Chung Hyeon Presbyterian Church, Seoul, S. Korea.

11

Rapid Church Growth in South Korea: Reflections

BONG RIN RO

Why is the Korean Church Growing so Rapidly?

Many Christians around the world have asked this question. The rapid church growth in Korea is well known through the news media. Articles with titles such as "Six New Churches Everyday," "Korea: Asia's First Christian Nation?" and "Church Growth Unlimited" have excited Christians around the world, particularly those who are involved in church growth studies. The Chung Hyeon Presbyterian Church is a typical example of how church growth has occurred in the urban situation.

The Chung Hyeon Presbyterian Church (CHPC) is one of the three large churches in Seoul, with over 10,345 members. It holds five services each Sunday. It is the largest congregation within the Presbyterian Church of Korea (Haptong). The two larger churches are The Full Gospel Central Church of Rev. Yong-Gi Cho which claims 250,000 members and the Yong Nak Presbyterian Church with 50,000 members which belongs to the Presbyterian Church of Korea (Tonghap).

Since coming to know this church I have attended the services a few times. I had the privilege of preaching at one of five Sunday morning services last April and also visited the new sanctuary which is being built to accommodate some 7,000 people. CHPC is certainly one of the amazing churches in South Korea, not only in terms of its size, but also in terms of its spiritual vitality and its organizational structure.

The Asia Conference on Church Renewal which met in Seoul in August 1982 states that the key to Asian church growth and renewal lies "in the hands of committed pastors who are able to mobilize the laity and capitalize on the contributions of church oriented para-church groups." It is the dynamic spiritual leadership of Rev. Chang-In Kim which God has used to build up this local church. The church's growth is the outcome of a team ministry as the senior pastor works with 27 associate and assistant pastors and 10 "Bible women". They mobilize the laity of the church through 16 Sunday school departments and many other departments.

The pastor's responsibility is to multiply his own effectiveness by training believers for the work of their ministries so they can together build up the body of Christ. The crucial issue, therefore, is: how can we produce more Spirit-filled pastor-trainers?

Contributing Factors to Korean Church Growth

1. *The Strength of the Local Church*

The strength of the Korean church rests in the local church. CHPC is a typical example. The Korean pastor works an eighteen-hour day from the dawn prayer meeting at 5:00 a.m. to late in the evening. In the New Testament church, believers met together for worship, fellowship, instruction, evangelistic outreach, and social service. God gave different people different spiritual gifts (Eph. 4:11–16), and He wants believers to utilize their gifts to build up the local church. The effective and Spirit-filled pastor is the key person who not only recognizes the gifts of his members, but also disciples the laity so they can contribute to the church. When each church is renewed spiritually under the effective leadership of the pastor, local church growth takes place.

Nevertheless, a strong emphasis on the local church can also produce negative effects. In fact, some critics of church growth in Korea criticise the Korean church for focusing too much attention upon the local church, so that the unity of churches has been jeopardized in cooperative programs. There is an urgent need for the Korean church to have a balanced view of the role of the local church together with the unity of churches and of para-church organizations.

2. *Abundance of Man-power*

Korea is the only country in Asia where an abundant supply of Christian workers is available. According to the government statistics, there are some 220 theological and Bible schools in South Korea which produce annually some 10,000 graduates. Half a dozen seminaries have student bodies of more than 1000 each. Thousands of students fail annually to secure admission to theological schools, due to the government quota system which limits the number of theological students.

The government reported that the number of churches in Seoul had increased from 2,050 in 1979 to 4,670 in 1981—a doubling of the number of churches in three years.

The president of a large Presbyterian seminary in Seoul told me last year that many of his 1,500 students had come to seminary for training after graduating from the top national university, and that successful professionals had left their jobs to train for the ministry. What can this be but the Holy Spirit working in the Korean church.

3. *Contextualization*

Christianity is Korean. The Philippines, with an 87% Roman Catholic and 4% Protestant population, is the only nation in Asia where Christianity has become deeply rooted. South Korea, in spite of its long history of Buddhism and Confucianism, is more than 20 percent Christian in its 39 million strong population. Crosses on top of all buildings are easily observable not only in the cities but also in small towns and villages.

Christian radio stations, TV programs, a "Halleluja" national soccer team, a presidential prayer breakfast, mass Christian gatherings in Explo '74, '76, and '80, and many other Christian organizations and programs, have made Christianity a part of Korean culture. Contextualization of Christianity has been taking place steadily during the past century of Christian mission in Korea.

The goal of the "Christianization of Korea" movement in the churches today is to increase the Christian population to 50 percent by 2000 A.D. Only dynamic faith in each Korean Christian will make the goal possible.

4. *Christian Stewardship in Tithing*

One important indigenous principle of missions, according to Nevius thinking, is self support. The CHPC's new building project, which will cost $15 million, is a vivid evidence of God's working in His church. Although Rev. Kim has met opposition from some segments of society and from other church leaders, the leaders of his congregation believe that it is the Lord's will to put up a new sanctuary in order to accommodate the increasing number of believers in his congregation.

The emphasis on tithing preached in Korean pulpits is certainly a very important factor in the growth of the church in Korea. Korean churches have used the money from tithing to spread the gospel not only in Korea but also around the world.

5. *Prayer Life of Korean Christians*

Certainly, the most important factor for the growth of the Korean church is prayer. Early dawn prayer meetings, all night prayer meetings, fasting, and many other prayer meetings at the church and in private homes have taught the Korean Christians to rely upon the Holy Spirit. Many pastors go up to prayer mountains to pray and fast for several days to renew their spiritual life just as Moses did at Mt. Sinai.

A Spirit-filled shepherd deeply influences his sheep in their spiritual life. How can God not bless His people when thousands of them continuously pray and cry out to God all night for His blessings?

Conclusion

CHPC is one of the best models of an urban church in Korea. The spirit-filled leadership of Pastor Chang-In Kim is crucial for the spiritual well-being of his congregation.

Its story exemplifies a principle well known from other places around the world: that when the Holy Spirit is allowed to work in the lives of pastors and believers, God works in the growth of the Church.

Dr. Bong Rin Ro is Executive Secretary, Asia Theological Association, Taichung, Taiwan.

12

Mizoram Baptist Churches in North East India

A Case Study

C. L. HMINGA

Introduction

This case study is focused on the churches in Mizoram, which have been under the care of itinerant pastors since the emergence of the church in that land some eighty years ago. The whole Mizo tribe, numbering now over 400,000 souls, left their traditional religion and embraced Christianity as their religion in a short span of sixty years, through sweeping people movements accelerated by waves of revival that swept the whole of Mizoram and the surrounding countries where there were Mizos.

The power of the Gospel has wrought the radical transformation of a warring, head-hunting people into one of the most advanced societies in India. Self supporting, self propagating and self governing churches have come into being. Those churches have been under the care of District Itinerant Pastors who have responsibility for several churches.

The First Five Decades

In the early 1900s when there were only a very few churches, the overseas missionaries and first pastors ministered to those congregations. When the number of believers grew, and more and more local village congregations came into being, it was necessary to train and appoint more pastors. Most of the early pastors were trained by the missionaries. They taught them in the Mission Headquarters for one or two months, and sent them out to evangelize unreached people with the Gospel. After a month on preaching tour they came back to the Headquarters and received further training for two or three months, after which they were sent out again. This process of training continued for three years after which they were well equipped to work full time.

The testing task of the early pastors was to travel on foot the whole day up and down the hills on jungle footpaths, conduct services at night, sit up till late at night singing Gospel songs with the people or answering endless Biblical and doctrinal questions asked by the people, and then move on to another village the next day or the day after. Sometimes the pastor had to engage in "power encounters" with staunch non-Christians. In spite of the love, encouragement and inspiration received from Church members he visited, the itinerant pastor would often return home exhausted. These pastors were expected to visit local churches under their care at least twice a year to administer the sacraments of Baptism and the Lord's Supper and to solemnise marriages. They also had to organise and preside over the annual gathering of Christians in their care, and to conduct a week's intensive Bible study course for the lay leaders who were helping them in the administration and worship programme of the local churches.

Each of the local churches was cared for in the absence of the pastor by the natural leaders who were accepted by the congregation and the pastor. These churches depended heavily on lay leaders who gladly and freely rendered their services to the church and the people. They were looked upon as leaders and expected to lead the people in worship, Christian living and Christian giving. They were required to give their tithes from the fruits of their labour. They did not receive material benefits but the love and respect of the people and the joy of the Lord. The Mizoram churches could never have been what they were and are today without the dedicated services of those lay leaders.

From the 1960s to Today

In the 1960s when most of the Mizos became Christians the need for more pastors was urgent. Thus 16 new pastors were ordained in South Mizo alone during the decade. During the seventies another 16 new pastors were ordained. Even then there were still vacant pastorates because some pastors were sent out as missionaries to other parts of India.

The churches in Mizoram still follow this pattern of itinerant pastoral ministry. However, in a rapidly changing culture they have to find new ways for a new age. The North Mizo Church (Presbyterian) has 65 itinerant pastors to care for the 413 local churches. The small presbytery formed in 1910 has grown into a Synod comprised of 12 Presbyteries. Some of their pastors have only three or four churches under their care. To assist the 65 pastors they have 1639 elders. The South Mizo Church (Baptist) has 23 itinerant pastors to care for the 233 churches and 823 elders to assist them. Most of the pastors still have ten or more churches under their care, although there are a few who have seven or eight churches. Although the number of pastors has increased, and the number of churches cared for by one pastor has thus decreased, the volume of work and responsibilities has grown massively. With the development of youth work, women's work and missionary outreach, the present pastors are in greater demand than the pastors of early years so that now there is talk of one pastor for one local church. This, however, seems unlikely in the near future.

In the pastorate in which I live, the pastor has ten churches under his care. Fortunately the villages are not too far from each other and so the pastor does not have to walk a long distance to visit any one of them. The ten churches are close to the Headquarters so that they have the privilege of being visited by Headquarters staff more often than are distant churches. The churches are trying to grow in every respect, in giving more both to the ministry in general and to the mission, and in building better churches for their worship of God. The youth group and the women's group equally cooperate and participate in the total ministry of the church.

Evaluating the Strengths and Weakness of these Churches:

There are three main strengths of the Mizoram Baptist churches.

The system is economical

The churches have centralised administration. On the one hand, tithes and missionary giving from all the local churches are sent to the Headquarters for the support of pastoral ministry and the mission work of the church. On the other hand, the Headquarters is responsible for the training and supply of itinerant pastors to care for the churches. If a local church appointed and paid its own pastor it would hardly be able to contribute to the mission fund and other projects. Moreover only very few churches would be able to pay their pastor. But by the existing system the small and poor churches and the bigger and richer churches have the same privilege of enjoying the ministry of a well trained, dedicated pastor under whose care they can all grow together.

It is expedient for mobilizing the whole church or denomination

If local churches were independent congregations or the pastorates were independent units, it would be far more difficult to mobilize the whole church denomination for the great task of world evangelization. For example, the Baptist Churches in other parts of North East India have more or less followed the principles and organization of the Baptist Churches in Western countries. Judging from my limited knowledge of those churches, they are much more independent than the Baptist churches in Mizoram and there exists a disparity between the weaker and the stronger churches and associations. This was more apparent in the case of the Assam, Manipur and Tripura Churches. I am inclined to think that it is difficult to mobilise the whole denomination in these areas.

No better pattern has been found in Mizoram

The oldest churches in Mizoram, the Presbyterian, Baptist and the Independent Church of Maraland, who adopted this model from the beginning, have continued with it because they have not found a better one. The younger denominations which appeared in Mizoram after Indian Independence have followed their lead.

But the system also has some weaknesses.

The churches do not get enough pastoral care

As we have already mentioned, the itinerant pastor depends greatly on the lay leaders of each congregation to care for the members. Most of the lay leaders are without professional training and are full time workers of one trade or another; thus they cannot be expected to give adequate Biblical and doctrinal teaching. Because of this, many church members are not firmly established in their faith. Thus they can be carried about with every wind of unsound doctrine. This weakness offers opportunity to those whose aim is "sheep stealing". Church statistics in North and South Mizoram reveal that many of their members have joined new sects every year.

Intimate personal relationships between the Pastor and the church members are lacking

An itinerant pastor who looks after ten or more churches cannot give personal attention or pastoral counselling to most of the church members. He has to depend on the lay leaders of the local churches for this important part of the ministry. If itinerant pastors have fewer numbers of churches in their care this shortcoming can be overcome to a greater extent.

It encourages itinerant preachers

One of the problems faced by the churches is the emergence of itinerant preachers who are self-styled evangelists. In churches where the pastor is seldom present, people are eager to hear guest speakers and so many people are going round the villages as preachers. These preachers often cause disunity and division in the local churches. They are doing more harm than good to the growth of the church. When new denominations and sects are increasing, the church ought to take appropriate steps to guard against this danger.

Practical Steps to Meet New Challenges

Revision of the organizational set-up

A wind of change is blowing everywhere. To cope with the changing situation and condition of the country it has been necessary to make organizational changes such as the reorganization of pastorates, Area Councils in the South, and Presbyteries in North Mizoram. To revitalize the whole church, necessary changes in the administrative organization also have had to be made. For example, what was one pastorate forty years ago will now be divided into five pastorates.

Training and employment of more pastors

With the education explosion and the intellectual enlightenment which followed, the expectations of village churches concerning their pastor were getting higher and higher. Increases in the number and quality of pastors have been demanded by the churches. The central administration has been trying its best to meet this growing need, though not satisfactorily. On the part of the pastors, there has been the desire and attempt to obtain higher qualifications. While this sounds good, it entails practical problems: some pastors have to care for two pastorates and the churches of such pastorates cannot help but suffer to some extent.

Training lay leaders

Since the normal programme of the local churches is in the hands of the lay leaders, these leaders need training in Biblical and doctrinal teaching and in church management. In South Mizo we have a regular programme of lay leadership training through a Bible School residential or mobile course. In North Mizo the Aizawl Theological College regularly holds a Mobile Theological School for lay leaders in the village churches. Besides these, the youth organization and women's organization of the Church have also been conducting leadership training camps or seminars. So the centre also has been alert to the needs of the churches.

Christian education or Sunday Schools

Sunday Schools deserve special mention because the strength of these churches has largely depended on the Sunday Schools, especially in the early years. Today every local church has a Sunday School. Introduction of Sunday School for all ages was a real source of strength for the churches. In a changing society where so many new things are being introduced, it has been necessary to review the programme and syllabus of the Sunday School to attract all age groups so that the Sunday Schools may continue to play a vital role as an evangelizing agent of the church.

Rev. C. L. Hminga is General Secretary of the Baptist Church of Mizoram, N.E. India.

SECTION IV

The Church as God's Agent for Conversion

13

The Church and its Unfinished Task of World Evangelization

WARREN W. WEBSTER

The Bible has a global perspective from cover to cover. In the book of Genesis we read of a time past when God made all things. In the book of Revelation we read of a time yet future when all things will be made new in Christ. In between we find revealed God's concern for the whole world which He loves by virtue of both creation and redemption.

Admittedly, much of the Bible is concerned with the outworking of God's purposes through a single people, but that particular story is suspended between the great cosmic accounts of the Creation and the Consummation which relate to all peoples.

The message and motive for world evangelization are not limited to a few isolated texts of Scripture. Rather they permeate the warp and woof of biblical revelation showing us a missionary God whose vision and concern from the very beginning extend to the whole world. The global range of divine concern as revealed in the Bible is the background for the Church's mission to the world.

The Church and its Biblical Mandate

The biblical mandate for world evangelization may be summarized in the words of four great commissions found in Scripture:

the commission to Abraham;
the commission for Israel;
the commission of our Lord;
the commission according to the Apostle Paul.

These representative declarations, bridging both the Old and New Covenants, unite in stressing the divine concern for all peoples on earth.

The Commission to Abraham

In Genesis 12:1–3 we see the early historical outworking of God's plan for the world through the call of Abraham as "the first missionary."

> The Lord had said to Abram, "Leave your
> country, your people and your father's
> household and go to the land I will show you.
>
> I will make you into a great nation
> and I will bless you;
> I will make your name great
> and you will be a blessing.
> I will bless those who bless you,
> and whoever curses you I will curse;
> and all peoples on earth
> will be blessed through you."

The "missionary call" has often been similar to that given to Abraham—to leave home and family, and to cross cultural frontiers, to go to the place of God's choosing, and to do so in obedience to the Lord of the whole earth.

God promised to make Abraham a great nation (*goy*). The promise included the provision that through him all peoples (*mishpachot*) of the earth would be blessed. The basic meaning of the Hebrew word *mishpachah* is "category, class, subdivision" as of a tribe or larger group of people (Numbers 26, Joshua 13, 15). In its most precise Old Testament definition it refers to a social group smaller than a tribe but larger than a household (Joshua 7:14 and 1 Samuel 10:20,21). Yet in three reiterations of God's promise to Abraham the Hebrew word *goyim* ("nations") is used interchangeably with *mishpachot* ("peoples, families").[1]

Both words underscore the unlimited range of God's interests and activities. This was one way of expressing the global dimensions of the promised blessing through Abraham potentially extending to all the branches or subdivisions of mankind.

The Commission for Israel

God intended that Israel as the covenant nation descended from Abraham should be "a light to the nations, that . . . salvation may reach to the end of the earth" (Isaiah 49:6). In Psalm 96:3 we find what has been called the Great Commission for Israel: "Declare my glory among the nations." It is clear from the beginning that God wanted his name to be known in all the earth, his "saving power among all nations" (Psalm 67:2).

The Hebrew word *goy* (pl. *goyim*) translated "nations" in these passages denotes a people considered either politically or racially. While the Old Testament does not contain any precise definition of nationhood or what constitutes a *goy,* the way the word is used suggests three major aspects: a common racial origin, some form of political structure or government, and possession of a territory of its own. The individual identitity of a *goy* was usually expressed through use of a common language as well.[2]

While *goyim* in the Old Testament frequently refers to Gentile nations apart from Israel, the singular form is applied to Israel also as a *goy* among the other *goyim* of the world (Genesis 12:2, 17:5, 18:8). It was before those other nations that Israel was to be a light and a means of spreading the knowledge of God to other peoples.

God's election of Abraham, and through him of Israel, was an act of grace. It was election for service, not merely for the enjoyment of God's favors. For the most part, however, Israel progressively compromised her mission in the world through disobedience and unbelief.

> The tragedy of Israel is that they mistook election for service, and election for favoritism. They clung to privilege but thought lightly of responsibility. They wanted to enjoy special treatment without undertaking their divine mission. Across the end of the Old Testament might be written the words: Mission Abandoned.[3]

There is a danger and a warning here for God's people in every age. Where the desire for privilege displaces the divine motive for service there is a danger that the people of God will slacken or fail in their mission to declare the glory of God—and the gospel of God—to their world neighbors.

Despite Israel's disobedience we find throughout the Old Testament that the divine foundation had been laid for the Church's mission to the world.

The Commission of our Lord

It is striking to note that the Gospels do not climax with the death, burial and resurrection of our Lord but with his giving of the Great Commission. The dominant theme of his post-resurrection teaching was his concern that men everywhere should hear the Good News. It is not surprising then that the Great Commission in one form or other is reported in each of the Gospels and in Acts.

The Great Commission is not an isolated command arbitrarily or artificially imposed upon the Christian faith. Dr. George Peters notes:

> It is a logical summation of the character of God as He is revealed in the Scriptures, of the missionary purpose and thrust of God as unfolded in the Old Testament, of the saving work of Christ, of the nature and work of the Holy Spirit, and of the nature and design of the church of Jesus Christ.[4]

In Matthew's form of the Great Commission our Lord explicitly commanded his followers to "go and make disciples of all nations." The four dimensions of his commission are outlined in the four "alls" of Matthew 28:19–20:

> It is based upon *all* divine authority.
> It reaches to *all* nations.
> It includes all teaching.
> It extends through *all* time.

We know that the Great Commission devolves upon believers in every era because of the Lord's specific promise, "I am with you always, to the close of the age." William Carey gave the classic reply to critics of his day who maintained that the Great Commission was given only for the original disciples:

> If the command of Christ to teach all nations extends only to the Apostles then doubtless the accompanying command in Matthew 28 of the divine presence must also be so limited. But it is specifically worded in such a manner as expressly to preclude such an idea—"Lo, I am with you always, to the end of the world." [5]

The command is coextensive with the promise. Since the promise was for all time so also must the command be.

In Matthew's account of the Great Commission the central emphasis is clearly on making disciples and the object of the discipling process is *panta ta ethnē,* "all nations". Before asking who these biblical "nations" are we should note a similar emphasis in the teaching of the Apostle Paul.

The Commission According to the Apostle Paul

Paul's Epistle to the Romans both begins and ends on a universal note. In the first paragraph he speaks of having received "grace and apostleship to bring about obedience to the faith for the sake of his name among *all the nations*" (Romans 1:5).

He closes the letter with a reference to the mystery of the gospel which was hidden for long ages past but is now "made known to all nations according to the command of the eternal God to bring about obedience to the faith" (Romans 16:25–26).

The fundamental thought here is that the gospel was revealed by command of the eternal God for one specific purpose: to bring peoples of all nations to obey the faith. The expression used to indicate the scope of mission is the same found in Matthew 28, *panta ta ethnē,* "all nations".

Who or what are the "nations" to be evangelized? The Greek word *ethnos* refers to a natural grouping. As such it may be used of a herd of cattle or swarm of bees, as well as for a tribe, nation or race of people. A biblical "nation" is more of an ethnic unit than a modern nation-state. Biblically speaking there are more "nations" to be evangelized than simply the 220 or so political nations and territories on the face of the earth, each of which may contain several or many *ethnē*. For example, in Senegambia there are at least 22 distinct ethnic groups, each with its own language, culture, world view and history and, to some extent, its own territorial distribution. Failure to develop different strategies for the evangelization of such ethnic units within modern nation-states has frequently resulted in missionaries being sent to evangelize countries in general rather than specific people groups or biblical "nations" (*ethnē*) within them.

Having recognized that there are some differences between biblical "nations" and modern "nations", we should be careful not to make too much of the distinction. Some have built a rather imposing missiological superstructure on an elaboration of *panta ta ethnē* which goes far beyond ethnic considerations to define a minutiae of people groups characterized by various sociological and occupational criteria. This may have value in formulating evangelistic strategies to penetrate all strata of society but it would be difficult to substantiate that such was the original meaning and intent of the Lord's command to "make disciples of *all nations*."

In the Septuagint *ethne* is the normal rendering of *goyim* ("nations") and has similar connotations of common origin, political structure, language and territory. Just as in the Old Testament *goyim* frequently referred to pagans or Gentiles, so in Hellenistic Judaism *ethnē* had become a technical term for Gentiles in contrast to the chosen people. As such, by New Testament times the term had come to have more of a religious than an ethnic designation.

> In view of this it is unlikely that *ethne* in Matthew 28:19 should be understood in the sense of separate ethnic units. It *could* bear that sense, but there were far more suitable Greek words to give expression to that shade of meaning: words such as *phule* (people as a national unit of common descent), *laos* (people as a political unit with a common history; this is the Greek word most frequently used for the Jews as a people), and *glossa* (people as a linguistic unit).[6]

It is interesting to recall that all four of these Greek words occur in sequence in Revelation 7:9 where we have a glimpse of the people of God at the end of history when the mission is complete:

> After this I looked and there before me was a great multitude that no one could count, from every nation (*ethnos*), tribe (*phule*), people (*laos*), and language (*glossa*), standing before the throne and in front of the Lamb.

Again *ethnos* is seen to be the more general and larger term for referring to nations and people, but in the end the smaller subgroups of mankind will also be represented in the great multitude to stand before the Lamb.

Finally, we may note from the Gospel parallels to Matthew 28:19 and related passages that *panta ta ethnē*, "all nations", is for all practical purposes a synonym for:[7]

holē hē oikoumenē	"the whole inhabited world"	Mt. 24:14; Mk. 13:10
holos (hapas) ho kosmos	"the whole world of man"	Mt. 26:13; Mk. 16:15
pasa hē ktisis	"the entire human world as created by God"	Mt. 16:15

The focus of these New Testament expressions, like the Hebrew terms examined earlier, is on a global mission to the whole world of mankind. The emphasis is not a methodological one which stresses a "people by people" approach to separate ethnic units—though that is not totally excluded. The central promise is that the Christian mission will reach geographically, culturally and religiously far beyond anything known up to that time—to the ends of the earth and the end of the age.

The Church and its Global Expansion

In pursuing the purposes of God and the commission of Christ how far has the Church progressed in its task of world evangelization? The growth of the Church and the influence of Christianity can be measured in several dimensions.

The Geographical Dimension

Geographically, the Christian faith has achieved near universal dimensions with churches on every continent and in nearly every independent nation. We live in an age when the Church of Jesus Christ is more widely planted and more deeply rooted among more peoples than ever before in history. In the last two hundred years since the rediscovery of mission on the part of evangelical Protestants, the Christian faith has literally exploded around the globe. Protestant and Roman Catholic missionaries have reached out to virtually every country to make Christianity the world's largest and most widespread religious faith.

Two hundred years ago less than one percent of the world's evangelical believers lived outside of Northern Europe and the eastern seaboard of North America. But in the last two centuries the Christian mission has spread in the non-Western world until now more than half of evangelical Christians are found outside of Europe and North America. Christianity can no longer be said to be a predominantly Western religion. Despite a decline of Christian influence and numbers in some parts of the Western world, the growth of evangelical believers in many non-Western countries continues at a rate higher than the rate of population growth in those areas. As a result, the center of gravity of evangelical Christianity is now shifting from the lands of the West to the rapidly growing churches of Africa, Asia and Latin America. There are now almost as many evangelical believers in Africa as in all of Western Europe.

In one sense there are few, if any, remaining geographic frontiers for the gospel if by that is meant hitherto unknown or unexplored areas where no Christian witness has ever gone. But there are areas, both large and small, where there may be no resident Christians or viable indigenous churches. Some of these areas are in lands formally closed to regular missionaries but potentially accessible to Christian travelers or "tentmakers" . Such barriers to the gospel are not so much geographical as they are political, religious or ideological.

Today there are Christians and organized churches in practically every country on earth though in some instances the Christians may be mainly foreigners or members of a minority ethnic community. There are approximately a dozen countries with *no known indigenous churches:* Albania, Mauritania, Libya, Djibouti, Saudi Arabia, Yemen, Oman, United Arab Emirates, Kuwait, Qatar, Maldives and Mongolia. All but Albania and Mongolia are Muslim states.

There are several other lands with *a few known indigenous churches* where the total of indigenous believers may be less than 1000: Morocco, Algeria, Tunisia, Somalia, South Yemen, Comoros, Afghanistan, Bhutan, and possibly Cambodia. In the case of Turkey and Iran the same situation pertains for the indigenous majority since most of the believers in those lands are from ethnic minority groups.

But surveyed geographically there are very few lands where the Christian faith has not taken root indigenously or is not, at least, represented by expatriate Christians. It can truthfully be said that the sun never sets upon the Church of Jesus Christ!

The Cultural Dimension

Over the years Christianity has spread on a global and cross-cultural scale to the point where it can no longer be accused of being either a Western or a "white man's" religion. The *World Christian Encyclopedia* reports that as of 1981, for the first time in 1,200 years, the Christian faith once again has a non-white majority. By A.D. 2000 the non-white races are expected to account for 60 percent of all professing Christians.[8] The races of mankind are all represented in the Church of Jesus Christ, though not equally or proportionally.

Ethnolinguistically, David Barrett analyzes 8,990 distinct people groups or cultures in the world and refers to some 4,050 as Christian cultures (defined as having over 50 percent church members). This leaves 4,940 non-Christian cultures (with church members under 50 percent). He notes that about 2,800 of the latter have been extensively evangelized by various means including Scripture translations, though response so far has been meagre. The remaining 2,100 cultures he refers to as "in varying degree unevangelized" which means with populations less than 60 percent evangelized, using his definitions. It is important to note that "unevangelized" and "unreached" are not necessarily synonymous. Of 2,100 "unevangelized" people groups Barrett says:

> These cultures are not however totally unreached by the gospel; many are found in largely Christianized countries, one in four already have Scripture translations in their own languages, many are exposed to Christian broadcasting in their languages, and many have small but significant churches of their own people. Less than half of these are unreached peoples.[9]

On Barrett's definition the only people groups that can correctly be called unreached are the one thousand or so whose populations are each less than 20 percent evangelized. Those one thousand relatively unreached people groups have a total population of 1.7 billion people among whom the percentage of church members would range as low as from zero to less than one percent. Unquestionably a significant part of the unfinished task of world evangelization must focus on new and culturally relevant attempts to communicate the gospel to those peoples.

The encouraging thing is that there are at least 8000 cultures or people groups which the Christian faith has to some degree penetrated, if not permeated. Perhaps that is what leads Barrett to observe optimistically that:

> The dimensions of the unfinished task of world evangelization are in fact very much smaller than contemporary Protestant and Catholic missionary organizations realize.[10]

Linguistically, Christians have seen significant progress in making the Word of God available in the languages of men. At the end of 1982 the United Bible Societies reported some portion of Scripture—at least one book—available in 1763 languages which are spoken by 97 percent of the world's people. This has been called the greatest achievement in language communication which the world has ever known. Neither the United Nations nor the Communists have ever succeeded in getting a message to so many people in so many languages.

Bibles or New Testaments are available in all of the world's major languages. The entire Bible has been translated into a total of 279 languages which are spoken by about 90 percent of the world's people. Actually just 75 primary languages represent the speech of 80 percent of the earth's population and all have the complete Bible. New Testament translations are available in 830 languages representing some of 95 percent of all speakers. In addition, a first-time translation of some portion of Scripture in a new language is completed on an average of every two weeks.

The work of Scripture translation has progressed to the point where only three or four percent of the world's population remain without so much as John 3:16 in their mother tongue; but that may represent between 150 and 175 million people. Some of those people may be able to use translations available in another language or dialect and so do not require a complete translation in their mother tongue. Nevertheless, it is calculated that Scripture translations are desirable in some 3300 additional languages. Currently more than three thousand Bible translators, including a growing number from the Two-Thirds world, are at work on new or continuing translation projects in nearly a thousand languages.

When it is stated that the Christian Scriptures are available in whole or in part in languages spoken by 97 percent of the world's population, it does not mean such a high percentage has been exposed to the Word of God or even knows that it exists. It only means that 97 percent could *potentially* obtain some Scripture in their mother tongue if they knew about it, desired it and could read and afford it. Even where Bibles or New Testaments are available in local languages, in many countries 90 percent or more of the people have never seen or owned a copy.

Annual distribution of Scriptures has risen steadily throughout this century, from 5 million Bibles and 7 million New Testaments sold or distributed in 1900 to over 36 million Bibles and 57 million New Testaments in 1980. Still there is a tremendous job of distribution yet to be done. In addition to the Bible Societies many church, mission and para-church organizations are deeply committed to Scripture distribution on a global scale.

One barrier to broader distribution of the written Word of God is the fact that there are nearly one billion adult non-literates, many of whom live in some of the least evangelized countries. In large areas of countries such as India, Pakistan and Bangladesh seventy or eighty percent of the people could not read a gospel portion if it were given them in their mother tongue because of the high rate of illiteracy. In such situations Christians are frequently found in the forefront of programs for encouraging adult literacy education.

Other organizations are active in mass media evanglism, which supplements the printed page in transcending linguistic barriers. In addition to Christian broadcasting, good use has been made of culturally sensitive films in communicating the gospel message. The film *Jesus*, dubbed into local languages, has proven effective with millions of people in audiences around the world. For those who have no Scriptures in their languages, or cannot read them, Gospel Recordings makes recorded messages available for evangelistic use in nearly 4,300 languages and dialects.

Culturally, it has been estimated by Ralph Winter that 80 percent or more of the world's people who do not profess the Christian faith live behind cultural barriers that prevent them from readily being able to grasp the significance of the gospel for themselves. They cannot presently be won by ordinary "near-neighbor" evangelism simply because they have no near Christian neighbors, or none who understand their language and culture, or none in their social stratum who can effectively communicate the gospel to them. The only way such unreached people will ever be effectively evangelized is for Christians somewhere to determine to cross those cultural barriers—whether language, caste, tribe, social class or economic strata—in order to communicate the gospel in ways the unreached can comprehend.

The Spiritual Dimension

"At the beginning of the 1980s, Christians of all kinds numbered 1,432,686,500, which is 32.8% of the world's population," according to the *World Christian Encyclopedia*. [11] This total represents all who call themselves followers of Jesus Christ—of all traditions and confessions, and all degrees of commitment. This includes Catholics, Protestants and Orthodox as well as independent indigenous churches and various sects. The total of such Christians increased enormously from 558 million in 1900 to 1,433 million by 1980. But during the same 80 years the Christian percentage of the world's population declined slightly from 34.4 percent in 1900 to 32.8 percent in 1980.

Some observers are surprised that the decline was not greater. Others are surprised that there was any decline at all in view of the manifold increase during the twentieth century in numbers of Christian organizations, workers, literature, broadcasts and Scriptures distributed. All of those factors supposedly contributed to the astonishing surge of Christianity in the Two-Thirds world from 83 million in 1900 to 634 million by 1980. Unfortunately those gains were largely offset by massive defections from organized Christianity in the West, due to the inroads of secularism, humanism, materialism and Communism during the same period. One might hope that the gains contributed primarily to the number of committed Christians while the losses came largely from the ranks of non-practising, nominal or marginal Christians; but the actual facts, if known, would probably not be quite so simple.

In any event there are more professing Christians in the world than "possessing Christians." From an evangelical perspective many of those that claim to be Christians still need to be evangelized so as to come to personal, saving faith in Christ. The great number of nominal, uncommitted or non-practising Christians remains a massive problem, pointing to the urgent necessity of re-evangelizing each new generation even within so-called Christian cultures.

Various attempts have been made to estimate the number or percentage of truly committed Christians—also known as believing

Christians, real Christians, converted Christians, born-again Christians, and so forth. David Barrett gives an approximate global total in 1980 of 420,000,000 born-again Chistians whom he defines as "those who have had, or claim to have had, an experience of new birth in Christ."[12] His global figure for Evangelical Christians is less than half that many and comes to about 190,000,000, or 4.3 percent of world population in 1980.[13] Somewhere in between the above figures Ralph Winter estimates the force available for world evangelization as "258 million true Christians" whom he defines as "those Christians who possess a genuine personal faith and are spiritually capable of winning others to that faith."[14]

No one knows for certain how many in any of the above categories are entered in the Lamb's Book of Life, but it is obvious that there is still much to be accomplished in world evangelization.

The Church and its unfinished task

We have seen that the Bible reveals a divine concern for the whole of mankind. In the Old Testament the people of God were to:

declare God's glory among the nations (Psalm 96:3);
be a light to the Gentiles, bringing salvation to the ends of the earth (Isaiah 49:6);
do this in order that through Abraham all peoples of the earth should be blessed (Genesis 12:3).

In the New Testament, Christ commissioned his followers to:

be witnesses to the end of the earth (Acts 1:8) and the end of the age (Matt 28:20);
go into all the world and preach the good news to all creation (Mk 16:15); and
make disciples of all nations (Matt 28:19).

The Goal

Over the centuries the people of God have pursued their biblical mandate with varying degrees of faithfulness and intensity. We have noted the spread of the gospel and the growth of the Church as the Christian mission has made progress geographically, culturally and spiritually around the world. Only when measured geographically does the goal of announcing the gospel to the whole world appear to be near fulfilment. Viewed from any other perspective—demographically, ethnically, linguistically or sociologically—the remaining task of world evangelization seems more formidable, though not impossible.

Events and progress in the recent past indicate that we are on the right track and that God's global program is moving according to his timing. Our mission will not be completed until history, as we know it, comes to an end with the return of Jesus Christ. He himself gave the eschatological sign of mission fulfilment when he promised: "This gospel of the kingdom will be preached in the whole world as a testimony to all nations, and then the end will come" (Mt. 24:14). The end of the age awaits the completed proclamation to the ends of the earth.

In trying to assess the extent of the task remaining we need to be clear that the biblical goal is world evangelization and not world conversion. Nowhere does the Bible teach that all people will respond positively to God's revelation. The record of biblical history and experience is that man as a free moral agent is at libety to either accept or reject God's Word once has has received it. Nevertheless, evangelical Christians are concerned that people everywhere should have an opportunity to understand in their own language and cultural setting how God's revelation can affect their present life and relationships, as well as their eternal destiny, in order that they can make a meaningful response. Through this process God is calling out "a people for his name" (Acts 15:14), which ultimately shall include some "from every nation, tribe, people and language" (Rev. 7:9).

In all its efforts for world evangelization the Church needs to remember that

> the decisive feature of Christian mission is not only conversion of men and nations, but obedient witness everywhere to the Lord who makes all things new, for *ultimately the goal of missions is the glory of God and confession of His sovereignty.*[15]

Understanding the Task

Before attempting a strategy for the unfinished task those involved must understand their objective. It is not very useful to talk about evangelism without some type of definition.

Dr. David Barrett in compiling the *World Christian Encyclopedia* includes a dictionary of carefully worded definitions which he has tried to employ consistently. His definitions, such as the following, merit study in order to understand and evaluate his conclusions:

> *Evangelism.* The activities involved in spreading the gospel.
> *Evangelization.* (1) The whole process of spreading the good news of the Kingdom of God. (2) The extent to which the good news has been spread. (3) The extent of awareness of Christianity, Christ and the gospel.
> *Gospel.* The good news of salvation and new life in Jesus Christ and the coming of the Kingdom of God.[16]

Researchers who define "evangelization" differently from Dr. Barrett may arrive at somewhat different conclusions concerning the nature and number of the "unevangelized," as well as the category of "evangelized non-Christians."

The Lausanne Covenant incorporates additional biblical and theological content which is helpful in describing "The Nature of Evangelism":

> To evangelize is to spread the good news that Jesus Christ died for our sins and was raised from the dead according to the Scriptures, and that as the reigning Lord he now offers the forgiveness of sins and the liberating gift of the Spirit to all who repent and believe. Our Christian presence in the world is indispensable to evangelism, and so is that kind of dialogue whose purpose is to listen sensitively in order to understand. But evangelism itself is the proclamation of the historical, biblical Christ as Saviour and Lord, with a view to persuading people to come to him personally and so be reconciled to God . . . The results of evangelism include obedience to Christ, incorporation into his Church and responsible service in the world. (Section 4)

The Lausanne Covenant should be studied in its entirety for it deals with important aspects of evangelical commitment to world evangelization.[17] In referring to the process of spreading the good news it points out that *evangelism and social responsibility* are not the same thing, but that neither are they mutually exclusive:

> Although reconciliation with man is not reconciliation with God, nor is social action evangelism nor is political liberation salvation, nevertheless we affirm that evangelism and socio-political involvement are both part of our Christian duty. (Section 5).

The 1982 Consultation on the Relationship Between Evangelism and Social Responsibility endorsed the declaration of the Lausanne Covenant that "in the church's mission of sacrificial service, evangelism is primary." The primacy of evangelism is logical rather than temporal. In point of time demonstrations of social concern frequently precede evangelistic proclamation. But evangelism is primary because it relates to the eternal destiny of people. Also, before you can have Christian social responsibility you must have socially responsible Christians, and they are the result of evangelism and discipleship.

Social action is seen as a *consequence* of evangelism, a *bridge* to evangelism, and a *partner* of evangelism. The report of the Consultation affirms:

> Seldom if ever should we have to decide between satisfying physical hunger and spiritual hunger, as between healing bodies and saving souls since an authentic love for our neighbours will lead us to serve him or her as a whole person.[18]

Evangelism and social concern "are like the two blades of a scissors or the two wings of a bird." They must not be confused or identified with each other in definition but neither should they be separated in practice.

In a similar way, *evangelism and conversion* should not be totally identified nor totally separated. Biblical evangelism intends conversion as one of its objectives, and desires to make disciples on as broad a scale as possible, but evangelism and conversion are not the same thing and must not be confused. People can be evangelized without being converted. As a result there are in every culture where the gospel has gone some "evangelized non-Christians" who, while understanding the gospel in varying degrees, have so far rejected it for themselves or not yet decided what their final response will be. The outcome of their decision may depend in great part on the presence or absence in their midst of a viable indigenous church in which new Christians feel at home.

Reaching the Unreached

One of the Church's primary concerns in its task of world evangelization is that of announcing the gospel in culturally relevant ways to those who have not previously heard or understood it. This includes focusing on totally unreached people groups as well as on the millions of unevangelized individuals within people groups where the Christian faith has already taken root.

One way of seeking to measure progress in the unfinished task is to determine the approximate size and location of unreached people groups. "People groups" have been defined both sociologically and ethnolinguistically. The ethnolinguistic approach used in the *World Christian Encyclopedia* takes note of common origin, language and culture in assigning everyone in the world to one primary people group based on ethnic, linguistic and cultural considerations. This works well in the majority of cases where racial and language lines are quite clear, but in melting-pot nations and the influx into massive urban centers some of the distinctions begin to blur as new people groups emerge. Nevertheless, this approach seems to offer the best possibility for measuring how far we have come and how much further we have to go in evangelizing the many and diverse peoples of the world.

Another approach to monitoring progress and planning strategies in world evangelization is sociological. One such commonly used definition describes a people group as "a significantly large sociological grouping of individuals who perceive themselves to have a common affinity for one another."[19] That common affinity may be due to race or language, but this definition also expands to include affinity groups whose loyalties are based on occupation, place of residence, age, social class, level of education, politics, hobbies or other shared interests.

This is a very flexible definition but also rather nebulous. It lends itself to open-ended proliferation of overlapping groups and subgroups. On this basis it has been estimated that there are some 16,750 unreached or "hidden" peoples in the world. This is really a symbolic number pointing to the need of getting the gospel to the many segments of world society that have either not heard the message or not yet significantly responded. From a sociological perspective there could well be 167,500 or more affinity groups needing to be penetrated with the gospel. The number 16,750 does not reflect any detailed research or correspond with any actual list. The lists that are available to us in the helpful series of directories delineate two to three thousand mostly ethnolinguistic people groups, many in various stages of early evangelization, but also include as "unreached peoples" the jeepney drivers in Manila, barbers in Tokyo, high rise apartment dwellers in Seoul and nurses in St. Louis. The fact that there are no churches among "jeepney drivers in Manila" or "nurses in St. Louis" does not mean that they are necessarily unreached, for there are many churches in most of the areas in which they live, and quite a number would, in fact, have connections with such. Special evangelistic thrusts and even Christian fellowship groups may prove useful among taxi drivers, barbers, apartment house residents and nurses, but it is very doubtful that separate churches are either needed or desirable for such affinity groups.

Similarly, a recently published attractive map titled "Peoples Groups of Mainland China" portrays 32 groupings based solely on sociological rather than ethnolinguistic criteria. The 32 people groups include such categories as "Children", "the Elderly", "Shepherds", "the Lost Generation", "the Military Forces", "Medical Personnel", "Coaches" and "Athletes", "Housewives", and "Undesirable"! Although such groupings may be useful for stimulating interest they have little value from the point of view of either research or strategy. Nor can such affinity groups be said to correlate closely with biblical "nations" and "peoples" in the way that the major ethnolinguistic people groups seem to do.

The greatest problem with the sociological approach to people groups is that any given person may belong to as many as eight or ten different sociological groupings. People can belong to both reached and unreached groups at the same time depending upon which sociological category is under discussion. This problem of overlapping classifications makes it very difficult to talk meaningfully about measuring progress in announcing the gospel to the world. For that purpose we need a definition of a people group that counts each person only once.

It seems that evangelistic progress is best measured in terms of the Christian presence within the major ethnolinguistic people groups in the world. But affinity or special interest groups reflecting relationships in society frequently provide a useful network for the spread of the gospel from person to person and should not be neglected in planning strategy.

In the current discussions on "reaching unreached peoples" one element of ambiguity arises from the fact that it is much easier to describe when an *individual* has been "reached" with the gospel than it is to say when a culture or *people group* has been "reached". Even in referring to individuals, however, when someone is said to have been "reached with the gospel" it is not always clear from that statement whether he has actually become a Christian or simply been exposed to the claims of Christ. The confusion is even greater when the reference is to "reaching" an entire culture or people group.

At this point the following definitions may be helpful in clarifying the categories of people groups, viewed from the perspective of evangelization:

> *untouched*—a population group that has never been explored, contacted or influenced by Christians. These are often primitive or aboriginal peoples.[20]
> *unreached*—an ethnic, linguistic or other people group within which there is no viable indigenous, evangelizing community of believers. (Where there is such a Christian community, that group can be said to be at least initially penetrated or minimally reached with the gospel whether or not their numbers and resources are adequate to evangelize the rest of their people without outside (cross-cultural) assistance. The remainder of the task of reaching those people is a matter of progressive evangelization whether totally from within the group or assisted by outside resources.)
> *unevangelized*—the state of not having the gospel known, understood or offered. (On Barratt's definition this term may be applied to ethnolinguistic cultures with populations of whom less than 60 percent have been evangelized.[21] Even in many "reached" cultures where the gospel has taken indigenous root the majority of individuals may be "unevangelized."
> *unincorporated*—not part of the body of Christ. (This term includes the category of "evangelized non-Christians" who may still be unconvinced, undecided and unconverted although they have been exposed to the gospel.)

In employing the above terms it should be noted that the number of ethnolinguistic cultures totally "untouched" by the gospel is comparatively small. Where Bible translators or other Christians are at work among such people they are no longer said to be "untouched" though they may be largely "unevangelized" and "unreached" in the absence of viable indigenous Christian witness in their midst.

The number of "unreached" cultures without a significant local Christian community of their own is somewhat more than the number of peoples totally untouched by the gospel. But of some 9,000 ethnolinguistic peoples Barrett regards as clearly unreached only some 636 groups have less than 0.1 percent of their population as church members. He further reports that in 394 of those people groups less than 0.01 percent of their population are members of any church. They are unreached peoples because they do not yet have a viable indigenous, evangelizing community of believers. Concerning the precise number which constitutes the dividing line between reached and unreached peoples Barrett comments:

> Even a church as small as 0.1% of a people can be a significantly evangelizing church; there are plenty of examples in history of a thousand Christians evangelizing their group or culture of a million people. But below this figure, the church is so small that it cannot reach very far by itself. This is the case with the 636 people groups just described. They have each no numerically significant evangelizing church, and they each live in countries with only a miniscule Christian presence. The gospel is therefore effectively hidden from them until outside influence can be brought to bear.[22]

However, the *responsiveness of the community* must also be borne in mind. In an open and responsive environment one real Christian in every thousand of a people can be a significant force for evangelism. But in hostile and repressive situations the evangelistic potential of such a small number of Christians is considerably less.

One of the bright spots on the world scene is the work of the Holy Spirit in raising up a growing force of non-Western missionaries for new thrusts in cross-cultural evangelism within their own nations and beyond. Within the last decade the number of missionaries arising out of the Two-Thirds world has increased dramatically from some 3,000 to more than 15,000. The role of the cross-cultural missionary, wherever he comes from, is not primarily to evangelize an entire people group. That is the task of the local people who are brought to Christ. The missionary's job is to create a cell which will then evangelize the group from within. While missionaries are used to plant churches, local believers multiply them. That is what makes both the planting of new churches and the renewal of previously existing churches so important in the task of world evangelization. David Bryant reminds us:

> Dynamic tension must always be maintained between church renewal and world evangelization. Each thrives on the other and drives us to the other, if kept in proper balance. Renewal prevents "burnout" in the task of mission. Mission challenges "cop-out" in the fruits of renewal.[23]

In trying to assess how far we have come in reaching the unreached with the gospel and in planning the next thrust for world evangelization, we need to begin by determining how far the gospel has spread in modern nation states and primary people groups. We already know in which of the world's 223 countries and territories indigenous churches are rooted. The dozen or so countries where indigenous believers are either nonexistent or very few in number should become objects of informed prayer on the part of Christians everywhere as strategies are laid for the advance of the gospel in such situations. In lands like Mongolia where there are few if any local Christians we do not need at this stage an elaborate strategy based on scores or hundreds of affinity groups within Mongolian culture. The prior need is to find ways of establishing a Christian presence in any part of Mongolian society where the gospel may begin to work from within. Later on as the

Church begins to grow in what is hoped will be a changing climate in such semi-closed lands, one of the concerns of the Church will be for reaching into the various people groups that make up its nation.

We know that with a few exceptions the Church has taken root in nearly every independent nation on the face of the earth. But we also believe that modern nation states are not the same thing as the biblical "nations" our Lord has commanded us to disciple. So our strategies must also include the 9,000 to 10,000 ethnolinguistic groups of which we are aware, in an attempt to locate and describe those in which the church of Jesus Christ is not yet represented by a viable indigenous, evangelizing community of believers. This should lead to efforts to penetrate with the gospel those unreached ethnic groups which are accessible, while focusing specific and determined prayer upon those which are not open to normal Christian witness for various political or cultural reasons. In the process of strengthening the Church and spreading its influence in places where it has already taken root, we need to assess more accurately the extent to which various sociological groups within each culture have no believers or churches in their midst and may require special, creative evangelistic methods tailored to those situations. We are concerned to reach unreached individuals, families and communities within supposedly "reached" people groups where biblical Christianity has already taken root, as well as to send missionaries to those almost totally unreached peoples among whom there are few, if any, indigenous churches. The goal is that in every primary people group there should be an indigenous community of believers able to evangelize their own people.

Tools for the Task

Many centuries before the apostle Paul was sent out from Antioch, there lived in the land of Greece a philosopher-scientist named Archimedes. It was he who enunciated the principle of the lever. He is reputed to have said that if he was given a fulcrum which was strong enough and a lever which was long enough and a place out in space to stand, he could move the world! Technically he was right, but he lacked the tools. What Archimedes lacked we as Christians have. For in the unshakeable promises of the inspired Word of God we have the world's strongest foundation. In prayer we have the world's longest lever, for prayer moves the hand that made the world. If we will go on using the Word of God as our foundation and prayer as our lever—energized by the Holy Spirit—we can go on moving the world until Christ returns.

Footnotes

1. Genesis 18:18, 22:18, 26:4.

2. See article under *goy* in G. Johannes Botterweck and Helmer Ringgren (eds.), *Theological Dictionary of the Old Testament* (Grand Rapids: Eerdmans, 1975), Vol. II, pp. 426–33.
3. Douglas Webster, *Local Church and World Mission* (New York: Seabury Press, 1964), pp. 59 and 61.
4. George Peters, *A Biblical Theology of Missions* (Chicago: Moody Press, 1972), p. 173.
5. William Carey, *An enquiry into the obligations of Christians to use means for conversion of the heathens* (London: Carey Kingsgate Press, 1961).
6. David J. Bosch in Chapter 18 of Wilbert R. Shenk (ed.), *Exploring Church Growth* (Grand Rapids: Eerdmans, 1983). Bosch expresses agreement with Walter Liefield's discussion on "Theology of Church Growth" in David Hesselgrave (ed.), *Theology of Mission* (Grand Rapids: Baker Book House, 1978), p. 175.
7. Bosch, *ibid.*
8. David B. Barrett (ed.), *World Christian Encyclopedia* (London: Oxford University Press, 1982), p. 9.
9. Barrett, *op. cit.*, p. 19.
10. *ibid.*
11. Barrett, *op. cit.*, p. 3.
12. Barrett, *op. cit.*, p. 819.
13. Barrett, *op. cit.*, p. 826.
14. "Unreached Peoples of the World 1983," a poster compiled by Ralph D. Winter and D. Bruce Graham (Pasadena: US. Center for World Mission).
15. Ian Breward in J. D. Douglas (ed.), *New International Dictionary of the Christian Church* (Grand Rapids: Zondervan, 1974), p. 667.
16. Barrett, *op. cit.*, p. 826 and p. 828.
17. "The Lausanne Covenant," published by the Lausanne Committee for World Evangelization.
18. *Evangelism and Social Responsibility: An Evangelical Commitment*, Lausanne Occasional Papers, No. 21 (Wheaton, Ill.: Lausanne Committee for World Evangelization and World Evangelical Fellowship, 1982), p. 25.
19. Edward R. Dayton, *That Everyone May Hear: Reaching the Unreached*, Second Edition (Monrovia, CA: March 1980), p. 25.
20. Barrett, *op. cit.*, p. 847.
21. Barrett, *op. cit.*, p. 19.
22. *ibid.*
23. David Bryant in an address before the Evangelical Foreign Missions Association in Chicago, "Concerts of Prayer; Waking Up for a New Missions Thrust", March 2, 1982.

Dr. Warren W. Webster, a former missionary to Pakistan, is Director of the Conservative Baptist Mission, Wheaton, USA.

14

The Local Church Reaches its Neighbourhood

ALFRED YEO

Introduction

A local church that does not reach out beyond the four walls of her building will die a natural death, because she fails to fulfil our Lord's unchanging Great Commission. The members of the local church must be filled with the fragrance and the beauty of the Lord. Evangelism should be an unorganised spontaneous natural "gossiping of the gospel" wherever the believers are scattered. The "chattering" of good news was continuous as a matter of life-style and privilege. The Early Church believers were Christ-saturated and people-oriented and not primarily program- or project-oriented. They looked for committed disciples, and not just converts or decision makers for statistical purposes.

God has designed and ordained local churches everywhere to be agents and centres for reaching out to the neighbourhood as well as far across the seas. Local churches do not exist for themselves but for the sake of those outside the churches. Evangelism must not stop at the proclamation of the Gospel. It is still insufficient just to lead the convert to make a decision for Christ. We need to go further by leading him to join a local church, a community of loving, caring, praying people, and not leaving the new disciple to be a "roaming catholic"!

Preferably, this local church will be a biblical (evangelical) fellowship where the Word of God is being expounded simply, clearly, regularly and faithfully. The new convert should be actively witnessing for the Lord, reproducing Christ in others, discipling others and leading them to join the church. In other words, evangelism must be church-centered. This is not an optional extra. Parachurch and evangelistic organisations must be serving the church in evangelism, not in competition with or duplication of the local church.

"Outreach" describes the strategy of early Church growth. In contrast 20th century churches organise parties, attractions, invitations, programmes, concerts, lectures, in an attempt to "drag in." Our Lord's Commission states categorically "Go . . . teach . . ." and not "Come . . . hear . . .". Early Church believers talked about the Gospel in bazaars, street corners, kitchens, and laundry areas. They had discussions publicly in theatres and schools of philosophy. Today, the Gospel is presented in sophistication in rented hotels, auditoriums and theaters or in churches and cathedrals on Sundays by ordained ministers or professional evangelists. We need to mobilise the total congregation in the active involvement of outreach.

In order that any active participation in witness may take place, the church must experience renewal from the Lord. The psalmist cried: "Renew me [or *revive me*], O Lord, according to Thy Word." The Church needs to catch the vision of the Risen Lord in all His redeeming love for us and His risen power which is at our disposal. Motivation to evangelism is the basic problem. Christians need to meditate on:

God's infinite love in sending His only Son;
Christ's substitutionary sacrifice on the Cross and the efficacy available to everyone who calls on Him;
The Holy Spirit's indwelling and empowering presence in us;
The eternal lostness of our loved ones, relatives and friends who do not know Christ;
The tremendously high privilege and honour to be chosen as the Ambassador of the King of Kings and Lord of Lords;
The overwhelming joy in heaven over one sinner who repents.

This should be our position in our active involvement in outreach, not merely on paper but in practice and reality.

Reaching Nominal Christians

In a large number of local churches there are many nominal Christians. They are very often a "thorn in the flesh!" Perhaps they were baptized or "Christianized" into the local church and confirmed and received into full membership of the church without a personal experience with the Lord. They have a form of religion without the power of godliness. They have not been born again of the Holy Spirit. Without regeneration there can be no renewal or revival.

Some Christians are backsliders without realising it themselves. If they are not in step or in tune with the Lord, they are backsliders. Sometimes this may be due to earlier discouragement or disappointment in their life. They are frustrated and have lost their faith. Some have experienced great misunderstanding from the pastor, leaders or members of the church and they are deterred from being involved in the church activities. They may go to church just once in a while to keep up a form of religion. Some over-enthusiastic Christians can become stumbling blocks to weaker Christians and so bring about their non-involvement.

Another category of nominal Christians is that which includes the divorced, the immoral, the adulterer, the Christian with a non-Christian partner. They feel guilty, rejected, and ashamed to return to church. Their circle of friends sympathises with them but the members of the church look down on them.

Another category of Christians includes the bedridden, sick, widowed and bereaved. They may feel lonely, helpless and neglected.

How do we reach out to nominal Christians? No amount of publicity of meetings, announcements and exhortation or preaching from the pulpit will move these people. They need a personal touch—a visit from the pastor or an understanding Christian, who will listen to their grievances, and sympathise with their sorrow, difficulties, shame and frustration. Normally one visit will not win them. Regular personal visits will win the confidence of these people. Counselling needs to be personal counselling and not in a group. Those who are prejudiced or have some misunderstanding with some members of the church need much explanation, reproof and reconciliation. Unless there is reconciliation there will be no renewal of faith.

Love will cover a multitude of faults. Love will lead us to forgive, to bear and forbear one another. Love will captivate, make them new converts and older Christians feel wanted and help them to feel the warmth and security in the fellowship. And we must pray for the spiritual results we long to see. Ultimately, it is God who keeps us in His power. He is able to save us from the power of darkness and translate us into the Kingdom of His dear Son. He is able to deliver us from the power of sin to the uttermost. On man's part we are to work out our salvation with fear and trembling for it is God who works in and through us for His own good pleasure.

Reaching Relatives and Friends

The Apostle Paul and Silas told the prison warden: "Believe on the Lord Jesus and you will be saved, you and your household" (Acts 16:31). They were predicting that if the prison warden put his trust in the Lord Jesus, he would be saved for eternity, he would be delivered from committing suicide and he would be spared from execution by the Roman authorities. This threefold deliverance, together with his constant hearing of hymm singing in prison and the reports from his prison officers of how Paul and Silas were talking to them about the Person of Jesus must have influenced him to put his whole trust in Jesus Christ. His wife, parents and children must have been astonished at his testimony and his transformed life.

The prison warden, still filled with shock, invited his two prisoners to his house for a meal. Paul and Silas must have testified to the family of God's marvellous work, while the warden's wife and neighbours' wives nursed the wounds on their backs. More neighbours must have gathered to see what was happening in the early hours of the morning. We are told that "the whole family was filled with joy, because they had come to believe in God" (Acts 16:34, NIV). The prediction of Paul and Silas came true. This prediction can be applied to many new converts from non-Christian homes. There is the possibility and potential for a whole family to be saved.

After the demon-possessed man at Gadara was healed by the Lord, he begged to follow Him as one of the itinerant evangelists on mission trips. Our Lord urged him: "Return home and tell how much God has done for you." So the man went away and told everyone how much Jesus had done for him (Luke 8:39). We can see how natural it was for the healed demoniac to witness to his home folk and the whole village of what the Lord had done for him. We should also have a spontaneous natural openness about the great things God has performed in our life.

Our individual home is the basic unit in our society. One percent of a child's time is spent in the Sunday School; seven percent in Primary School; and 92% under the influence of the home. So the influence of home is vitally important.

Reaching out to a believer's own family for Christ was a very natural and spontaneous practice in the early Church. Paul told Timothy to see that the widow had the priority of putting her faith into practice among her children and grandchildren, "for this is pleasing to God" (I Timothy 5:4). "If anyone does not provide for his relatives, and especially for his immediate family, he has denied the faith and is worse than an unbeliever" (5:8). The provision here refers to material needs. But as Christians, we do not only provide material needs for our children and relatives, but also spiritual food. Furthermore a widow's first good deed that is worthy of praise is that she brings up her children well. In former days and in certain traditional families in the twentieth century, a household includes aunts, uncles, cousins, grandparents and in-laws. When one person becomes a Christian, we should not regard him as the *only* Christian, but simply as *the first* in the family. There are many families concerning whom we can testify to the truth that through the first Christian in a non-Christian home, the rest of the members can be led to the Lord. It could happen through a child or an adult, illness or death, accident or happy occasion.

We can seize every opportunity to make Christ Jesus known to our relatives and friends. During the celebration of grandfather's birthday or a wedding anniversary, a thanksgiving service can be held before dinner for many relatives and friends. The Gospel can be presented at the service. On a number of occasions this writer has been asked by the bride and groom to preach at their wedding service as they desired their family and relatives and friends to hear the Gospel. In small groups we can invite neighbours, relatives and friends to tea or dinner. We can show an appropriate Christian video-tape, followed by a discussion. There could be an evening of singing or listening to music, depending on the taste of the relatives.

We can be instruments to gather friends of certain common professions together. Members of the Armed Forces can meet separately from factory workers. High School students will meet separately from the ladies. Music lovers can meet on their own. Appropriate speakers or discussion leaders can be invited to help the separate groups to know more of Christ.

Reaching Out Cross-Culturally in the Neighbourhood

The reaching out to friends discussed in the previous section will naturally include people of other cultures in our day-to-day encounters. Special efforts should also be made to reach out to people in the mission field which is at our door step. In European countries, North America, Australia and New Zealand, "Chinatowns" are found in many big cities. Thousands of Chinese are living, working or meeting there for food and even cinema shows. Greater efforts should be made to get Chinese Christians to work with Westerners in these "Chinatowns". Chinese restaurant workers are not able to attend church on Sundays. Special efforts should be made to conduct recreational and spiritual gatherings for them on weekdays.

In Melbourne, the Greek population is the second largest to that of Athens. Christians in Australian churches can encourage Greeks to meet in their church premises.

Thousands of Pakistanis and Indians are found all over Western countries. Western local churches must help organise get-togethers in their style and cultural pattern. Western churches can offer their church premises, material help and lots of prayer and encouragement.

Today, most cities of the world are cosmopolitan. People of different cultures and origins have migrated and are making the new cities their own. Some people stay only for a short period of time because of work or study or business.

In Singapore alone, thousands of sailors call in from Russia, Indonesia, China, Japan, and Korea. Thousands of tourists from all over the world fly into the city. Thousands of Japanese are being employed in Singapore on a contract basis. A Japanese Christian Fellowship has been formed to witness to them.

A European couple invited other Europeans working in Singapore to their home for friendship and Bible Study. A German service was organised in one of the local Presbyterian churches. In the same church, Indonesian services are being held regularly to witness to the thousands of Indonesians living locally. There are a number of Indian churches in Singapore.

The existing local churches should open their church doors to other language groups to allow them to conduct services. Sharing church premises may present some problems, but at least in the initial stage, for the sake of outreach, local church boards should consider sharing their building with other language groups. Financially it is impossible to build a church for every language group in an area. In one church in Singapore three languages are used in a single service: English, Tamil and Hokkien. One church has introduced ear-phones for simultaneous translation from English to Cantonese and Hokkien. This method will save time and interruption of the service. In another church, three services are held one after another on Sunday morning—English, Mandarin and Foochow.

Reaching the Political Rulers

Every Christian is potentially a prophet. The function of prophets in the Old Testament was that of foretelling and forthtelling. In the New Testament the prophets' role was that of proclamation and prediction. An example of this was Agabus who is noted for his prediction in Acts 11:28, 21:10–11.

In the eighth century B.C., contemporaries such as Amos, Micah, Hosea and Isaiah stressed the essential righteousness and morality of God's nature and the attendant ethical implications for the nation and communities. If the people were to take their covenant relationship with God seriously, they were obliged to consider the justice of God and the punishment of evil. Amos and Hosea spoke out strongly against the people's idolatry and immorality in the name of religion. Micah denounced the social injustice, the human degradation, the false prophets, and the rulers of Israel. The prophets predicted that God would use a pagan nation to punish God's own guilty, wayward, stiff-necked nation.

The local church that is alive and relevant for today's generation must have an active, vibrant prophetic role to play. The church must be sensitive to the government's policies regarding various religions. We are to be careful to listen in order to discern what God is saying to us through national issues and situations. Evangelical Christians, fellowships and churches should not remain in guilty silence, but should speak up on the issues positively.

The Church can draw the attention of the government to the disparity of wealth, to social injustice, exploitation of children, racial discrimination, sexual immorality, pornography, polygamy and drug abuse taking place in communities. If one local church fails to draw the attention of the authorities, other churches can reinforce the effort.

Reaching Out Through Preaching

The Early Church was born as a result of the resurrection of our Lord Jesus Christ. God had transformed the seemingly tragic Good Friday into a triumphant Easter Dawn. Proclamation comes out of jubilation, experience, witness and conviction of the truth regarding the person and work of Christ.

Through the heralded proclamation of the Good News, God is pleased "to save those who believe" (I Corinthians 1:21). John the forerunner was a good example of a herald, proclaiming the coming of the Messiah, calling the people to repent and be baptised. Our Lord went about Galilee, "preaching [*kērysso,* 'to herald'] the Gospel of the Kingdom" (Matthew 4:23). Christ committed the solemn responsibility to His disciples, "Preach (*kēryssete*) as you go, saying: 'The Kingdom of heaven is at hand' " (Matthew 10:7). Paul twice told the timid Timothy that he had been appointed a preacher (*kēryx,* "herald"), an apostle and a teacher (I Timothy 2:7, II Timothy 1:11).

The proclamation (*kērygma*) always leads to an appeal for response. Proclamation and appeal are designed together and cannot be divorced. We have not completed our task if we proclaim the Gospel without an appeal for decision. It is equally wrong, or more wrong, to appeal for conversion without first presenting faithfully the facts of Christ. We need to reexamine our evangelistic methods.

God has given us the ministry and the message of reconciliation (II Corinthians 5:19). We are heralds, and ambassadors for Christ. The manner of our appeal in the ministry of reconciliation should be determined by God's urgency and solemnity, his determination and drive: ". . . as though God were entreating through us, we beg you on behalf of Christ, be reconciled to God." Such condescension on God's part in trusting frail vessels, such as we are, surely should motivate great compulsion and deep commitment to His Commission.

As the Church we must remind ourselves of what God has accomplished *for us* at Calvary and be renewed in obedience to God's working *in and through us*. It has pleased God to make His appeal through man's preaching to enable man to see God's eternal plan and purpose, God's loving kindness and tender mercies, the true meaning of life and spiritual values. The solemn responsibility of proclamation is immense. Richard Baxter wrote in his "Reformed Pastor" in 1656: "How could'st thou speak of life and death with such a heart? Should'st thou not weep over such a people and should not thy tears interrupt thy words? Should'st thou not cry aloud and show them their transgression and entreat and beseech them as for life and death?"

Must the whole Church be involved in the ministry of proclamation? In the teaching of the Word, only a few believers have the gift. But in sharing the message of Jesus Christ as a herald, an ambassador, every believer must be involved.

Reaching People Through Prayer

Churches today are spending too much time talking about prayer instead of praying. Many Christians are organising prayer conferences instead of praying. At prayer meetings we spend more time listening to announcements than in praying. Our Lord exhorts that men ought everywhere to pray and not to faint. Our Lord knows better because we are not fighting "against flesh and blood, but against principalities, against powers, against rulers of the darkness of this world, against spiritual wickedness in high places" (Ephesians 6:12). And so in prayer we enter into the spiritual realm, that of struggling against the power of darkness. We are God's co-workers in His dominion, in His Kingdom. The evil one will not make things easy for us. We need to cling to the faithfulness of God. In His providential sovereignty and through the triumph of the Cross, we can become more than conquerors through Christ who loved us.

Church prayer meetings should not be merely presenting to God our shopping list of needs and requests. They should also be times of worship and praise, and meditation on His Word, His revealed will and His purpose for us. The answers to some of our requests have already been revealed in His Word. Sometimes we do not need to pray about it —God has already spoken!

Church prayer meetings should be very much the people's prayer time, and not a chance for the pastor or elders to display their praying skills. Everyone present should be encouraged to pray aloud. In many Chinese churches, the prayer time on Sundays or weekdays is spent in praying aloud simultaneously. Those churches which do not practise praying in this way might feel disturbed and unable to concentrate. But they can do it in other ways. Those who are shy when praying in large groups can be encouraged to pray aloud in small groups.

All the members of the church should learn to pray for others. Besides praying generally for the nation, for the government, for peace, for the church, for crusades and conferences, they should be prepared to visit relatives and friends, homes for senior citizens and children, hospitals and prisons, and pray with people in need.

In the course of visiting certain church members in hospital, it would be good to talk to the other patients in the same ward or room. Even if the other patients are Buddhist, Hindu or Muslim, they will welcome prayer for their recovery. Such intercessory prayer is personal and individual. This is pre-evangelism. If we take time to chat to some of them, this will encourage the patient who is a Christian to break the ice in chatting about the Lord Jesus. Soon after the prayer, if the patient becomes well sooner than expected, he will be more open to attend church and listen to more of the gospel and its healing power. The normal concept of believers is that the pastor's prayer is more effective, real and direct to God, and the prayer of the laity is not as holy and powerful. Only the pastor's prayers can secure answers from God. This is a fallacy.

The Church's ministry of prayer can support the pastors' preaching. The preachers must not be afraid to covet the prayer of the congregation in their preaching. As the congregation pray sincerely to God, the venue will be filled with the Divine Presence. Non-Christians attending the meeting will be moved by reverential awe at the presence of God. As believers become conscious of the holy presence of God, the non-Christians will sense His reality. As the messages are bathed in prayer, and proclaimed in the unction and power of the Holy Spirit, lifting up Christ Jesus, men and women will be drawn to Him. The Apostle Paul requested prayer that he might be able to speak the Word boldly, rightly, simply, clearly and freely without fear or favour (Ephesians 6:19–20). Paul exhorts us to "persevere in prayer," with a wakeful mind and thankful heart (Colossians 4:2–4). Paul requested open doors to preach the Word. Opportunities to witness for the Lord need much prayer support and should not be taken for granted. Paul urged the Ephesian Christians: 'Give yourselves wholly to prayer and entreaty; pray on every occasion in the power of the Spirit. To this end keep watch and *persevere*, always interceding for all God's people . . ." (Ephesians 6:18–19 NEB).

Rev. Alfred Yeo is Executive Secretary of the Evangelical Fellowship of Singapore.

15

Evangelistic Strategies for the Local Church

TISSA WEERASINGHA

Introduction

The early Church did not depend on special evangelistic programs as we know them today. The accent was on witnessing casually in the course of one's daily routine, wherever and whenever possible. Often, special evangelistic thrusts last only for the special period and then are shelved. While I would not discount the efficacy of crusades, door-to-door outreach projects and so on, it is evident that the impact of them has been rather limited. As far as local church outreach is concerned, a method is required which demands far less organisational and financial capacity, while at the same time being more durable. People to people evangelism on a daily basis, where they are, is one of the most effective Biblical strategies. However, in order for this to become a reality, on-going education is needed in how to share one's faith with the Hindu, Buddhist, Muslim, secularist, animist, and so on. Much of this training should be imparted at the services where the larger gatherings of the church take place, in addition to the special personal evangelism training courses conducted in any growing church. Learning to share one's faith is not a "special kind of training" but part and parcel of the nurturing process of new Christians. This education should be built into the development process of the new believers.

In people to people evangelism, we shift the focus from one highly specialized person or method, concentrated at a limited time in the calendar of the church, to a "grass roots" non-specialized, almost no-cost, year-long enterprise.

Meeting Felt Needs is the Key to Credibility

"Felt needs" are the immediate needs of which the people we contact are conscious. These needs are to be distinguished from "basic needs" such as food, clothing and shelter, and the "ultimate need" which is salvation in Christ. Felt needs may relate to emotional needs, sickness, demon possession, marital trauma or any such conflict which causes anxiety and fear which is unresolvable without recourse to special means of help.

How does the outreach of the local church relate to ministry to felt needs? Most people when initially contacted are not interested in hearing about their spiritual condition, nor are they disposed to believe what is said. Moreover, there is a credibility factor that affects the acceptance of the message, no matter how articulately that message is being communicated to them. It is precisely at this point that ministry to felt needs comes into play. Our Lord fed the hungry, healed the sick, cast out demons, in His initial contact with them. So did the apostles and disciples on their missions. This initial encounter opened the doors for a further clarification of the Gospel in its holistic dimension and often led to repentance and faith on the part of those ministered to.

Felt needs are met through the spiritual gifts ministry of the body. All believers are asked to discover and capitalize on the spiritual gifts with which they have been invested (Romans 12:6–8). The discovery of one's spiritual gifts is the key to one's self-identity and identity in the local church. And both these identities are related. Wholesome Christians are the greatest "public relational" asset of the church of Jesus Christ. They are the key to local church outreach.

The Multi-Congregational Church in the Urban Setting

The fulfilment of the Great Commission has a crucial relationship to population mobility trends today. In the understanding of this relationship, we may see the vital necessity and priority of urban evangelization. In Third World countries, especially where rural development is not accelerating at the rate it should be, the city is going to continue to be the powerful magnet. This will make overcrowded cities prime candidates for pollution, crime and hostility.

Most national governments facing urban overpopulation are frantically speeding up rural development and building satellite towns around the city to divert the population excess. When people discover the frustrations of city life, they may migrate to the satellite towns, depending on their mobility level and the state of the economy. Urban evangelization will be a key to the transmission of the gospel everywhere. As people migrate, the gospel will "migrate" with them.

The multi-congregational church is an effective structure for evangelism in the context of social and ethnic pluralism. The multi-congregational church model is a composite of different congregations which retain their uniqueness and diversity of worship while functioning in the larger context as a single integrated body of believers. Although each congregation retains its own style of worship, all congregations are under an integrated leadership structure and belong to one membership roll. This facilitates outreach in the sense that it caters evangelistically to all different kinds of people within its evangelistic radius, thus becoming a multi-faceted missionary outreach. Each ethnic group has its own worship which does not intimidate the others linguistically since only one language is used in each service.

There is one co-ordinating pastor responsible for the total program, but additional staff to supervise the various congregations. The church board is structured in such a way that there is adequate representation from all the congregations. The concerns of each congregation are dealt with in the context of the total enhancement of the church. The youth fellowship, ladies' fellowship, and the men's fellowship are organised across the three major congregations. All three congregations meet separately except at the monthly prayer meeting when all gather for a meeting that lasts for four hours.

The membership roll is one, and all members belong, not to the congregation primarily, but to the church. All finances go into the common church fund although offerings are counted separately for each service. Expenses of each congregation are met as the need arises and not according to the total collected from each congregation.

The Home Cell Unit for Nurture and Outreach

Many churches have a bigger back door than front door. Although people visit the church and even make professions of faith, the drop out rate is phenomenal. In order to avoid this it is necessary to create a structure within the church which acts as a net and prevents the "escape" of new Christians. The home cell system acts as an effective structure to contain new Christians as well as being an outreach in the community. In 1982 our own home cell network increased from 17 to 40.

The overall supervisor of the network is the pastor. This is necessary for providing leadership, motivation and vision. The total membership of the church is divided into several districts or areas over which area leaders are appointed. The area leaders' responsibilities include periodic visitation of the home cell units, and solving problems relating to physical facilities, and similar issues.

The Format of the Home Cell Unit Meeting

The home cell unit meeting includes Bible teaching, prayer for various needs of people present, singing and fellowship. The Bible study material is standard material which is given to the leaders during the weekly training sessions held in the church. This material is prepared and taught by the pastor. Every home cell unit meeting is at the same time a teaching as well as evangelistic meeting. Fellowship, nurture and evangelism are of equal importance in it. Attendance records are kept and when members are absent they are visited. In this way every member in the church who is part of the home cell unit is shepherded. It is made clear to all worshippers that participation in the home cell unit is a prerequisite to adequate pastoral care. Those not participating are considered as not requesting pastoral care from the church. There are home cell units for women and youth as well as mixed meetings. Some are bilingual, but most are monolingual; and the leaders may be either men or women according to their gifts.

Evangelism is done in and through the home cell unit and people are recruited for the church service. Although on Sundays expository Bible teaching is given, at almost all of the services people make commitments to Christ. The secret is that their heart attitudes have been already prepared at the home cell unit the previous week. Therefore, although an "evangelistic message" as such is not preached, there is a ready response for salvation. If people attend the church as visitors and make commitments, they are immediately recruited into the nearest home cell unit to their home and the leader becomes their "pastor". Therefore, not only does the home cell unit serve as a channel to the church, it also serves as a net for the church.

Spiritual Weapons for Spiritual Warfare

We know that all the resources of the enemy are arrayed against the church as it seeks to evangelise. Not only are the minds of men blinded by Satan, but communities and nations are under his grip. In many nations of the world, belief in guardian deities is widespread. Not only are there national deities, there are also local gods to whom the people are subject. These gods, whom we understand to be demonic powers, are a hindrance to the advancement of the Gospel. They are the enemies of evangelistic outreach. Communities where there is demon possession, sorcery and witchcraft have to be dealt with at this level if there is to be any successful outreach. Evangelistic outreach is not merely witnessing verbally to one's faith but also involves a prior victory gained in spiritual warfare.

And so, prior to undertaking any systematic penetration of a community, it is necessary to win the battle on our knees. Spiritual victory must precede the physical penetration. Since prayer is a great mystery we are able to experience its dynamics better than we are able to understand its technicalities.

Rev. Tissa Weerasingha is pastor of Calvary Church, Colombo, Sri Lanka.

16

Church Planting Among The Nomadic Turkana People of Northern Kenya

A Case Study

EARL ANDERSON

Northern Kenya is a semi-arid land comprising perhaps slightly less than half of the land of Kenya. The population is very sparse, mostly nomadic, perhaps half a million people. These are members of various tribes (Somali, Boran, Rendille, Samburu, Turkana, Pokot) and some smaller tribal units. This study will be concerned with evangelism in Turkana.

Evangelism in Turkana was Pioneered by Missionaries

The first contact for the Gospel in the district of Turkana, which borders Sudan and Uganda, was in the late 1940s. It was made by an Africa Inland Mission missionary, Tom Collins. He learned the Pokot language very well as he made gruelling treks on foot to contact the villagers. He often stayed with them for a week or two, living as they lived. Later he was able to cover greater distances by using a four-wheel-drive vehicle. Another worker, Dick Anderson, took up the same kind of work as Tom had been doing, mostly by vehicle. His zeal was tremendous. Messages were usually of the open air variety when in government centers, market places or trading centers.

In 1959 a site was chosen in Turkana which was to serve as a medical center and base for evangelism. At this point it may be asked why the church did not commence its settlements in conjunction with the government centers. Experience in pioneering work among so-called primitive people had led missionaries to go out to the rural areas. There, people were less harrassed by the problems of urban living, such as drunkeness and sexual promiscuity. Also tribal leaders were less sophisticated and more receptive than in the big centers. It was found to be easier to reach the people in rural areas first.

Various short term helpers, usually of other tribes, accompanied the doctor. These did some good work, but most of them did not stand the rigors of safari life and the climate. The Turkana ate all sorts of things which the more sophisticated southern Kenyans could not stomach.

The 1960s saw certain church centres being established, mostly manned by non-Turkana Africans. The evangelist usually had a place selected for him where an air strip could be made, in order that a supply of food and essentials could be maintained. At intervals MAF (Missionary Aviation Fellowship) flew the Doctor to these posts.

Experiments with Turkana Itinerant Evangelists

When young Turkana men were converted they learned to read, usually in Mission schools. An effort was soon made to use these lads as evangelists, the idea being that they could communicate easily with their own people. However, their knowledge of the Bible was limited and their foundations in the Gospel shaky. Their backsliding was a sorrowful experience for the leadership. However, an effort was then made to equip these young evangelists for itinerant evangelism. The idea was to follow certain groups in their moves from water hole to water hole. This method produced difficulties. The evangelist was usually a young single man. He had no wife to build the small igloo type of palm-leaf house. He had no donkeys to carry his goods. If he should get donkeys, who would herd them? The people were too poor to produce food and housing for him. Since the evangelist had a slightly better education, he would not live as they lived in any case. A Christian was always recognised by his refusal to participate in pagan practices. Thus he was unable to participate in many local events. And so it became evident that a better method of evangelism was to set up a place at a watering point where the evangelist could wait for the people to come. This method is, to a large extent, the practice today. Nearly every permanent watering point has a Christian witness available. Later, when schools became fashionable, it was evident that evangelists or pastors should be posted to each school area for reaching the local children.

Since the tribe is nomadic, the result was that sooner or later each person could come within reach of the Gospel, as long as watering points were adequately staffed.

Itinerant evangelism, as the Turkana Christians saw it, was an evangelism based on centers from which day trips to villages would be made. Each evangelist returned to his center for the night. Even when the number of local Turkana Christians became significant in the 1960s, they felt that they were too different to be able to live with the local people. It was not simply that the missionaries expected higher standards of the evangelists. Government officials expected evangelists to be an example of better living. Owing to the climate, local men wore very little. Women were covered from the waist down to their knees with skin skirts. The evangelist was at least partially clothed, thus becoming different. This forced a separation all the way through living conditions, even to food. This in turn meant an evangelist needed funds to live differently. Often money was provided from outside sources, such as missionaries using assistance funds, or other AIC churches sending support. The distances are so vast from one point to another that the evangelist had to have the means to get around. This was generally too great an expense, and so evangelism through centres and schools became the emphasized method.

Peter Mwaluko, from the Ukamba tribe, became the first African missionary of the Africa Inland Church. He was stationed in a center established to teach the Turkana people to fish in Lake Turkana. This centre was started at Kalokol in the 1960s. A marvellous job was done reaching fishermen, pupils in the school and others operating at Kalokol as workmen, helpers, or inquisitive tribespeople. Peter lived as simply as he could, subject to hygiene, in a palm frond house. He did his best to reach others. He emphasized the change the Gospel made when accepted—a change which was not only spiritual, but evidenced itself physically. (In the early days a change of apparel often resulted from some contact with the Gospel, but after the Government took over the schools and promoted the wearing of clothes, this change was no longer automatically an indication of an interest in Christianity. Latterly it had to be shown by evangelists that clothing had no necessary connection with conversion.)

The efforts of Peter Mwaluko at Kalokol have borne fruit. Much of the leadership in Turkana has sprung from his work. His contacts can be traced in outpost work, in many phases of church work, and even in some Government posts.

Confrontation with tribal customs

Christianity brought cultural changes right from the start. A difficulty with using local lads as evangelists appeared when the age of puberty called for tribal rites.

This was a terrific problem as it entailed non-Christian deeds such as acceptance of spirits to be placated and the like. A Christian was not reckoned a Turkana.

The peripatetic evangelist found himself at night out under the stars cooking his own meals, which were often then begged by the locals. One of the most frustrating problems facing evangelists and missionaries was the prevalent idea that once a thing was asked for, it had to be given! There was a reason for begging. Economic ties through begging were a partial assurance against an economic set back. A man could turn to anyone with whom he was on begging terms for help. Among the early hazards of evangelism was the thought that if a man became a Christian he could have all the different things an evangelist had. The idea was prevalent that out there somewhere was a god, or church, or group who would supply everything if one agreed to become a Christian. This assumption was tested many times. When the expected supply didn't come the individual was greatly upset, sometimes becoming an enemy of the evangelists. Right from the start it became evident that even a semi-educated local evangelist was still so far removed from his people that a barrier existed.

Ministry Patterns of the Evangelist and the Pastor

As small church centres developed in the rural areas of Turkana some of the Christians began to look for work in the administrative center of Lodwar. Christian boys from the secondary school needed shepherding and this led to the construction of a church in Lodwar. In the 1970s work in the town of Lodwar was commenced and a church building erected. Peter Mwaluko became its pastor.

Government policy—in effect if not deliberately—has been to foster static centres of population around permanent water, with projects providing a means of livelihood. At these centers Christianity usually has a witness—a mission station, a church, a school, a health center or, in case of extreme need, a feeding center.

There needs to be a definite understanding of the difference of the roles of pastor and evangelist. The itinerant pastor has the care of church activities, and may have a number of churches in his care. All these he must visit, and cater to church and Sunday School needs. On the other hand the evangelist breaks new ground. He tries to reach the unconverted wherever they may be found. He is often the first contact a tribesman has with the Gospel.

Experience shows that the evangelist has difficulty in getting the emphasis in the right place. The spiritual message is initially nearly always lost in the physical aspect, such as "What do I get now? What will my relatives think?" This attitude is well illustrated by an old lady at Kalakol who, when a visiting speaker asked for a show of hands for salvation, answered, "Well, I have put up my hand four times now, and I still have not received a dress."

Poverty-stricken people think primarily of the material realm. Although normally the nomad learns that somewhere, somehow, life may become easier. The physical amenities of medicine, food and clothing are powerful stimulants to cause a nomad to compromise his culture. However, the gospel goes further than the physical. The physical need must often be alleviated first. To preach to a hungry person usually produces no spiritual results. This is why so many societies in evangelistic work find that they get bogged down in the social aspects of the Gospel without making much impression on the spiritual problems.

As to Turkana, it can be stated that there have been an unusually large number of backsliders, or perhaps the confessors never understood enough for them to make genuine commitments to the Lord. Herein lies a problem which arises from the use of new or untrained evangelists. There is always the temptation to send the new convert out to reach his own people. Perhaps the underlying idea is that employing him will give him a source of income, thus alleviating the unacceptable matter of giving to him when no work has been done. So "food for work"—evangelistic work—becomes a so-called "happy" solution. The problem here is that the new evangelist is inclined to preach a gospel of "accept the Lord and you'll get support".

Results of Itinerant Evangelism in Turkana

The work in Turkana got off to a very slow start. The years of gruelling, patient trekking done by Tom Collins showed few visible converts. Dr. Anderson, after a long period of itinerant evangelism, established the hospital at Lokori as well as many centres in the surrounding area. Gradually these have gone on growing from the seed planted. Now there are over two thousand baptized believers scattered all over Turkana and 14 church centres.

The position of the church in Turkana is slowly changing. The disappointments caused by the backsliding of most of the first Bible School students is no longer experienced. In the 1970s a number of middle aged couples became the backbone of the church. Most of them are uneducated, but they have learned to love the Lord and obey Him. Also there are some educated Turkana in employment with Government or other groups, who are strengthening the church. However, the district church council has no more than two Turkana members.

Itinerant evangelism in Turkana could be carried out best by expatriate missionaries with vehicles and equipment. A local evangelist lacked the funds and education to be able to own a vehicle, something which would, in any case, have estranged him from the local people. It was expected that expatriates would be different, whereas educated local evangelists engendered jealousy and so lacked rapport. It would be impossible to assess how much was accomplished in the spiritual realm by all of the itinerant evangelism carried out in the beginning days in Turkana. However, introducing the Gospel all over Turkana was carrying out the Great Commission. Certainly, placing life on the line was a good thing, yet permanent and lasting decisions for Christ appeared meager.

Non-Turkana evangelists tended to be settled in centers, later becoming pastors who operated a circuit for visitation, teaching and baptizing converts, serving communion, performing weddings, and other church activities. It is difficult to assess their contribution on an itinerant basis. They became and still are a very stable factor in the Turkana district church.

Turkana young people, finally, were sent to and graduated from Bible Training Schools operated by the Africa Inland Church in other parts of Kenya. These graduates were welcomed to the work in the 1970s but the majority of this relatively small number have had to leave the work of the church and have gone into secular employment. The hope was ultimately to use these men as pastors, but to this day no Turkana has been ordained. Evangelists now usually have a home center and travel on foot, or by vehicle to surrounding areas. Now cultural difficulties are not so pronounced. Evangelism is still a necessary and emphasized method of proclaiming the gospel. However, new irritations are being experienced in the realms of finance, education and relations with churches. Also, security is sometimes a problem; but the Government is doing its best to alleviate this.

Conclusion

Evangelism in Kenya has shown that trying to adjust to local culture and custom is becoming less important. Education, medical services, economic changes in life style and running businesses—plus the everyday exchanges with other tribespeople and other cultures—has definitely lessened the stress on local tribal moves. However, there are two ideas almost universally held in common by most Africans. The first is that it is desirable to make no major religious or cultural move unless there are a large number willing to go along with the change. This attitude appears when the evangelist preaches that "each one shall stand for himself before God." A communal spiritual awakening is wonderful, but the ultimate reality of the Gospel is the fact that accepting Christ as Saviour is an individual choice.

A second concept is the view that any religion of any consequence will command the total life style. The idea is that the religion must dictate the total living of the individual. That is why African evangelists tend to become legalistic and lay down the law as to clothes, eating, behaviour, and attitude to government and church. We occidentals tend to worry about enculturating the Gospel—whereas the African has tended in the past to change to a culture as close to the Bible as possible. This is seen in many of the sects in Kenya where clothes, business and total life style attempt to copy what they believe to be a Biblical way of life. Looking for commendable status in old tribal customs is a recent innovation, and probably the result of the training of a new crop of Africans overseas. Their desire to understand and explain their culture is very natural and generally commendable. What the long term result of this will be cannot yet be predicted.

In assessing what has been accomplished in the Nomadic North, it is amazing, regardless of mistakes, indifference and lack of funds. Also we are humbled when we see where we have failed when we might have accomplished more. Itinerant evangelism is still a way to reach the lost, so we need to encourage it, but with wisdom, courage and prayer.

The changes we find today in culture, and the results of education, make an evangelistic ministry on an itinerant basis far more possible. The burden of funds for evangelism is more and more a responsibility of the indigenous church. The church is getting concerned about spiritual depth. Prayer is needed that this may become a permanent attitude which will bring motivation for attainment and glory to God.

Dr. Earl Anderson is a missionary in Kenya, serving the Africa Inland Church.

SECTION V

Churches as God's Agent for Social Change

17

The Church And Its Mandate For Social Change

TOKUNBOH ADEYEMO

Since their conference at Bangkok in 1973 the preoccupation of evangelicals has focused on the mission of the Church in the world—its definition, its clarification and the call for its implementation. Numerous books and articles have written on the subject.[1] Several conferences and consultations have been held.[2] A number of new evangelical humanitarian agencies have evolved while the older ones have doubled, tripled, or quadrupled their budgets over the years.[3] The subject of the poor, the oppressed and social justice has received almost unparalleled attention.

The Church's Identity

Happenings all around the world have by and large dictated the agenda for the Church. In some instances the Church has lost its identity in the course of its service. This must be rectified. If one message should ring out from this conference, it is the clarion call of the 1937 Oxford Conference: "Let the Church be the Church." This is not the time to split hairs on Abraham Kuyper's distinction between the Church as an institution and the Church as an organism—useful as the distinction may be.[4] Suffice it to say that biblical data never singles out the Church in an institutional form. The Church arises and exists neither by nature nor by historical human decision, but as a divine *convocation*. The initiative eternally belongs to the Lord, who says: "I will build my Church." Here Calvin's military conception of the Church as *la compagnie des fidèles* is apt. A company usually comes together on the basis of a command and not on that of a free agreement. To the first disciples the Master said: "Follow me and I will make you fishers of men!" And since Pentecost the Holy Spirit has been calling together repentant sinners, infusing them with new life and assembling them unto the Lord. It is accurate to describe the Church in the Greek term *kuriakon,* since it belongs to the Lord. It is purchased with His own blood (Acts 20:28) and sanctified by the Holy Spirit (Eph. 4:30). By the transforming power of the Holy Spirit, the Church is constituted "a chosen people, a royal priesthood, a holy nation, a people belonging to God" (1 Pet. 2:9).

David Bosch describes the Church as "the community of believers, gathered by divine election, calling, new birth, and conversion, which lives in communion with the Triune God, is granted the forgiveness of sins, and is sent to serve the world in solidarity with all mankind."[5] We cannot speak of the Church without establishing it wholly on the work of the Holy Spirit under the Lordship of Jesus Christ, who assures His followers of His attending presence where two or three of them are gathered in His name (Mt. 18:20). By gathering or assembling here and there (an idea derived from the Greek word *ekklēsia,* "those called out"), the Church automatically becomes visible. Without undermining the reality of the spiritual unity of all believers in Christ, it is clear that predominantly *ekklēsia* in the New Testament applies to a local assembly of people who profess faith and allegiance to Christ.[6] "The first congregation was a visible group, which caused a visible public uproar. If the Church has not this visibility, then it is not the Church."[7] Since *ekklēsia* can be used (and, in fact, is used in Acts 19:32, 39, 41) of other human assemblies and societies, the Church has been predicated as one, holy, and catholic in the Apostles' Creed.

Credo unam ecclesiam emphasizes the unity of the Church. Because it testifies to one Lord, one faith, one baptism, one hope, one Spirit, and one God, the Father, the Church is an indivisible unit (Eph. 4:4–6). Though parlous differences exist within the Protestant Church (not to speak of the situation between the Protestant and the Roman Catholic or the Orthodox Church), by virtue of its foundation, Jesus Christ, its commandment, its commission, and its goal, the Church essentially is one.[8] It differs from all other societies in that its many branches are not duplications of a standard pattern.

The Church is holy—*sancta ecclesia.* It is "set apart" in the world and distinguished from all earthly societies. The Church is the communion of saints. This does not mean that it is an assembly of perfect people (consider, for example, "the saints of Corinth"). Rather, its holiness is due to the fact that it is indwelt by the Holy Spirit through whom it is able to testify to man's ultimate concerns. By the same Holy Spirit the Church possesses the propensity to be holy. Hence the admonition: "Be ye holy in all manner of life for I am holy" (1 Peter 1:15–16). The Church signifies separation from, as much as it signifies solidarity with, the world. In the words of David Bosch, "The Church is a foreign body in the world . . . Without a faithful and sustained contact with God the

Church loses her transcendence. Without a true solidarity with the world she loses her relevance."[9]

Thirdly, the Church is catholic or universal—*ecclesia catholica*. In Christ there is neither Jew nor Greek, bond nor free, male nor female, for all believers are Abraham's seeds and heirs according to the promise (Gal. 3:26–29). Colin Morris sees the Church's universality as "a protest against the fragmentation of humanity into groups and sects and tribes."[10] The Church recognizes (or at least should recognize) no barriers whatsoever. The catholicity of the Church means that through the whole of history its inner core of identity remains the same. It cannot alter its nature. Though there are different forms in the main denominations and though there are weaknesses, errors and perversions, there are not substantially different Churches. (However, we can legitimately speak of true and false Churches.)

To the three predicates of the Church—one, holy and catholic—the Nicene Creed adds a fourth, namely "Apostolic". *Ecclesia apostolica* means the Church founded on the witness of the Apostles. By this confession both the historicality of the Christian faith and the authority of the Scriptures are affirmed. As an organism built upon the foundation of the apostles and prophets, Jesus Christ himself being the chief cornerstone (Eph. 2:20), the Church speaks authoritatively about the unchanging message of God's love and judgment in contemporary accents to man's ever-changing situations from the standpoint of solidarity.

This new community, one holy, catholic and apostolic Church, is primarily a worshipping community. God's declaration has not changed: "Let my people go, so that they may worship me" (Ex. 8:20). From east and west, north and south, the gathering together of all believers in Christ is first and foremost unto the Lord. This encounter with the risen living Lord in worship not only reveals the true nature of the Church in the light of God's perfections, but also revives the Church and sharpens the sense of its responsibility in the world. The Church cannot afford to exhaust itself in self-serving. If it does, it smacks of death. It may have been called to worship the Lord; it has also been sent to serve the world. The Master says: "As the Father sent me into the world, even so I send you into the world" (John 17:18; 20:21). Herein lies the blueprint for the Church's social responsibility in the world: to fulfil that for which Jesus Christ was sent in the power of the Holy Spirit.

The Church's Manifesto

If the Church's social responsibility derives from and fulfils that for which Christ was sent, it is only appropriate that we look at the Master's track record. Two main passages attract our attention, Luke 4:18–19 and John 17. In the former passage, which is a quotation from

Isaiah 61:1–2, Jesus enunciates His mission in terms of proclamation, healing and liberation. In the latter passage, He summarises His time with His disciples in terms of manifesting God's name to them (verses 6, 26); discipling them (verses 8–18); and equipping them through a process of sanctification (verse 19). When we survey the overall teaching and practice of Jesus and of His Apostles, six areas of the Church's social responsibility can be identified.

Confessing Jesus Christ as Lord

Jesus, at the end of his earthly ministry, says: "I have manifested your name unto the men whom you gave me out of the world" (John 17:6; also in verse 26). To manifest God's name literally means to show God's person and perfections so that man may know Him and enter into an intimate relationship with Him (see Ex. 6:3). By the words He spoke and the works He did, Jesus Christ revealed His Father (John 14:9–10).

Similarly, the Church is charged with the responsibility of revealing Jesus Christ as Lord. This is a resurrection mandate! For death could not kill Him; the grave could not hold Him; Satan could not destroy Him. In triumph Jesus arose from the dead and He lives forever more! This cannot be said of any other man including religious teachers such as Mohammed, Buddha and Confucius. "God has exalted him [Christ] to the highest place, and has given Him the name that is above every name, that at the name of Jesus every knee should bow, in heaven and on earth and under the earth, and every tongue confess that Jesus Christ is Lord to the glory of God the Father" (Phil. 2:9–11). In this divine declaration, God does not exclude any part of the created universe from the domain of Christ's Lordship. Neither does He exempt any creature—for He says "every tongue". The Lordship of Jesus Christ extends to, and covers, all of life and its daily reality.

Lordship means ownership. The maker of any object is its owner and therefore its lord as long as the object has not been sold or given away freely or willed to somebody else. By the act of creation Jesus possesses and controls the "title deed" to all things and all beings—whether a communist Chinese, a socialist Frenchman, a secularist Englishman, a religious Indian or a superstitious African. "For by him all things were created: things in heaven and on earth, visible and invisible, whether thrones or powers or rulers or authorities; all things were created by him and for him" (Col. 1:16, see John 1:3). As Lord, He has both *dunamis* and *exousia* to control and shape the destiny of His subjects. To the Lord Jesus has all authority in heaven and on earth been given (Matthew 28:18). Moreover, by the act of redemption provided for all, Jesus is Lord. For with His precious blood every believer is redeemed from the empty way of life handed down from the forefathers (1 Peter 1:18, 19).

Simply stated, confessing Jesus Christ as Lord means complete surrender to Him. It means total obedience to His commands. It means absolute allegiance to His reign. This has far-reaching implications. In communist Russia, confessing Jesus as Lord may mean coming into conflict with the powers-that-be with consequent imprisonment. It sometimes means that in Marxist Ethiopia. In apartheid South Africa it may mean condemning the inhuman racial discrimination and identifying with the poor and the powerless. In the totalitarian regimes of many of the Latin American and African states, it may mean civil disobedience to unjust rules and corrupt structures. In the affluent secularist West, it may mean a radical examination of our lifestyle and values and an unequivocal denunciation of atheistic humanist tendencies and theories. In all cases, it means testifying that the ultimate supreme reality with power and authority is Christ, not Caesar. Doing so may mean death. It may mean hatred and severe persecution by the world. Since the Church, the one holy catholic apostolic community, is not of the world any more than Christ is of the world (John 17:14), it is bound to be hated in the fulfilment of this responsibility (John 15:18–20). But the one to fear is not the one who can kill only the body but the one who can kill body and soul and cast it into eternal hell. When the disciples were forbidden to speak in the name of Jesus, they responded: "Judge for yourselves whether it is right in God's sight to obey you rather than God. For we cannot help speaking about what we have seen and heard" (Acts 4:19–20). The Church is responsible for standing up and being counted for Jesus at whatever cost.

Proclaiming Good News

Announcing his mission, Jesus proclaimed: "The Spirit of the Lord is on me because he has anointed me to proclaim good news to the poor, freedom for the prisoners, recovery of sight for the blind . . . and the year of the Lord's favor" (Luke 4:18–19). On the occasion of Jesus' sending out of the twelve apostles and the seventy disciples (Luke 9:1–6; 10:1–12), one of the assignments given to them was that of preaching the good news of the kingdom. This commission was repeated after the resurrection and recorded by all four Gospels (Mt. 28:19; Mk. 16:15; Lk. 24:17; Jn. 20:21). The Church runs like a herald to deliver the message. "It is not a snail that carries its little house on its back and is so well off in it, that only now and then it sticks out its feelers, and then thinks that the 'claim of publicity' has been satisfied. No, the Church lives by its commission as herald."[11] This is a Pentecost mandate! As the Spirit of the Lord was upon Christ anointing him to proclaim with power, so has the Holy Spirit been poured out upon the Church to do likewise. The Spirit was not given to the Church for private enjoyment. For the Master says: "You will receive power when the Holy Spirit is come upon you, and you shall be witnesses unto me both in Jerusalem, and in all Judea, and in Samaria, and unto the uttermost part of the earth" (Acts 1:8). This responsibility is the missionary or evangelistic task of the whole Church.

This news is particularly good because it is primarily for the *ptōchoi*, the poor. Like *ani* in the Old Testament, *ptōchos* in the New Testament is commonly used to denote a person who is bowed down; one who occupies a lowly position; one who ducks away in fear. He is a man who has to try to live completely without means and is therefore reduced to begging in order to stay alive. According to Boerma, the Spanish word *humilhados* describes the condition better. "The *humilhados* is the humiliated one who can no longer stand upright because of economic and social pressure."[12] Boerma rightly reasons that *ptōchos* like *ani* describes a relationship and not necessarily a contrast with the rich. The relationship is that of a poor man and a man of violence, the powerful, the oppressor, who puts the poor in his lowly position and keeps him there. The poor is made a marginal man with the fate of having nothing. This is the kind of structural evil manifest in our economic systems and orders which are tailored to make the rich richer and keep the violent oppressors in power while the poor are only made poorer but also kept in perpetual begging, reduced to charity.[13]

The Church is not only called to seek God's kingdom, but is also sent to pursue its righteousness, its justice. G. von Rad writes: "There is absolutely no concept in the Old Testament with so central a significance for all relationships of human life as that of *sedaqah* (justice/righteousness).[14] According to biblical data justice can be described as "fidelity to the demands of a relationship"; it is a concern for the marginal people in society, the widow, the orphan, the alien, the poor, the refugees. In the Book of Job and in Proverbs the just person preserves the peace and wholeness of the community. Such a one "upholds the weak hands and him who was stumbling" (Job 4:3–4), cares for the poor, the fatherless and the widow (Job 29:12–15; 31:16–19; Prov. 29:7) and defends their cause in court (Job 29:16; Prov. 31:9). In the Psalms the just person is the one who calls upon Yahweh as a source of strength with a confidence which is based on faith in the justice of Yahweh, that is, Yahweh's fidelity to his promises. Yahweh rewards according to justice (Ps. 18–20); leads in the path of justice (Ps. 23:3); delivers according to His righteousness (Ps. 31:1) and vindicates in justice (Ps. 35:24). Throughout the rest of the Old Testament Yahweh is proclaimed as just and righteous (2 Chr. 12:6; Neh. 9:3; Jer. 9:24; Dan. 9:14; Zeph. 3:5; Zech. 8:8). He looks for justice and righteousness (Isa. 5:7). He challenges his people "to seek justice, encourage the oppressed, defend the cause of the fatherless and plead the case of the widow" (Isa. 1:17). To do this is to do the right; it is to be Godlike, "for the Lord God executes justice for the fatherless and the widow and loves the sojourner, giving him food and clothing" (Deut. 10:18).

Like the prophets of old who were called to speak not only on behalf of Yahweh, but also on behalf of those who have no voice in society, the church is mandated to proclaim: "Let justice roll down like waters and righteousness like an everflowing stream." The Kingdom message calls for justice and mercy and faith (Mt. 23:23). Take for instance the message of John the Baptist in Luke 3:7–14. To his audience, a "generation of vipers" (v. 7), people who lived in self-satisfaction, pride and deception, John shouted: "Produce fruit in keeping with repentance!" "Fruit in keeping with repentance" means *just action* to John. In verse 11, he calls for fair and equitable sharing of wealth with the needy. In verses 12 and 13 he condemns all forms of corruption, calling for honesty and justice. And in verse 14 he denounces all forms of violence, militarism and oppression. John preaches against both personal sins and the structural evil of the system represented by both the civil servants and the soldiers who came to him. He addresses both individuals and the authority of the powers-that-be. The Church cannot and must not do any less. By the power of the Gospel the rich must be liberated from their greed, selfishness, pride and self-satisfaction while the poor must be liberated from their poverty, ignorance and hopelessness. The Gospel calls for fairness, justice and equity. As it is a dream to expect any system or structure to change without changing its individuals, it is equally unrealistic to assume that changed individuals will automatically transform any system. Both must be addressed in the proclamation of the Gospel.

The New Testament community was a loving and caring fellowship. "No one claimed that any of his possessions was his own, but they shared everything they had . . . There were no needy persons among them" (Acts 4:32–35).[15] The Jerusalem Council put no demand on Paul and his team in the settlement of the Jew/Gentile salvation controversy except this: "that they [the Jerusalem Church] would have us remember the poor" (Gal. 2:10). Paul did not ignore that demand of the gospel (see 1 Cor. 8:9; 9:1 ff.) He also taught that one called as a slave should not be troubled. However, if he can gain his freedom, he must do so for this is part of the Gospel emphasis (1 Cor 7:21). To the Apostle James, the gospel demands visiting the fatherless and widows in their affliction as well as keeping oneself unspotted from the world (James 1:27). John describes it in a ritual sacrificial language of dying for others (1 John 3:16–18). As Christ, through his incarnation, identified with humanity in its sin and helplessness to lift it up, so must the Church in words and deeds responsibly enter into the lives of men proclaiming the good news of God's kingdom and pursuing its righteousness (Mt. 6:33).

Healing the Brokenhearted

Almost invariably in the Synoptic accounts of Jesus' ministry, preaching and healing go hand-in-hand. The Matthean account uses the threefold formula of teaching, preaching and healing while Mark and Luke simply speak of preaching and healing (Mt. 4:23; 9:35; Mk. 1:34, 38; Luke 4:40, 43, 44). One word that stands out in Christ's healing ministry is "compassion". Translated from the Greek word *splagchnizomai* which comes from the same root as the word translated as "bowels," compassion is love in action. When the Greek word is translated into English, it is usually accompanied by action verbs such as "moved" or "filled" to convey the real meaning of the concept. Compassion is something that wells up from within—down deep at the gut level—and propels one into action. It was compassion that made Jesus heal every sickness and disease (Mt. 14:14); cleanse the lepers (Mk. 1:41); give sight to the blind (Mt. 20:34); raise the dead (Lk. 7:13); and feed the hungry multitudes (Mt. 15:32). Jesus was moved to compassion by the world's pain and sorrow, especially that of those who were gripped by demonic affliction (Mk. 9:22; Luke 7:13). The sight of a leper, banished from the society of his fellow-men, living a life which was a living death of loneliness and universal abandonment called forth Christ's sympathy and his power to heal. He also saw the world as a confused mob without any sense of direction. That moved Him no less to compassion. It is only logical that, when he sent out His disciples, He should give them power to heal. Luke records that "they departed, and went through the towns, preaching the gospel, and healing everywhere" (Luke 9:6).

Another word which aptly describes Christlike compassion is "altruism" which has been defined as "regard for, and devotion to, the interest of others." No other story has so vividly drawn out the demands of this ministry as the parable of the good Samaritan (Luke 10:30–37). His response was triggered by a lawyer's question, "And who is my neighbour?" In this parable Jesus draws our attention to some of the qualities of altruism that should mark the Church's healing ministry. Altruism sees beyond the accidents of race, tribe, colour, nationality and even religion, to peoples made in the image and likeness of God. Neighbourly concern ceases to be drawn along tribal, class, national or racial lines. People are seen no longer as objects to be exploited or things to be used but in their true humanness as creations in God's image for whom Christ died. The good Samaritan saw, not a Jew (though the unfortunate traveller was one), but a man in need.

Next, the good Samaritan risked his life to save the wounded. The Jericho road was notorious for armed robbery. (This may be part of the reason why the priest and the Levite did not stop to help the wounded man.) Instead of asking: "If I stop to help this man what will happen to me?", Christlike compassion asks: "If I do not stop to help this man, what will happen to him?" What matters is not one's personal security but the other's redemption. In the words of Bonhoeffer: "The Church is the Church only when it exists for others."[16] One can say that the ultimate measure of a church is not where it stands in moments of comfort and convenience, but where it stands at times of challenge and crisis—as in Ethiopia, Namibia, South Africa, El Salvador, Nicaragua, Northern Ireland, the Middle East, or Vietnam. Furthermore, Christ-like healing ministry demands involvment. With his own hands the good Samaritan bound the wounds of the man, set him on his own beast and paid the hospital costs from his own pocket. This is much more than the wounded may deserve. Compassion is fellow feeling for the person in need. It is the bearing of another's pain, agony and burdens—in doing which, Paul says, "the law of Christ is fulfilled" (Gal. 6:2). From this point of view missionary services—medical, agricultural, orphanages, development—cease to be doing something *for* the recipients and become something done *with* them for the sake of Christ and of His kingdom. It is this property of compassion that can make one love his enemies, bless those who curse him, do good to those who hate him and pray for those who despitefully use and persecute him (Mt. 5:44).

St. Basil, styled "the Great", a hermit theologian and one of the Cappadocian Fathers, created a whole complex of charitable institutions during the 4th century. Around his church building and monastery arose a whole new city consisting of hotels, almshouses and hospitals for infectious diseases. The bishop himself took up residence there. The establishment was regarded as a threat to the state; but at the risk of his life Basil rejected the objection. During the great famine of the year 368, he organised free meals not only for his people but also for the immigrants, foreigners, pagans and even the infidel children of Israel. He is quoted as saying: "You commit as many injustices as there are people with whom you avoid sharing what you have."[17] To Basil, as well as to other Church Fathers, "charity" meant giving what one had, and not what one had left over (see Mk. 12:44).

The Church has been invested with the power of the Holy Spirit and blessed with material resources, including scientific competence, and charged with the responsibility of healing wounded humanity. This takes the Church out of its comfortable environment, and places it in market places, on the highways and by-ways, in ghettos, in prison cells, in refugee camps, in rural as well as urban centres—wherever people are; people wounded and bruised by the scourge of sin and the violent brutality of man against man. It rules out evangelism at arm's length and speaks of "release" rather than "relief". There are few better examples than the ministry of Mother Teresa which has been internationally recognised as a ministry of healing, a significant link in the chain of peace.[18] But her work must not be the exception. The Church of Jesus Christ all over the world is under obligation to respond to human need with Christlike compassion.

Liberating the Bruised

The task of setting the oppressed free involves power-encounters. By the fall of Adam, humanity came not only under God's curse but also under Satan's control. He is the one who blinds the minds of unbelievers (2 Cor. 4:4). He is a murderer from the beginning, a liar and the father of lies (John 8:44). He is a deceiver, a destroyer, dwelling in wickedness, holding mankind in bondage and death (Heb. 2:14–15; Eph. 2:2–3). He is the accuser of the brethren (Rev. 12:10). And from His entrance into the world in human flesh right through to His exit from it in triumph, Jesus Christ waged war against the Devil. The Apostle John says, "The Son of God was manifested that he might destroy the works of the devil" (1 John 3:8). The author of Hebrews writes, "Since the children have flesh and blood, he too shared in their humanity so that by his death he might destroy him who holds the power of death—that is, the devil—and free those who all their lives were held in slavery by their fear of death" (Heb. 2:14–15). The Apostle Paul also employs this warfare motif to describe the victory of the cross. He writes: "Having disarmed the powers and authorities, he [Jesus] made a public spectacle of them, triumphing over them by the cross" (Col. 2:15).

Realising the nature of the warfare, Christ never sent His disciples out without equipping them with power and authority. Power to drive out evil spirits (Mt. 10:1,8); power to liberate mankind from demonic and human oppression—all this has been made available to the Church by Jesus Christ in the Holy Spirit. The Church has been called to side with God in the battle against God's enemies, against all the demonic forces and activities under the leadership of Satan. The Church is engaged in a battle of good against evil; of light against darkness; of life against death; of order against chaos; of sight against blindness; of law against anarchy; of righteousness against wickedness; of Christ against anti-Christs; of God against God-substitutes. No wonder the Apostle Paul says, "We wrestle not against flesh and blood, but against principalities, against powers, against the rulers of the darkness of this world, against spiritual wickedness in high places" (Eph. 6:12). Although these elemental spiritual forces of evil employ human beings—individually or as a group— in the execution of their atrocities, the Church errs if it fails to recognise the invisible, intangible forces behind the human agents.

Any form of wickedness, unrighteousness and oppression—socio-economic, cultural or political—is of the Devil, and the Church in partnership with God is responsible for destroying it. In some instances evil takes the form of ignorance, disease and poverty as among millions of Indians, Africans, and Australian Aborigines. It is the Church's duty for Christ's sake to provide functional education and modern medical facilities, and to share God-given material resources in such situations.

At times evil takes the form of religious and traditional superstition, myths and magic. The Church should confront such circumstances with the liberating truth of the Gospel. The entrance of God's word brings light. "You shall know the truth, and the truth shall make you free," says Jesus. The force that ignited the Reformation fire of Luther and Calvin during the 16th century and set the people free from religious bondage was the Word of God given back to the people in the language they could understand and at a price they could afford. In today's society, the more rampant form of wickedness is structural evil taking the form of discrimination, violence and exploitation. This dehumanising monster manifests itself in institutions where power and privilege are shared along racial, tribal or sexual lines with total disregard for individual worth. It is also seen in cases where position is assumed and maintained by violence against the wish of the people. And it can be seen where the economic order is tailored so as to deprive and exploit the unfortunate masses. In all of these cases Christ's righteousness calls for unequivocal denunciation.

The prophet Nathan withstood king David to his face, condemning him for the atrocity he had committed against Uriah (2 Sam. 12:1–12). William Wilberforce fought relentlessly against the odds for the abolition of the slave trade in the 19th century. Martin Luther King, Jr., was assassinated in his struggle against racial segregation in the southern states of North America. Lord Shaftesbury dared to stand for justice for the poor in the midst of the Industrial Revolution of the early 19th century. All these men in some way shared in God's desire that justice should reign and that the oppressed should be released. Speaking of their heroic example, Francis Schaeffer comments: "These men did not do these things incidentally, but because they saw it as a part of the Christian good news."[19]

Discipling the Nation

The fifth responsibility of the Church is that of making disciples of all nations. Discipleship can be defined as persuading people to forsake their ignorance, indifference, scepticism, pride, corruption, wickedness or any other vices, and to embrace Jesus Christ as Saviour and Lord joining the fellowship of His Church. During his three and a half years of public ministry, Jesus concentrated on discipling his band of twelve Apostles. He invested his life, time and resources in the lives of the Twelve. And this although he knew that He had the whole world to reach. The strategy that the Master used was that of one-to-one pouring of His life and vision into the lives of His disciples. With this accomplished, in anticipation of the cross before Him, He had the right to say: "I have finished the work which you gave me to do" (John 17:4). Discipleship satisfies and glorifies God. It is more than conversion; it is an addition to the Church through geometrical progression. Discipleship makes every believer responsible and reproductive.

Three things mark the discipleship process of Jesus Christ with the Twelve. First, He taught them God's words. In John 17:8 and 17:14 He underscores the importance of doing this. He recognises that their conversion has been wrought by nothing but God's words. Their establishment in faith depends on how much they give themselves to God's words. So also their growth and maturity. God's Word is their only offensive weapon against the Devil. Judging by the Gospel accounts, in addition to His public ministry of the word, Jesus must have spent many hours in serious study, explanation and application of God's word with His disciples privately. At the end of this successful ministry he commissioned them, saying, "Having gone, make disciples of all nations, baptizing them . . . and teaching them to obey everything I have commanded you" (Matthew 28:19–20).

The term *mathētēs* literally means "a learner" in contrast to *didaskalos*, "a teacher". In a more technical sense, a *mathētēs* is an apprentice, one who patterns his thought and actions after that of his master.[20] To be another's disciple is to pledge to abide in that person's teaching and copy his lifestyle. Jesus implies this in His invitation to His disciples, "Follow me"; "Learn from me"; "Abide in me"—He did not invite them to a set of rules and regulations, but to Himself. To be like Jesus became the consuming desire of the Apostles. As early as the period of Acts 6, they had determined their priority, namely "to give ourselves continually to prayer and to the ministry of the word" (v. 4). We read that daily in the temple, and in every house, the apostles did not cease to teach and preach Jesus Christ (Acts 5:42). The Apostle Paul, writing years later, instructed his disciple Timothy to continue in the tradition of disciple-making (2 Timothy 2:2). The practice of this teaching responsibility is tragically deficient in most of the Church in the Third World.

Secondly, Christ prayed for his disciples, both those who have believed and those who will believe later (Jn. 17:9, 11, 15, 17, 20). He prayed for their oneness, their security and their purity. His prayer served as a "fire-extinguisher" to extinguish the problems of divisions, personality clashes and immorality which later cropped up and which would have killed the Church. The Church must take her prayer responsibility seriously. Further, the Church has been called to intercede for the world—a task which the world does not carry out for itself. The Reformed Ecumenical Synod Committee on the Church and its social calling addresses this issue as follows: "The Church makes an appeal to God who loves the world and sent his Son to save it. The Church asks for the advance of the gospel, for the work of the Spirit in the hearts of men, for the improvement of evil situations, for the settlement of conflicts, for the removal of such evils as oppression, racism, war, for the guidance of the rulers of this world and those who are responsible for political, social, economic decisions, for peace and prosperity."[20] This assertion is supported by the quotation of 1 Timothy 2:1, 2.

The third thing that Jesus did for his disciples was to keep them (Jn. 17:12). This responsibility can be described as providing adequate and proper pastoral care for the fold. Of what use is our evangelism and missionary outreach if we lose four for every five won? In his *World Christian Encyclopedia* (1982), David Barrett documents the fact that the massive gains made by Christianity across the Third World throughout the 20th century have been sadly offset by massive losses in the Western and Communist worlds over the last 60 years. "In the Soviet Union, Christians have fallen from 83.6% in 1900 to 36.1% today. In Europe and North America net defections from Christianity —converts to other religions or to irreligion—are now running at 1,820,500 former Christians a year. The loss is much higher if we consider only Church members: 2,224,800 a year, i.e., 6,000 a day. It is even higher if we are speaking of only church attenders every year, some 2,765,100 Church attenders in Europe and North America cease to be practising Christians within the 12 month period, an average loss of 7,600 every day." This is frightening! The Church needs to face her responsibility of keeping disciples. If any leave, it should not be because of our negligence.

Equipping the Saints

This naturally leads us to the sixth responsibility of the Church, namely, equipping the saints for the work of the ministry. This task is particularly directed to gifted leaders in the Body of Christ. The Apostle Peter charges his colleagues, the pastors for example, to feed the flock of God, taking the oversight of it, not by constraint but willingly. James speaks similarly to the teachers in his epistle. Paul addresses the evangelists with a similar emphasis in his second epistle to Timothy. The message cannot be missed. A wise leader—either at home or on the mission field—is one who reproduces himself or herself in others even as Christ is reproduced in him or her.

In the New Testament, three pictures are given to help us understand the business of equipping the saints. The first one is contained in Mark 1:19. Here we have an account of James and John with torn nets. Attempting to fish with a torn net is a futile exercise. And so they have to sit down and mend their nets before any fishing operation can take place. The Greek word *katartizō* translated 'to mend' is the same word as "to equip" in the Ephesians 4:12. Here is the message: unconfessed sins in the life of a Christian make him or her as useless in God's business as a torn net. Sins must be dealt with in order for God to use us. In many churches today discipline has become a thing of the past. This must be corrected.

The second picture is contained in Galatians 6:1. Here we have an account of an offence leading to a broken relationship in the Body of Christ. With the word "restore" we are given a picture of a surgeon who takes a broken bone and puts the two pieces together in a cast until they heal. By this process, he restores the broken bone to its normal function. The word "to restore" here is the same word as "to equip" in Ephesians 4:12. In the Body of Christ, unless broken relationships (sometimes denominational relationships!) are restored, the Church cannot fulfil her mission in the world. As long as there is jealousy and quarreling and division among brethren, their credibility is tainted, their effectiveness impaired and their growth hindered.

The third picture comes from 2 Timothy 3:17. Here, the expression "thoroughly furnished" comes from the same root *katartizō* and conveys an image of a ship that has been made ready to undertake a voyage. All that the ship needs for its journey has been provided. In a similar way, all Scripture is God-breathed and useful for teaching, rebuking, correcting and training in righteousness so that the man of God may be thoroughly equipped for every good work. Unless you and I are well equipped in the way described here, and unless the Church is thus equipped, we become irrelevant in today's world and useless for the future. And this means total failure in our business for the Lord.

The Church's Equipment

But the Church need not fail and should not fail. The Master has made adequate provision for her success. Christ's equipment for the Church is three-fold: the Holy Spirit, the Word of God, and the heroic examples of faithful saints. As a politician depends upon public opinion in his career, as a banker depends upon the circulation of money to remain in business, and as a military general depends upon soldiers in warfare, so does the Church depend upon the Holy Spirit for her life and mission. Our Lord Jesus Christ was conceived of the Holy Spirit; was baptized by the Holy Spirit; was driven to the wilderness by the Holy Spirit; was anointed to preach by the Holy Spirit; performed miracles by the Holy Spirit; was enabled to endure pain by the Holy Spirit; was raised from the dead by the Holy Spirit. And before he parted physically with his disciples he promised them not two things but one—the coming of the Holy Spirit in all his fullness! The Holy Spirit comes with *power*: power to proclaim the good news of the kingdom; power to heal the sick; power to raise the dead; power to drive out evil spirits; power to cleanse leprosy; power to give peace to the troubled hearts; power to make the crooked straight. What we need today is a demonstration, not just a definition, of this power! Jesus says:

"You will receive power when the Holy Spirit is come upon you, and you will be my witnesses." Is this power operative in our church today? Is it evident in our ministry? If not, we need to go to Jesus in repentance.

The Holy Spirit also comes with *fruit*: the fruit of love, joy, peace, patience, kindness, goodness, faithfulness, gentleness and self-control. As the Church yields its life to Him, He (the Holy Spirit) reproduces Christlikeness in it. This nine-fold fruit is condensed in Ephesians 5:9 into three clusters consisting of all goodness, righteousness and truth. Against such there is no law.

Furthermore, the Holy Spirit comes with *gifts,* diverse in their nature and operations, but uniform in their purpose namely—that each recipient may do business with his gift for the Lord and make profit (1 Cor. 12:7). To every servant or disciple is given a *mna* and the master expects the *mna* not to be kept safely salted away somewhere but to be used wisely and to make profit. At his return He will ask His disciples individually not how well they have kept their gift but how wisely they have used it and what gains they have made.

The second piece of equipment the Church has for her business is the Word of God. This was not promised but given by the Lord while He was still with His disciples. In that Olivet prayer where the Lord summarised His earthly ministry, He said, "I have given them the words you gave me and they accepted them" (John 17:8, 14). Because of this word, He says, the world is going to hate the disciples. Why? Because God's word is truth coming against all lies; it is light coming against all forms of darkness; it is righteousness coming against wickedness; it is compassion coming against exploitation; it is peace coming against violent turbulence! Everything about God's word is good, wholesome and perfect. It stands in antithesis to this world's values, controlled by the Devil. This is why the world hates the Church. And any Christian who will live godly in Christ Jesus, we are told, shall be persecuted (2 Tim. 3:12).

But the good news is that the word of God is dynamite. It is called the sword of the Spirit, an offensive weapon against any attacks. By it enemies have been put to flight; the oppressed released; the sick healed; the seekers saved and the Church made victorious. The apostles were not ashamed of it—they knew it was the power of God unto every man's salvation. They committed their lives to it and charged their disciples to do the same. We cannot be exceptions.

The third piece of equipment for the Church's business consists in the heroic examples of faithful saints down through the centuries. Can the Church forget Noah, Abraham, Moses, Joshua, Jephthah, Samson, Deborah, Rahab, Esther, David, Daniel, and the prophets, the apostles, the Church Fathers, the Reformers, the Revivalists, the pioneer missionaries and the contemporary saints? For their faith many suffered imprisonment and many were martyred. On the other hand, God wrought many signs and wonders through them. Kingdoms have been conquered, justice administered, lions' mouths shut, the fury of flames quenched, darkness dispelled, and wickedness punished. Their stories are not recorded in Scripture just to fill up the pages. Rather, their discipline in prayer and fasting, in faith and work, has become a rich source of inspiration and motivation for the Church.

Conclusion

In conclusion, let the Church be the Church—one, holy, catholic and apostolic, and its social responsibility will take its rightful place. As the Church lives out the Gospel let its manifesto be:

> The Spirit of the Lord is upon me;
> He has saved and sanctified me;
> He has called me to worship Him;
> He has sent me . . .
>   to confess Jesus as Lord
>   to proclaim goodness to the poor
>   to heal the brokenhearted
>   to liberate the bruised
>   to disciple the nations
>   to equip the saints
> In preparation for His return!

Shalom and Maranatha!

Footnotes

1. These include: John R. W. Stott, *Christian Mission* (1975); Orlando E. Costas, *The Church and its Mission* (1974); Ronald J. Sider, *Rich Christians in an Age of Hunger* (1977); Samuel Escobar and John Driver, *Christian Mission and Social Justice* (1978); Conrad Boerma, *Rich Man, Poor Man and the Bible* (1979); David J. Bosch, *Witness to the World* (1980); Waldron Scott, *Bring Forth Justice* (1980); Jim Wallis, *The Call to Conversion* (1981); Christopher Sugden, *Radical Discipleship* (1981); and Francis A. Schaeffer, *A Christian Manifesto* (1981).

2. Significant conferences and consultations on the subject since LCOWE (Lausanne, 1974) include: Basel: "Church and Nationhood" (1976); Bulawayo: "Rhodesian Congress on Evangelism in Context" (1976); Madras: "All India Conference on Evangelical Social Action" (1979); Pretoria: "South Africa Christian Leadership Assembly" (1979); Melbourne: "Thy Kingdom Come" (1980); High Leigh: "Consultation on Development" (1980); High Leigh: "Consultation on Simple Lifestyle" (1980); Pattaya: "Consultation on World Evangelization" (1980); Grand Rapids: "Consultation on the Relationship between Evangelism and Social Responsibility" (1982).

3. Groups such as World Vision International, World Relief, Compassion, World Concern, Christian Aid, Food for the Hungry, and TEAR Fund have all expanded and doubled their budgets.
4. This distinction is quite common in Reformed circles. Louis Berkhof has vividly explained the distinction in his *Systematic Theology*, pp. 567 ff.
5. David J. Bosch, *Witness to the World* (Atlanta: John Knox Press, 1980), p. 222.
6. See Robert L. Saucy, *The Church in God's Program* (Chicago: Moody Press, 1972), pp. 11–18; Gene A. Getz, *The Measure of a Church* (Ventura: Regal Books, 1975), pp. 12–21; and Charles C. Ryrie, *A Survey of Bible Doctrine* (Chicago: Moody Press, 1972), pp. 140–150.
7. Karl Barth, *Dogmatics in Outline* (London: SCM Press [English translation], 1949), p. 142.
8. The five stanzas of Samuel S. Wesley's "The Church's One Foundation" sum up the unity and essential oneness of the Church in a beautiful poem. Stanza two reads: "Elect from every nation, yet one over all the earth; her charter of salvation, one Lord, one faith, one birth; one holy name she blesses; partakes one holy food; and to one hope she presses, with every grace endued."
9. Bosch, *ibid.*, p. 222.
10. Colin Morris, *Church and Challenge in a New Africa* (London: The Epworth Press, 1964), p. 142.
11. Barth, *ibid.*, p. 147.
12. Conrad Boerma, *Rich Man, Poor Man and the Bible* (London: SCM Press [English translation], 1979), p. 7.
13. Ronald J. Sider's *Rich Christians in an Age of Hunger* (1977) is a shattering critique of the systems. Also Jim Wallis' *The Call to Conversion* (1981) makes fascinating reading.
14. G. Von Rad, *Old Testament Theology*, translated by D. M. S. Stalker (New York: Harper and Bros., 1962), Vol. 1, p. 370.
15. This voluntary sharing of possessions among the Christians in Jerusalem was prompted by their love for the Lord. What is said of that community—that there were no needy persons among them—cannot be said of the Church today. Among us, in our church, are not only needy persons but destitute and oppressed fellow believers. This is sad. The Church today needs to heed the call to live simply so that others may simply live.
16. Dietrich Bonhoeffer, *Letters and Papers from Prison*, edited by Eberhard Bethge (New York: Macmillan, 1953), p. 382.
17. Hans von Campenhanse, *The Fathers of the Greek Church* (New York: Pantheon Books, 1959), p. 86; also St. Basil: *Homilias*, VI, 7, MPG, T, XXXI, Col. 276–277.
18. The vital ministry of Christian humanitarian agencies such as World Vision, World Relief, World Concern, Food for the Hungry and a host of others cannot be overlooked. As Tom Sine asserts in his book *The Mustard Seed Conspiracy* (1981), the Church holds in its hands the weapons to change the future for Christ.
19. Francis A. Schaeffer, *A Christian Manifesto* (Westchester: Crossway Books, 1981), p. 65.
20. W. E. Vine, *Expository Dictionary of New Testament Words* (McLean MacDonald Publishing Company, n.d.), p. 318.

21. Reformed Ecumenical Synod, *The Church and its Social Calling* (Grand Rapids: RES, 1980), p. 21.
22. David B. Barrett, ed., *World Christian Encyclopedia* (Nairobi: Oxford University Press, 1982), p. 7.

Dr. Tokunboh Adeyemo is Executive Secretary of the Association of Evangelicals of Africa and Madagascar and Chairman of the WEF Executive Council.

18

The Redeemed Gospel Church, Nairobi, Kenya

A Case Study

MOROMPI OLE-RONKEI

Introduction

The history of the Redeemed Gospel Church in Kenya dates back to 1974 when it was started in the slums valley of Mathare. The Church is an independent Pentescostal Church which has now established several branches throughout the country, with Mathare as its headquarters.

Mathare Valley is not only the largest ghetto in the city of Nairobi, but also the filthiest and most crowded inhabited area. It brings together a conglomeration of the destitute, the uneducated, the unemployed, widows and orphans, the poverty stricken and the hopeless. The population is above 100,000 while the birth rate is one of the highest in the country. With no proper source of income, the population have had to turn and look for other alternative means for their livelihood.

Women have resorted to alcohol brewing and prostitution while the young men have organized themselves into robbery gangs.

The state of the valley can only be described as pathetic and desperate. Above all, the inhabitants need the Gospel; they also need food, shelter, clothing, proper sanitation and love. But who is to give it to them?

In presenting this paper, I wish to analyse two areas of concern, the social aspects and the problem of evangelism. This will enable us to clearly see the two faces of the valley and how they have been married together.

Social Problems Facing the Valley

During our early days of operation in the valley, there was a very high resistance to the gospel because of social problems. It was very hard for a prostitute to give up her immorality while it was the only way of survival for her family.

Initially, the church started on strict Gospel proclamation. That was not effective. It overlooked the felt need of the people. But when it changed its strategy and reached out in compassion, people began to listen. The result has been phenomenal. Combining social concern with evangelism has taken the church to the people and brought the people to the church.

Housing

The houses in the valley are built of mud walls with corrugated iron sheets for the roofs, while others are made out of polythene materials which suffer leakages when it rains.

Although piped water is available, the people have to purchase it from a public tap. There are not many taps, and the families which are not living next to them have to travel to get their water. The water supply cannot be guaranteed all year round as the pipes sometimes break down, especially during rainy seasons.

The public toilets which are scattered throughout the valley are not only few in comparison to the population, but also extremely dirty as there is no organized cleaning system.

A major concern with housing is the inability of many families to afford the rent. The church has come to the aid of such families by providing them with building materials to erect their own small houses. The church has now turned this into a loan scheme, where the families, once settled, begin to repay the loan in small instalments without any interest. Extra rooms would normally be built for rent, and this begins to act as a regular source of income for the families.

The valley has no electricity, and the dwellers use kerosene lamps to light their houses. Once it is evening, the valley is in total darkness.

Fire Outbreaks

A major problem concerning the housing situation in the valley is the constant outbreak of fires, which render thousands of families homeless.

The type of house built in the Valley is highly vulnerable to fire, and since all the houses are joined together, fire can spread at great speed. The cause of fires has never fully been identified. The blame usually falls on children who had been playing with fire. Critical analysts think that fires may be started by the landlords, in the hope of having the squatters evicted, which would enable them to build bigger houses for rent. This, however, has no official confirmation.

The Church, aware of such atrocities, has organised herself to offer as much help as she can. Material help has been given in the construction of houses, supplying the people with blankets and clothing, food and household utensils. The Church normally does this in close co-operation with the local authorities.

Health

The health conditions in the Valley are deplorable. The number of people in each tiny house is very high. The roofs leak making the floors muddy in rainy seasons and dusty in dry seasons. Things such as soap are not viewed as necessities, but as luxuries. Heaps of garbage rot everywhere while people defecate on the pathways and beside their houses rather than risk travelling to the toilets at night.

The Church has been limited in the amount of help it can offer in these areas. One area of help has been to assist in transporting serious cases to the hospital.

Earlier, the Church ran a clinic, and through it was able to carry out regular medical check-ups, especially on children. This activity however was terminated due to shortages of funds, but presently prayers have been intensified and appropriate action is underway to resume the activities of the Clinic once more. The need is for qualified personnel to carry out the check-ups and attend to immediate cases, and for a viable transport system to transport urgent cases to bigger hospitals.

The Church has also taken action to introduce "Health Scouts". These are young children from the age of about ten onwards, who are taught hygienic methods and then in turn teach and apply them to their family situations. This is a good example of how a church has applied II Tim 2:2 into a social situation, and the results have been amazingly positive.

The Circle of Poverty

According to research carried out in the Valley, its poverty dates back to colonial times. Many of the families had husbands either in detention or killed during the Mau Mau rebellion. Other poor families that could not afford to stay in other areas of the city due to high rents moved into the Valley. With no employment and no source of income, the people were driven by necessity to look for alternative ways to survive. The women resorted to prostitution and the brewing and selling of alcohol. Their daughters followed in their footsteps, and hence there was a common saying, "Like mother like daughter."

Likewise, the boys who have not had any form of education felt that they would never be employed. They organized themselves into gangs which indulged in thuggery and other forms of violence. Alcohol became their refuge. Therefore, as is the case for the daughter, for the boys—"like father like son".

However we cannot generalize and say that the entire population leads this type of life. There are families that carry on clean honest businesses and lead decent lives despite being in the Valley.

Training Offered By The Church

Education

Through education, it is possible to break this vicious circle of poverty. The Church has opened doors to help provide education for the children from the Valley.

Currently, there are two nursery schools with a total of over six hundred children. Plans to expand are underway, which will call for the building of extra classrooms and the recruitment of more teachers. The children will eventually move on to primary and secondary schools, from which graduates will seek to secure employment and help move their families from the ghettos. Through donations from charitable organizations, the church is able to sponsor most of the children through to their secondary school education.

There has also been the establishment of a special school that caters for children who are already too old to start primary school. This special programme enables them to learn various trades that will help them in the future. It also gives them the opportunity to choose and specialise in one particular trade in which they feel they are gifted.

Library

As the educational program continues to flourish, the Church has seen the need to erect a library. Plans are currently being formulated to turn the idea into a reality. In this context, the library will serve not only as a resource center, but also as an educational center that will attract more children to read. With poor lighting conditions in their homes, the students will have a quiet place to study and can study until late evening.

Vocational Training

To cater for those who are not in a formal school or special school, the Church saw the need to establish vocational training.

A vocational training institute has been established within the valley, currently offering courses in tailoring, carpentry and leather-craft. These courses run for one year after which the students sit for a Government Trade test. With their graduation certificate, job opportunities within the city become much more likely.

Future plans for the expansion of the institute include mechanics, engineering, welding, book-keeping, secretarial and home economics courses. Meanwhile the Church is involved in sponsoring students to study these courses in other institutions in the city.

Self-Employment

As people from the Valley come to receive Christ as their Lord and Savior, their lives are transformed and they begin to seek alternative occupations. The idea of self-employment through small scale business was therefore introduced by the Church.

The Church undertook to sponsor candidates and start them off through a loan scheme. The loan is paid back in instalments over a period of time without any interest. The loan idea was introduced as a motivational drive in order to encourage people to work hard at their businesses. Such small businesses include selling fresh vegetables or charcoal, running a small kiosk to sell foodstuffs, operating a small shop, selling clothes, or vending paraffin.

Through such programmes, many families are now able to support themselves, meeting all their domestic needs without much difficulty.

Finance

Since it is an independent church, the Redeemed Gospel Church obtains much of its income from local contributions. However, charitable organizations that have come to recognize and approve of the good work and efforts of the Church have contributed generously. Tear Fund (Netherlands) and World Vision International (Africa Region) have been great supporters of the Church and its projects.

The Church and Evangelism

The Redeemed Gospel Church is nine years old. In that short period, the Lord has blessed her ministry with the establishment of four churches within Mathare Valley, eighty throughout the country and two in neighbouring Uganda.

Behind this amazing story of success lies much prayer, dedication and proper management of both the spiritual and social problems of the people.

Seminars and Conferences

The Church has seen the need to organize seminars and conferences for the training of local pastors and Church elders. These seminars, emphasizing the development of the whole person, and the meeting of physical and spiritual needs, also help in equipping laymen with appropriate leadership skills.

On a lower scale, there are training programmes for youth. These teach lessons in clear communication and presentation of the Gospel—especially to the Valley's population—and follow-up methods. It is from this group that Sunday school teachers emerge.

Outreach Programs

Apart from visitation or door to door evangelism, we have two other outreach programs. First, we have open air street programs. We divide ourselves into small groups and then hold meetings on various street corners. We conduct five such meetings in a week. These draw from 100 to 1000 people in a meeting.

Second, we have big open air crusades. These draw from 5,000 to 10,000 people. These occasional meetings go on for three to five days. After such a big crusade we stage one-week follow-up campaigns, and teaching on discipleship.

To support the evangelists and to act as catalysts to attract people to meetings, rallies and crusades, three singing groups have been established. The objective of these groups is to convey the message of the Gospel to the community through music and songs.

As a result of the youth training programs, there were many committed and enthusiastic young men who felt the inspiration of the Holy Spirit to go out and spread the Word. With their acquired skills, they teamed up in twos or threes and in the evenings and weekends moved from house to house sharing the love of Christ.

Large weekend witnessing programes are also organized where a group of over three hundred young men "invade" an estate, and in twos go from house to house.

Such a large operation would normally be carried out after a week-long period of prayer and preparation.

With many people accepting Christ as their Lord and Saviour, a strong follow-up program is essential. The youth training program includes strategies on follow-up. Trained young men are therefore always present during street preaching, rallies and crusades. They take on the job of discipling the new converts and helping them grow in the Faith.

Young Children

The Church has not forgotten the little ones. Programs to cater for them have also been formulated. Every Saturday and Sunday, they meet for games, music and Bible stories and studies. Eventual membership of the Church's Young Ambassadors singing group becomes an ambition for them. Through programs of this nature, the church is raising young dedicated Christians whose lives are fully given to the Lord.

Literature and Films

For most of the world, literature is a very powerful weapon to change and influence the minds of men. In Mathare Valley, this does not apply due to the low literacy level. For the Redeemed Gospel Church, literature has had to take a "back seat". The situation is changing however, and the use of literature is increasing year by year.

The Oscar-winning film "Chariots of Fire" did not pass unnoticed in the city of Nairobi. Films have an undeniable impact on their audiences, and this has led Christians to consider seriously the use of motion pictures as an evangelistic tool.

The Redeemed Gospel Church has started a film department whose responsibility it is to provide films that carry a Christian message. The large crowds that come to watch the films are challenged with the Gospel before they depart, and this has yielded fruit much above the Church's expectations.

Counselling

The lives of the people from the valley are plagued with numerous social ills. Having realised that counselling is offered by the social workers of the Church, the people come for advice.

Counselling is available both to the Christian and to the non-Christian. This has opened yet another avenue for the presentation of the Gospel to those who are not Christian. This covers the areas of marriage, family life (parents and children), and of Christians living amidst drunkards and prostitutes.

Conclusion

The evangelistic road through the valley has not been an easy one. Resistance to the Gospel has been and still remains strong. Most people are not ready to change their way of life for Christianity.

The Church's condemnation of sin and vice in the valley has produced violent reactions, even including death threats to the evangelists.

But in all of it the Redeemed Gospel Church relies upon the word of our Lord Jesus Christ, who said, "Lo, I am with you always, even unto the end of the world." (Matt. 28:20)

Mr Morompi Ole-Ronkei is a member of Nairobi Baptist Church and a staff member of AEAM, Nairobi, Kenya.

19

First Alliance Church New York USA

A Case Study

EUGENE McGEE

Introduction

First Alliance Church was the inner city mother church of the Christian and Missionary Alliance. But from 1964–1981, for many reasons, her membership was dropping alarmingly. The church was located in Times Square until 1971 and this area had become the pornographic center of the city. Peep shows, live sex shows, male theaters, pimps, prostitutes, drug addicts, homosexuals, and muggers made the neighborhood dangerous. The white adults attending the church were largely couples without children and single people. The church had practically no children except a few from the poorer classes who were brought into the church by compassionate individuals. In addition to these problems the church was pastored by a man who lived many miles away.

As a result of this declension, a feeling of malaise permeated the body of believers. New York City itself was losing thousands of jobs each year. The streets were becoming more and more dangerous. One member of the church had been mugged seven times! The Sunday evening attendance had dropped to only 50 people for the four years 1970-1973.

In 1970, the congregation moved into a beautiful renovated building in a much better location. In spite of better facilities and position the church declension continued, but to a lesser degree.

In January of 1973, a new full-time pastor was called; but the year saw a drop of five people in the Sunday morning attendance. The church now faced a seemingly unsurmountable problem. About one-third of the contributing members worked for the denominational headquarters which was to complete its move to Nyack, New York, in the summer of 1974.

Unless something dramatic took place the church was certain to become financially unviable. If it survived, it would be because it was the mother church of the denomination, and the officials of the denomination thought its value to the denomination was worth the necessary support. This situation was not at all appealing to the members, the church governing board, or the new pastor. After much prayer and consideration a new program was presented to the board by the pastor.

Preparation For Programming The Church For Growth

A study of what the local church had done for the past ten years was made. (Not only the pastor but also the people needed this information. The knowledge that records are kept and publicized is the first step toward an interest in church growth.)

The next step was the preparation of the people for church growth. Church growth without preparation is extremely dangerous from a number of points of view. One pastor of another church learned this the hard way. The church had suffered a severe split before he became pastor, and much of its leadership had gone. Among the 27 new families and individuals who came into the church in the first year were many qualified people who were almost immediately thrust into positions of leadership by the church people. Before long a rumor swept through the church that "all these new people are taking *our* church away from us." Preparation for church growth must impart the fact to the church that new people mean an end to the status quo. In an urban church growth situation, with the influx of large numbers of people from different cultures coming into a church, preparation for church growth is imperative. In May of 1974 a program of education for church growth was launched. The program was two-pronged:

1. A series of 13 sermons on church growth was given and eventually the congregation was thinking and talking about church growth. This led to an atmosphere of expectancy.
2. Wednesday evenings for several months were devoted to a study of the purpose of the church, the goals of the church, and the means of achieving the goals. These meetings were chaired by a very able layman of the church.

Out of the Wednesday evening meetings came a statement of the purpose of the church which was formulated by the people. Each person was asked to bring in a statement containing what he believed to be the purpose. Since the people were involved in the *purpose defining process,* they were automatically committing themselves to the attaining of the goals inherent in their statement of purpose. Once the people were committed to the idea of church growth, major changes were acceptable if they could be demonstrated to be goal-reaching innovations.

The needs of the surrounding culture were studied. The first question was, "What changes are to be made?" The answer to that question had to come from God. The first change the new pastor instituted was to revive the monthly nights of prayer. The people were called to a night of prayer and praise to the Lord. As many as could would remain until six in the morning; anyone could leave at his convenience. The monthly nights of prayer have continued to this day, and out of them have come the major programs of the church.

Since it is Christ's church which He purchased with His own blood, should any of His leaders attempt to change anything without first of all finding out what He wants done? Presumptuous change can bring dissension; prayerful change will bring cooperation.

A Cinema Club and a School Bus

While in France for six years, the pastor had been involved from time to time with France *Club Ciné*. A significant film would be shown by the Club, and a panel of experts would then comment on its various aspects. Why not try this, he thought, in New York City? The people of New York love the theater and the stage. Why not use this tool? The Cinema Club was an instant success and led to some other very important changes in the church's outreach.

A gifted, dedicated Portuguese young man, who was working as a parking lot attendant, had come to New York from New Bedford, Massachusetts. He had actually come to New York much in the spirit in which Jonah ran to Tarshish. He was attempting to get away from the amount of "church work" that had been expected of him in his home church. But in Harlem he saw so many young men given over to drugs, alcohol, and the like, that he began to witness on the street corners. Within a short time, he had about thirty people meeting in his apartment. He had led most of them to Christ. Most of them were Hispanic, from the Spanish Ghetto of the Upper East Side. What was he to do with them? He began to look for a church.

One day he picked up an advertisement for the Cinema Club in a Christian bookstore, and decided to bring his group to the film. When they all arrived in the neighbourhood and saw the church was mostly white people, some wanted to leave. "That's whitey's church; they don't want us!" Their leader, called "Chaplain", told them, "We are going in. All they can do is throw us out." But far from being thrown out, they were amazed at the warmth of the welcome. Especially the children and young people were delighted with the "do-it-yourself-sundaes" which were the refreshments that followed the film and the panel.

About three weeks later, Chaplain and all his young people walked into the Sunday morning service and took the pews at the very front on the right side. No one at the time realized it, but the Holy Spirit was providing the missing ingredient which either stunts or kills an inner-city white church—*children*.

Before all this happened, the pastor had been praying for a church bus. A new full-size school bus had been part of his vision for the church before accepting the call. He had no idea of where he would park it. The church has no parking lot, and parking spaces are limited and very difficult to find. Yet the vision was from God, who had already made His provisions for parking. One woman, who was an heiress of the Champion Spark Plug fortune, heard of the need of the bus for the church across the street from the hospital where she was dying. One day when the pastor was visiting her, she asked how much money was needed. When told, she took out her checkbook and wrote a check for the new bus. Inquiries at the local police precinct eventually brought to light a City law which permits the parking of school buses in front of school property no matter what the parking ordinances may be! The glistening new bus was parked in front of the church and named "Sparky" in honor of the woman who had given most of the money. Her nickname as a teenager in Toledo had been "Sparky." "Sparky" has now brought thousands of kids to church, and has been joined by two other school buses, "Mr. Tebbs" and "Simpson". The advent of children into the church life immediately brought to light the need for a better Sunday School system. In 1973, the Sunday School averaged about thirty-five to forty people. It met at 9:30 a.m. The church choir also rehearsed at that hour in the Sanctuary. Where to find space, and where to find qualified teachers? This dilemma brought about another change of even more drastic proportions. The proposal now facing the church Governing Board was a complete change of the church meetings.

Changes in The Church Sunday Schedule

The Church in 1974 was following the schedule used by most evangelical churches in the USA: Sunday School at 9:30 in the morning; worship at 10:45; evening evangelistic service at 7:00 p.m. The new proposal was to change the Sunday School to 2:00 p.m. and the evening service to 3:00 p.m. These changes would:

1. Make more space available for Sunday School as the Sanctuary would now be available.
2. Allow choir members to be available as teachers.
3. Permit a larger attendance at what used to be the evening service—since people could simply stay on till the afternoon. (Parking spaces are almost impossible to find on Sunday evenings.)

Once these changes were in force another development took place which also supplied an element missing in most city churches. One day, as the pastor was doing his own grocery shopping in a wholesale grocery outlet, he saw a huge plastic sack full of "chop suey" makings. He decided he would cook a Chinese dinner and invite any of his flock who desired to eat with him in the "Blue Room" of the church. About twenty people thus ate lunch together, and split the cost, which worked out at 35c. each. It was a successful start, and the pastor then prepared three more dinners for the people. By this time, he was praying for someone to take over, as the crowds were increasing both at the church and at dinner each Sunday! A woman came after the fourth meal, and told the pastor, "You should not be cooking for us. I'm taking over!" The church now had the second missing ingredient. The dinner between Sunday School and church gave the people a *social life*, something which they had never experienced at church before. People began to know each other by first name. Visitors were given their first meal without charge and the pastor was able to meet many of them immediately instead of having the burden of calling at their apartments.

The people were now coming at 11 a.m. and spending the day in the church. The change-over was difficult at first. Many of the saints were used to a Sunday afternoon nap, but soon their lives adjusted to the new program and the word began to spread that the church was growing. 1974 saw the departure of the headquarters people, but the year itself revealed a program that was now geared to meeting the needs of the people.

Radio and Cable TV Ministries

A young man who was studying journalism at Columbia University came to the pastor and said, "Pastor, you should be on the radio with your messages." Church finances were so poor that the pastor thought it impossible. In March of 1974, he received an invitation from a local station to go on the air at 8:30 a.m. on Sundays. The pastor put the letter aside and forgot about it. Three months later the time was still unsold, and the station renewed its offer. This time the pastor took it to the Church Board. They agreed it would be a good means of outreach, if the money could be raised. A Sunday was set aside and pledges taken from the congregation to raise the necessary amount. The young man who had pushed the idea made a pledge of $25.00 per week. When the amount fell short by $50.00 he upped his pledge to $75.00 per week. This was a real sacrifice on his part. His $300.00 per month for the first year helped the radio ministry to be born. In a large city, outreach for a downtown church on a citywide basis is one of the keys to growth.

In answer to prayer, a man gave a complete set of black and white cameras to the church. After a year of black and white programming over the Manhattan Cable system, color cameras were added. Many new people have been attracted to the church through the television ministry. Time is furnished free and all the cost lies in the purchase of tapes and equipment. However, equipment is expensive.

New Lay Leaders Come Forward

People are the greatest asset to church growth. When the pastor first came to the church and saw the condition of the Sunday School, he looked for a person with the gift of organization. He was directed to a woman of outstanding talents. Her husband was a prominent executive with Metropolitan Life, and she was active in many areas of New York life. After her election to the Sunday School, the School won national first prizes for increases in attendance for two years consecutively. Sunday School attendance went as high as 100 in September and averaged 63 for the year. The Sunday School has increased dramatically, and two years ago (in 1979) a 9:30 a.m. Sunday School was added to the church schedule. This Sunday School is for adults and young adults only. Sunday School at 2:00 p.m. continued to be for all ages.

The second person who had an important impact was the Director of Music. He had objected to any kind of music on Sunday morning except the classic anthems. He was horrified when the pastor asked a musical group from a college to sing one number. When the pastor did this a second time, he sent in his letter of resignation. Just before his resignation was to take place the Lord touched his heart and he agreed to stay on until another director could be found. This took five months. During that period, he had a new experience of God's forgiveness and the filling of the Holy Spirit. When the new director of music came in, he turned over to him his choir and his salary, and remained on for two years as church organist. This demonstration of dedication to the Lord by a most accomplished musician who could have sold his services easily to another church was not lost on the church. His unselfish example inspired the whole church to greater involvement.

People who come into this fellowship at any of its meetings seem to be struck with a supernatural sense of God's love for them. The Holy Spirit manifests Himself in the midst of His people in filling their hearts with love for all who come to the church. The congregation is a cross section of the human race, financially, socially, and racially. People are held together in this situation, not because they like each other, but because they love each other with *agapē* love. Those with racist tendencies would feel uncomfortable in this church.

The church has been constantly growing. The Sunday School has now reached the limits of its expansion. Property costs being what they are in this area, only a major miracle could give us more space.

Preaching and Home Bible Studies

The present pastor spent many years in Youth for Christ work. In this time he had frequent opportunities to see many churches and hear numerous preachers. One fact stood out. Preachers of expository sermons stayed longer in their parishes, and built solid churches over a period of time. He decided to concentrate on Biblical exposition. Having begun in Genesis in 1973, the church is now studying the last few chapters of Isaiah. Too much emphasis cannot be placed on the ministry of the pulpit. The church growth, both in grace and in numbers, is tied to some degree to the pulpit ministry. The saints are hungry for the Word. Sinners need the Word. Where the Word is preached, things happen.

In 1979, in one of the all night prayer meetings, the pastor was praying over New York City's millions. "Lord here are eight million people, and You love each one of them, and so few of them are being reached with your Word. What do You want us to do?" The startling answer came to the pastor: *"I want a Home Bible Study on every block in New York City."*

This revelation came to the pastor over and over. *God wants a Home Bible Study on every block in New York City!* How can that be accomplished? If He wants it, He can bring it to pass! The pastor was led to ask the Board to authorize a new program for 1980. The goal was thirty Home Bible Studies by the end of the year. One new Study a month would be begun for the first three months; two a month for the next three months; and three a month for the rest of the year. Since there were already three Home Bible Studies at the beginning of the year, this would total up to the thirty. At the end of 1980, the goal had been reached. Other churches began to join with us in the movement to place a Home Bible Study on every block in New York City.

A Big Step of Faith—Daily TV

Returning from the National Religious Broadcasters Conference in Washington, the pastor was even more certain that God had called him to this goal of a Home Bible Study on every block. In the following Sunday morning service, God was present in mighty power. A Christian man who had come to New York from Los Angeles to open a New York office for his advertising agency was present.

Afterwards he invited the pastor to lunch. At lunch he told the pastor, "I have just contracted for the time 7:00–7:15 a.m. Monday through Friday on WWDJ [a powerful station which covers the New York Area]. I am sure I can sell this time with a single phone call to one of the national religious broadcasters. It is a prime time on a prime station; but I was convinced by your Sunday morning service that you should have this daily radio broadcast, if you are to have a Home Bible Study on every block in New York City." When he mentioned the amount necessary, the pastor looked crestfallen. The church was celebrating its Centennial (it was already $10,000.00 behind its budget) and this broadcast would call for additional thousands of dollars each month. He took it first to the church for prayer and then to the

Governing Board. After the proposal was presented, one member spoke for it, but the second speaker, a very strong and influential man, spoke against it with much vigor. At this point the pastor felt sure that the radio broadcast was lost. But a surgeon on the Board then stood and told the Board that he believed the offer was of God and that they should accept it. The motion was carried by a very narrow margin. The man who made the strong opposing speech ended his support for the church and shortly left for another church. God, however, miraculously supplied the need for the radio broadcast, and the response to it was prompt. Requests for the Home Bible Study Starter Kit have poured in from all over the area. This ministry is now incorporated separately from the church and is carried on as a ministry to the entire area of New York City.

But why lengthen the cords so far? Why not concentrate on the immediate neighbourhood which, in this instance, numbers many thousands? First Alliance's neighbourhood is unusual. It is predominantly Jewish with a mix of Roman Catholics. It has the highest *per capita* income in New York City and, as might be expected, the city's lowest crime rate. It is an area of anonymous high rise apartments. In short, a difficult area for evangelism. So First Alliance simply casts its net wider.

Rev. Eugene McGee is pastor of the First Alliance Church (CMA), New York, USA.

SECTION VI

Parachurch Agencies Serve the Church

20

The Relationship Between Church and Para-Church: Biblical Principles

NOEL JASON

What is the para-church? Part of our biblical understanding of the Church's nation and mission—just as much as the local church is? Or is the para-church a greedy competitor, encroaching on the functions of the local church, and taking them over in countries where there are few indigenous resources at the disposal of the churches?

This is one of the critical issues with which we need to struggle. The bedrock on which all other theological insights are to be founded is a clear understanding of God Himself as revealed in Scripture. For it would be meaningless to analyse the identities of the local church and the para-church agencies without setting them in the context of God's scenario for the redemption of the world. Furthermore, since it is in him we all live and move and have our being (Acts 17:28), the question of identity is relative to awareness of the sovereign Lord who is the sole bestower of identity (Rom. 4:17; I Pet. 2:10).

What is "para-church"? The term, judging by the responses to a questionnaire issued, is of recent origin and of limited currency. A Canon of a missionary-sending diocese in the Church of England candidly confessed to not having come across the term before! There was also evidence of anger, resentment and disillusionment—between local churchmen and para-churchmen. A layman painted a word-picture of his "mainline church as a rotting tree generating humus in which the mushrooms of parachurch agencies grow and thrive."

There was also evidence of some confusion between para-church and sectarian churches. For there were several who did not make this important distinction, such as one theologically trained lay-leader who wrote that para-church groups were "entities with no roots historically or traditionally; they are departures from the main-stream of the Church, and they spring up whenever undue importance is given to any one aspect of the Christian faith". Her attitude is typical of many who belong to main-line denominations, and is an implied condemnation.

The preposition "para-" is a Greek word that has come into use in the English language, and has supplied the basic idea to many compound words. According to the *Oxford Dictionary of the English Language*, when *para* is prefixed to a noun, it either describes a status or function ancillary to that of the noun, or denotes a modification of the substance.

More light could be sought by reckoning with the potential of *para* in the Greek language itself, although it is almost certain that whoever coined the term never stopped to consider the Greek language possibilities of *para*. In the Greek, with its radical sense of "beside", *para* (depending on the three possible cases it can take) is capable of conveying "movement from the side of" (to be secondary); or, "movement by the side of" (to be equal); or, "to remain by the side of" (to rest). Thus, if *para* is conjoined to "*church*" and interpreted strictly etymologically, the following affirmations concerning the para-church could be made:

(i) *In status, the para-church is subordinate to the local church.*

But in the light of the teaching of the New Testament, which insists that that in the Christian life no service is lowly or mean, how does one understand "subordination"?

It is subordinate in its deference to the local church. In so far as the members who constitute the para-church are bona-fide members of the local church, it could be pointed out that there is a basic loyalty to the local church. For this reason, the para-church does not seek to usurp the rightful place of the local church in the life of the Christian community. Nor does the para-church aim to supplant the ecclesiastical presence and practices of the local church.

It is subordinate because of the delegation of responsibility it has received from the local church. For sometimes the local church itself constitutes these autonomous bodies in order that special needs in Christ's world may be quickly and effectively met, as in the models both of the Lord first sending his disciples where he himself was about to go (Luke 10:1) and of the apostles appointing deacons for table-distributions (Acts 6:1–6).

(ii) *In being, the para-church is equal to the local church.*

Para indicates that the para-church stands, or, better still, moves by the side of the local church.

(iii) *In function, sometimes, the para-church is a judgement on the church.*

Among the respondents to the questionnaire, there was a young Sunday School teacher who stated with candid clarity that the para-church aims to carry out those functions which, in its opinion, the local church is unwilling or unable to discharge effectively or adequately.

(iv) In achievement, the para-church finds its rest, in God's economy, by the side of the local church. Ideally, the para-church comes into being in order that the outreach of the church may be strengthened; and that effectiveness of service may be enhanced. The para-church strives side by side with the local church, and can find justification for its existence only in the mission of the church. Its reward will be the same as that of the local church, when the Lord of the Church will say to them both, "Well done, good and faithful servants; enter into the joy of your Master" (Matt. 25:21).

Causes of Discord

At the risk of seeming neo-Platonic, it must be admitted that, when all is said and one, a gulf still exists between the ideal and the real. It is all the more sad, because it is Christ's two arms, as it were, that we are now discussing. Fear, distrust criticism and hostility between the para-church and the local church often come to the surface, and the resultant publicity is both damaging to the witness of the people of God and dishonouring to the glory of God. Let us examine the causes of discord.

(i) *Competition* Competition can be good or bad, depending on the attitudes assumed by the competitors. If the motivation stems out of a desire to excel in Christ's service, that is, a theocentric striving after excellence for excellence's own sake (Phil. 4:8, 9) then it is as it should be. If, on the other hand, the competition is geared only to the setting up of impressive track-records, it is self-exalting and Christless.

(ii) *Covetousness* Among the things which may not even be named among saints, Paul lists covetousness (Eph. 5:3); nevertheless it is one of the major causes for the incompatibility of the local church and the para-church. Covetousness, in this context, is two-fold.

There is the coveting of roles. The local church covertly desires to be the para-church, while the para-church is often openly ambitious to become the church.

There is also the uglier coveting of rewards—pecuniary, or in terms of position. The local church often lusts after the income of the para-churches, especially if the wealth is generated abroad, and envies the popularity and the liveliness of the para-church. The para-church, for its part, longs for the stability and the structure of the local church. International recognition and perennial globe-trotting, which are the established prerequisites of para-church, often fuel the fires of covetousness in the less well known and the more down to earth churchmen.

(iii) *Criticism* A loving administration of home-truths never hurt anyone permanently (Eph. 4:15, 16), but uninformed, biased, public and private criticism—ecclesiastical interdicts concerning the para-church, and sweeping generalizations about the local church's deadness or indifference—can only widen the rift between the two tangible expressions of the love and righteousness of God.

Some Guidelines for Interaction

In conclusion, six guidelines for the improvement of the inter-relation and joint action of the para-church and the local church may be set forth:

(i) Unity: The first step in building a meaningful relationship between the para-church and the local church is the mutual recognition of the fact that the God who raised up his Church to be the expression of his image, likeness, and re-creative power is also raising up many "helpers" for the local church; thus the local church should offer the para-church its priority, structure, polity and security (see Eph. 5:28, 29), while the para-church should bring to the local church the power of deeper dedication, specialist knowledge and adaptability.

(ii) Maturity: When the Spirit rested on them, Eldad and Medad were prophesying in the camp, and an outraged Joshua begged Moses to forbid them. But Moses said to him, "Are you jealous for my sake? Would that all the Lord's people were prophets, that the Lord would put his spirit upon them!" (Num. 11:26–30).

Moses knew the demands of God's service, and was glad for all the assistance he could get. When that maturity is attained, there is no need for the local church to fear for the loss of its own identity, nor for the para-church to suffer restraint and persecution.

(iii) Diversity: To The Sons of Thunder who sincerely believed that everyone should toe their line, Jesus said, "He that is not against us is for us. For truly I say to you, whoever gives you a cup of water to drink because you bear the name of Christ, will by no means lose his reward" (Mark 9:40, 41).

Should we not recognise that there are varieties of service, but they are performed for the same Lord who inspires them all (I Cor. 12:5, 6)?

(iv) Humility: John the Baptist's disciples loved their master dearly, and could not bear the thought of the rising popularity of the Rabbi of Galilee. "All are going to him," they complained to John. But the Baptizer epitomised the code of conduct for Christian service in beautiful simplicity: "He must increase," said he, "but I must decrease" (John 3:25, 30).

That, coming from a man whom Jesus described as "the greatest one to be born of a woman", is really staggering. What matters is that they all should go to Jesus. If, in that process, the local church and the para-church get little or no share of the limelight, does it matter one little bit? "Not I but Christ" is a permanently relevant motto for the servants of Christ.

(v) Flexibility: If Paul were interviewed, and some one asked him to comment on his "technique", I am fairly certain that he would say something like this:

"For though I am free from all men, I have made myself a slave to all, that I might win the more. To the Jews I became a Jew, in order to win

Jews; to those under the law, I became as one under the law—though not being myself under the law—that I might win those under the law. To those outside the law, I became as one outside the law—not being without law toward God but under the law of Christ—that I might win those outside the law. To the weak, I became weak, that I might win the weak. I have become all things to all men, that I might by all means save some." (I Cor. 9:19–22)

When John Wesley decided on this strange way of "preaching in the fields" where the people were, a monolithic church frowned with the ponderous dignity of ecclesiastical disapproval, but it was his flexibility that brought him face to face with the masses who heard him gladly.

(vi) Urgency: The Apostle Paul says,

"Besides this you know what hour it is, how it is full time now for you to wake from sleep. For salvation is nearer to us now than we first believed; the night is far gone, the day is at hand. Let us then cast off the works of darkness and put on the armour of light; let us conduct ourselves becomingly as in the . . . day . . . not in quarrelling and jealousy" (Rom. 13:11–13).

Local church. Para-church. O the depth of the riches and wisdom and knowledge of God! For from him and through him and to him are all things. To him be glory for ever. Amen.

Dr. Noel Jason is pastor of a Church of South India congregation in Madras.

21

The Relationship Between Church and Para-church: A Theological Reflection

PABLO PÉREZ

The Para-Church Situation: A Brief History

Many have argued forcefully that the para-church idea originated in the church of Antioch, in the activity recorded in Acts 13, where the so-called "apostolic bands" for missionary activity came into being.[1] This argument appears to have been advanced with the intention not only of establishing the biblical basis for the para-church organization, but also of placing it as early as possible in the history of the Church. At the same time, and no less importantly, it is used to demonstrate the clear distinction between the para-church enterprise and the local church. Wagner thus says that "the church was the church, and the mission was the mission right from the beginning." [2]

Winter develops this by claiming that the Roman Catholic monastic orders from their very inception represent an even clearer model of high motivation, strong commitment and almost spectacular results in carrying out the mission of the Church. They, in turn, are but the forerunners of the modern missionary movement initiated by William Carey and J. Hudson Taylor in successive stages of development. Both Winter and Charles Mellis have pleaded for the establishment of orders on the Catholic model in Protestant circles so that there can be a positive move toward the evangelization of the world in this generation.[3]

Others, however, have not only challenged this idea but have outlined what seems to me a more realistic explanation for the development of the para-church agencies. George Peters, approaching the subject from a missiological point of view, states that a mission/church dichotomy "is not sound biblically, theologically or pedagogically" since it is

> not known in the Bible. It does not fit into the *body* structure of the church;

> neither into the fellowship of the saints, nor into the co-laborer and fellow-laborer practice of the apostles. It must be recognized that the sole Lordship of Christ in the church argues at least as strongly for the unity of mission and church as it does for the individual responsibility of each member.[4]

Orlando Costas also takes exception to Winter's ideas and structural scheme when he says:

> I see three basic problems with Winter's approach. (1) It militates against the historic-universal character of the church. (2) It makes a universal generalization out of a historical particularity. (3) It makes a theological principle out of a missiological failure.[5]

A host of similarly minded writers vigorously and effectively opposes any dichotomy whatsoever, arguing mostly on the basis of the unity of the Church and issues related to it. The fact that the decade of the 1970s (and also now the 1980s) has witnessed a literal avalanche of para-church agencies speaks eloquently of the impact of the writings of the "dichotomists" on an increasing number of enterprising Christians, and especially on the directors and executive secretaries of these agencies, both young and old.

Coupled with all of this is the fact that some people claim that the real beginning of the para-church organizations and their missionary activities, in the form in which they are known at the present, should be traced no further back than the founding of the Society for the Propagation of the Gospel in Foreign Parts, in Great Britain, in 1701; while many more point to 1792 as the actual beginning, because of the work then started through the vision of William Carey.

All of these dates and events have significance not only for the Biblical support and the historical validity they may give to these agencies, but also for the degree both of autonomy and accountability of many of their actions—two very crucial issues in church/para-church relationships. The validity of these claims is crucial if the problem is to be solved.

The Nature of Para-Church Agencies

Even the most ardent supporters of the dichotomy between church and para-church do not seem to be very interested in understanding the essential nature of these agencies. It is candidly stated that "the essential nature of the Protestant foreign mission (para-church) agencies often eludes even the serious researcher."[6] This same author proposes:

> What we will call the "essential nature" of any given agency will be described by comparing the home support base or internal structure of the mission with the field activity or external structure of the mission.[7]

On the other hand, if "the church was the church, and the mission was the mission, right from the beginning," how can the para-church agencies be "intrinsically related to the church—not as abnormalities, but rather as legs are related to the body"?[8]

Wagner adds:

> . . . the best success in world evangelism has usually come from situations in which the church or churches have permitted, encouraged, and supported the formation of specialized *missionary agencies* to do their missionary work.[9]

This view argues that these agencies should have a separate identity, and should be allowed a degree of autonomy and absence of structural relationships with the church. They should also be allowed to pursue their own directives derived from the personal encounter with the Lord of their members.

Yet autonomy is dangerous. As we can readily discover from the pages of the history of the Church, not every burning desire nor the fondest dreams of individuals can be interpreted as being a firm foundation of missionary activity in the sense of furthering the gospel of Jesus Christ and establishing his Church throughout the world. Witness to this are the Crusades, the voyages of the Portuguese and Spanish explorers of the 15th and 16th centuries, and the conquest of the Americas by the Spanish crown. Certainly no one will ascribe para-church status to any of these undertakings, even if they all seem to have some of the same characteristics that give rise to para-church agencies nowadays: a sense of mission born out of a vision with an accompanying call from the Lord; a sense of compassion for the unbelievers still in darkness; a firm commitment to accomplish the task seen clearly in that vision and call; fund-raising efforts and consequent appeals based on the commitment and the prospect of attaining the intended goal and thus serving God and civilization.

Sad to say, the very pragmatic consideration that the para-church agencies are doing efficiently what the church as a whole has not been able to do, seems to be more important than trying to determine their nature. If there cannot be found a Biblical basis for this nature, are these agencies to disappear from the picture or should we learn to live with these "abnormalities"? Perhaps we should agree with George Peters when he says that:

> the Bible presents broad organizational principles but not defined organizational patterns. These broad principles certainly provide authority for the organization of missionary societies and justify their continued function.[10]

The Structure of Para-Church Agencies

Ralph Winter's discussion of the fundamental structures of missions as "vertical and horizontal", or "modalities" and "sodalities", is by now very well known in mission circles; the two elements distinguished are "the warp and the woof" of the Christian movement. Simon Barrington-Ward adopts Vincent Turner's terminology in describing these two as "structures and *communitas*."[11]

Such thinkers seems to echo William Carey's plea for "means" (voluntary societies, sodalities, para-church agencies) to be used in the spread of the gospel, in his now famous *An Enquiry into the Obligation of Christians to use Means for the Conversion of the Heathen*. Yet they reflect, on the one hand, a very close link with current terminology used by social scientists in their description of social groupings and their structure; on the other, a very strong influence from moods and conditions of the prevalent social reality in the United States and, more specifically, of the business world.

George Peters, for one, states that:

> . . . most early British and continental missionary societies were organized on an interdenominational basis or only loosely related to a denomination . . . The trading companies rather than ecclesiastical bodies became the pattern of organization, legislation and operation. Such development was most unfortunate and worked itself out negatively in at least three ways:
>
> First, it left many of the larger churches passive and uninvolved in missions.
>
> Second, it set up a trade-company type of mission administration and complex with the mission societies becoming autonomous agencies alongside autonomous church bodies, thus introducing a dichotomy on the home base.
>
> Third, it related the churches of the mission lands to a missionary society rather than to a mother or sister church of the sending countries.[12]

J. Alan Youngren suggests that one peculiar interpretation of Paul's style of leadership, especially prevalent in para-church agencies, can be explained by the typically American frontier view of life. He suggests that:

> Four characteristics of the frontier mind we Americans inherit still serve to increase our enthusiasm for the parachurch alternative: (1) less respect for tradition and traditional social structures; (2) communalism—an attitude favoring the autonomy of one's own community or group; (3) self-reliance and an independent spirit; (4) infatuation with almost anything new.[13]

Ralph Winter adds:

> . . . despite wide diversity in organizational details, there are certain sweeping common denominators which hold true for virtually *all mission structures* . . . the conscious and unconscious *parallel* is not to *civil government* but to the *Catholic orders*, the *military, and* the structure of *private enterprise*, in that order.[14]

The vast implications of this dictum are still to be fully discovered, not only for the effect it is having on present-day missionary work throughout the world, but also for its potential effect on the nature and form of the Church in the future.

The foregoing are expressions of writers and missiologists from the so-called First World. At the same time a serious indictment is made of the para-church agencies by Vinay Samuel and Chris Sugden, from Bangalore, India. In their *Christian Mission in the Eighties—a Third World Perspective* they compare these agencies to multinational corporations and thus call them "multinational mission agencies." Their thesis is that in many areas these multinational mission agencies are actually preventing the effective mission of the gospel in the contexts where they operate.

They state:

> We find that parallels exist between some aspects of some multinational business corporations and some multinational mission agencies which give us a helpful tool to analyze and understand some of the activities of these agencies.
>
> Some strategies for Christian mission are based on a global organization promoting a clearly articulated verbal message. The goal is to make this message as widely available as possible, preferably to people who have no relationship with national Christian groups (E3 evangelism) . . .
>
> In the multinational strategy, local centers are bases for distribution. Even if they are production centers, they produce the identical product to the master copy and distribute it locally. The criterion of their performance is whether they distribute the product effectively. If they do not, then the franchise is moved to a new company.
>
> We discern the same spirit in the ecclesiology (or lack of it) in current mission strategies. The church is defined as a distribution center . . . If the national church is not an effective distribution center for the product of the mission agency, then it is bypassed . . .
>
> A multinational corporation acts as a parasite on the leadership resources of a country . . . So at no expense to itself, the multinational corporation attracts some of the most capable leadership . . . We discern a similar pattern in church leadership. The mission agencies can pay larger salaries than the national churches. So they attract capable, well qualified young men from the church training colleges . . . This well educated articulate leadership, with loyalty to the message and the method of the mission agencies, then forms the "national evangelical leadership" with no accountability to the church in the country, and no base in local churches and denominations. They represent no national church bodies and are accountable to none. They are evangelical pirates . . .
>
> Among multinational corporations we find an inevitable growth toward covering the whole market, or dividing the market up on a global scale . . . We discern similar trends in the Christian world. Relief and development agencies move into evangelism and church planting, theological education and leadership training, mission research and literature publication. We find agencies dividing up the market between them and regarding particular territories as their own sphere of influence.[15]

And so they conclude:

> In our comparison of multinational mission agencies with the muitinational

business corporations we have noted the following negative points. First, multinational mission agencies tend to by-pass and weaken the national church. Secondly, their overriding commitment is to maximize the marketability of the gospel. Thirdly, their sales approach reduces the gospel and runs counter to the spirit of the incarnation.

Whether one agrees with the aforementioned description or not, there is no doubt that the parachurch agencies usually evidence a close relationship to one particular culture at a particular time in its history. It can be effectively argued that such a relationship or borrowing has taken place throughout the centuries of church history. Yet the undiscerning approach that is being taken today by many mission agencies, boards, and missionaries should sound a note of warning as to their work and the form and nature of the church they are planting.

Types of Mission Agencies

One should not think that para-church agencies are all the same. They vary both in method, function, structure, and purpose, as well as in the degree of relationship they maintain with the church and with each other. Of course, they could all be classified as either "church-related" or "service-related," as some missiologists have maintained. But there are other ways of classifying too.

Winter suggests there are basically four types of para-church agencies:

Type A, Denomination-administered and funded;
Type B, Denomination-administered, but funded by direct designated giving;
Type C, Denomination-related but autonomous;
Type D, Unrelated to any one denomination.[16]

In terms of this division, it is easy to see that, at the present time, Type D societies are on the increase. It is estimated that somewhere between 6,500 and 10,000 parachurch groups are in existence in the United States alone,[17] and the number is likely to increase. And these are precisely the groups that command most of the attention because of their "thoroughly independent approach to ministry."[18]

I would like to suggest that these Type D agencies can be perceived even better under a different system of categorization, based on these agencies' own objectives and self-designed programs. These would include:

Specialized agencies. Those which strive to offer special services to existing groups and churches but have no desire to plant churches, and are not designed to do so. The group includes World Vision, the different Bible distribution groups (World Home Bible League, the Bible Societies, and the like), leprosy missions, Missionary Aviation Fellowship, and a host of others performing a wide variety of very necessary ministries in support of the work of the churches.

One cannot forget that both the YMCA and the YWCA were originally established to be an arm of the church in its ministry to young people.

It is no secret that in most places these organizations have followed their own programs and are not directly related to any type of church work. On the other hand, the British and American Bible Societies were not originally established to help the churches, but rather to distribute the Scriptures where they were not known. That in some cases churches resulted from these efforts was rather accidental to the original purpose. Moreover, such groups as the Christian Medical Society, as well as some others which provide fellowship for professionals, artisans, technicians, and some others fall into this category and, so far, have helped many to find their Christian identity, especially in some parts of the Third World.

At the same time, it is to be remembered that the Sunday School, though not originally conceived as a para-church in the modern sense of the term, but with many of the characteristics of one, has become an integral part of the church to the extent that it no longer has its own separate program. Much the same can be said about special-emphasis ministries, such as the Christian Endeavor Movement, which have sometimes become parts of denominational structures and are under the supervision of their governing bodies in several parts of the world.

Finally it should be acknowledged that, in general, these groups show the least resistance to good relations with the churches, depend heavily on subsidy from them, and tend to make their financial statements public, thus showing a degree of accountability for their labors.

Ambivalent agencies. Though this term is rather inadequate, it includes those groups which do not have the intention to establish churches, but, because of special circumstances and unforeseen needs, eventually do so among the special group to whom they minister. They then have to undertake all the different aspects of the ministry of a church, become busy in church development, and are distracted from their main task.

This has been the case with the Salvation Army in several parts of the world, although in some others its denominational activities are separate from its other services. Some rescue missions have followed this pattern in one way or another, but for different reasons. In some instances, groups identified with Campus Crusade for Christ and Inter Varsity have also taken this route.

Evangelizing/church planting agencies. Again it is difficult to find the appropriate term for an agency that engages in active evangelization with the view of establishing a church which will be turned over to the jurisdiction of a denomination already in existence in that district. This has usually been the procedure followed by the Wycliffe Bible

Translators with very satisfactory results. In some other cases groups with a particular denominational inclination incorporate their churches into the local structure most similar to their ideals. This is the case with most churches started by the Conservative Baptist Foreign Missions Society, as observed from personal experience.

Church (denomination) planting agencies. In the majority of cases these agencies have every intention of establishing strong churches which are sound in doctrine and zealous in evangelism. The resulting churches are usually independent in nature, with a strong similarity to Bible churches in the United States (if not specifically called so), self contained in many aspects, and rather exclusive in their relationships with existing denominations. If they multiply, a full-fledged denomination arises usually bearing the name chosen for them by the mission agency that established them, or even the name of that agency. Examples of these are many, but the Central American Mission (now CAM International), with its Central American Churches;[19] the Latin America Mission, with its Bible churches; and the Inter-American Mission, with its Inter-American churches will serve the purpose.

Para-Church Agencies and their Mission

Para-church agencies may have a stormy relationship with the local church. They may first offer their services to complement the work of the church in some areas of particular weakness; then they become competitive for the support from the church in finances, personnel, prayer concern, and other areas of common interest; in some cases they then become antagonistic by setting up their own program as of primary importance over against the programs of the church. The church, in turn, proceeds to assert itself, especially in the area of authority, closing the doors to all formal relationships with these agencies. Many a church declares itself to be the entity approved by God since the church is specifically mentioned in the Scriptures as the body being uniquely related to Christ, to God the Father, and to the Holy Spirit. Obviously, no such mention is made of the para-church agencies—Jesus never said, "I will build my para-church."

Why, then, have para-church organizations proliferated as they have?

Stephen Board, though not a theologian himself, ascribes the flourishing of para-church organizations to three characteristics of evangelical churchmanship, which he explains briefly. These are:

> First, our roots. In the immediate past we learned from the fundamentalist movement a certain disenchantment with the institutional church. Many of us are converts "out of" one church and into another; hence we tend to regard the church as a failure . . . All of the parachurch agencies have floated on the top of this ecclesiastical revulsion . . .

Second, American evangelicals tend to be "low church" in ecclesiology (church doctrine). We are able to get by without a strong emphasis on the sacraments, and our Reformation heritage speaks of the priesthood of believers . . .

This leads to a third characteristic of evangelical churchmanship: it is pietistic . . . we emphasize a heart experience with Christ first and a solution to thorny church questions later on, if ever. As pietists we tend to be individualists. And as pietists we are "the church within the church" . . .

Finally, we are pragmatic. If our church cannot do the job, we'll turn to someone who can.[20]

Towards Interdependence

In the many writings that have touched on the subject of church/para-church relationships there have been numerous valid and well-intentioned suggestions for the solution of the problems represented by it. Unfortunately, there is little evidence so far that these have been heeded at all.

A highly commendable effort in this direction has been made by the Commission on Evangelical Coöperation in its *Co-operating in World Evangelization—A Handbook on Church/Para-Church Relationships*, published by LCWE. The Commission found "*over one hundred areas of conflict* or friction, either between church and para-church, or between the different Christian organizations themselves." That number was reduced and in turn classified under five main categories, as follows:

(i) Dogmatism about non-essentials and differing scriptural interpretations (Matters of theology, conviction, terminology, tolerance).
(ii) The threat of conflicting authorities (Matters of validity, mandate, accountability, fear).
(iii) The harmfulness of strained relationships (Matters of attitude, prejudice, personality, fellowship).
(iv) The rivalry between ministries (Matters of goals, duplication, specialization, "umbrellas").
(v) The suspicion about finances (Matters of fund-raising, publicity, overheads, overseas aid).

What are we to do in the face of so many problems? I would like to suggest three courses of action.

1. *Work toward a sound ecclesiology.* This demands serious exegetical work, one that does not ignore historical and doctrinal formulations or the influence of culture, both local and "imported". This demands also that no one be excluded from the church universal on the basis of affiliation with seemingly conflicting structures, nor given a second class status because of involvement in any particular activity, or lack of it.

2. *Make special efforts to work toward true accountability.* This means that even if churches have a certain degree of self-determination and

can dispose of their resources almost at will, they should consider themselves under the primary guidance and judgment of the Scriptures rather than cultural pressures, faddish trends, or denominational programs and directives. Self-government does not mean immunity, much less impunity.

On the other hand, para-church agencies should not be content to have the seal of approval of the recently formed Evangelical Council for Financial Accountability as sufficient evidence of their honesty and integrity. Rather it should be a shame that such an agency with such a name should have the final word on a para-church ministry's credibility and acceptability.

3. Great care should be given to the training para-church workers receive, since most of them attend Bible colleges, seminaries, and liberal arts colleges or universities which are interdenominational and independent. In most cases a person's attitude toward the Church and ecclesiology is shaped by these institutions and can thus become a determining factor in future ministry and relationships with the Church.

May the Lord allow us to see the day when churches and para-church agencies walk together in harmony, assisting each other in true interdependence, trusting each other as equal members of God's family, and being committed to each other in the bond of unity.

Dr. Pablo Pérez, formerly Principal of the Mexico Bible Institute, is a pastor of an Hispanic Church in Dallas, USA.

Footnotes

1. Ralph Winter and Peter Wagner state such views in their various writings. They are also supported by Warren Webster, the General Director of the Conservative Baptist Foreign Mission Society, in his chapter "The Messenger and Mission Societies", in *Perspectives on the World Christian Movement*, ed. Ralph Winter and Steven C. Hawthorne. Pasadena, CA: William Carey Library, 1981, pp. 763–769.

2. In *Stop the World, I Want to Get On*. Glendale, CA: Regal Press, 1974, p. 48.

3. Winter, in his "A Plea for Mission Order", in *The Warp and the Woof*, South Pasadena, CA, William Carey Library, 1970, pp. 26–30; Mellis, in his "Missions as 'Orders'" in *Missions in Creative Tension*, ed. Vergil Gerber, South Pasadena, CA: William Carey Library, 1971, pp. 63–64.

4. George W. Peters, "Mission/Church Relations Overseas", Part I, in *Missions in Creative Tension, op. cit.*, p. 205.

5. Orlando E. Costas, *The Church and its Mission*. Wheaton, IL: Tyndale House, 1974, p. 171.

6. Fred. E. Edwards, *The Role of the Faith Mission*. South Pasadena, CA: William Carey Library, 1971, p. 19.

7. *ibid.*
8. Wagner, *op. cit.*, p. 46.
9. *ibid.*
10. George W. Peters, *A Biblical Theology of Missions*. Chicago: Moody Press, 1972, p. 224.
11. In J. Alan Youngren, "Packaging or Partnership? A model for true church growth", *The Churchman* Vol. 95, Number 3, 1981, pp. 249–263.
12. G. Peters, *op. cit.*, pp. 216–217.
13. In "Parachurch Proliferation: The Frontier Spirit Caught in Traffic", in *Christianity Today*, Nov. 6, 1981, p. 39.
14. Winter, "The Anatomy of Christian Mission" in *The Warp and the Woof*, pp. 12–13.
15. V. Samuel and C. Sugden, *Christian Mission in the Eighties*. Partnership in Mission, Asia; Bangalore, 1980, pp. 17–24.
16. Ralph D. Winter, "Protestant Societies and the 'Other Protestant Schism' ", in Ross P. Scherer, *American Denominational Organization*. Pasadena, CA: William Carey Library, 1980, p. 203.
17. Youngren, *op. cit.*, p. 203.
18. *ibid.*
19. The designation was perfectly suitable for churches in Central America, but when they started planting churches in Mexico, the name became "Bible Churches". I have no information on what has happened in Spain, where CAM-International has been active for more than 10 years.
20. In "The Great Evangelical Power Shift—How has the mushrooming of parachurch organizations changed the church?", *Eternity*, June 1979, pp. 18–19.

22

Vision of the Future —A Non-Institutional Church in Argentina

A Case Study Report

J. NORBERTO SARACCO

Introduction

It is common in Latin America to hear complaints and frustrations expressed by pastors and church members a few months after an evangelistic crusade has ended. Generally, the result is not proportional to the effort. The great multitudes that filled the stadiums melt away as if by magic once the last meeting is over. But when we find a ministry that has united multitudes, and these multitudes have remained faithful and even grown through the years, our hearts are moved. This is the case with *Vision of the Future*, perhaps one of the most important evangelistic movements of the last decade in Latin America.

General Description

Vision of the Future is an entity created by the Rev. Dr. Omar Cabrera in 1972 under the motto: "The greatest power in the world is the power of faith in God." It has been at work for a decade.

"*Vision of the Future*" is a phrase which the Rev. Cabrera heard as a revelation from the Lord one morning at 2:00 a.m. when he was asking God what work he wanted him to do in Argentina. Vision of the Future is not limited to a denomination. Its objective is to take the saving and liberating power of God to men in every way—reaching the spiritual, intellectual, physical and economic areas of life.

In September 1972 a series of meetings took place in the city of Parana, capital of the province of Entre Rios. The publicity read "Faith meetings for people of all religions". There the power of the Lord was manifested. People were healed of cancer; many had their legs made longer and others their hips set. Blind people recovered their sight and invalids went out of the meeting walking normally.

Parana was only the beginning. Hundreds of cities and towns began to be visited by this ministry. Whether in the comfort of well-appointed rooms, or in the open air, whether with freedom or facing terrible opposition, the preachers saw thousands receive God's touch on their lives. At present, Vision of the Future has seven evangelistic teams, 90 workers and more than 450 volunteers—the name given to persons of both sexes who help in different tasks in the preaching centers. The full-time staff in the central office has grown to 32 persons. Nine church buildings have been erected with a capacity for more than 1000 persons each, and 20 properties have been bought. 15 vehicles have been acquired, including some buses to transport the teams. It is important to emphasize that all of this has been done by local offerings. Vision of the Future has no ties with any foreign organization.

In 45 preaching places the Word is ministered monthly to 100,000 persons. In addition, people are reached through 45 radio stations and an average of 15,000 letters are answered. There are 150,000 names on the mailing list of those who are sent information, or from whom correspondence is received.

A fundamental element in this ministry is literature. Literature and radio programs constitute the two areas through which people are constantly receiving teaching and discipling. Booklets are distributed which speak of specific subjects, such as "Fear", "Alcoholism", "Worry". Rev. Cabrera has published four books, *How to Receive and Maintain Healing*, with 150,000 copies in print; *The Wonderful Law of Abundance*, 200,000 copies; *How to Face Adversity*, 60,000 copies, and *Secrets of Prayer*, 25,000 copies, Mrs. Marfa Cabrera, wife of Rev. Cabrera, writes *Daily Breath*, a series of daily devotional lectures of which 40,000 copies are printed every three months.

These figures demonstrate the dimensions that this ministry has achieved in only ten years of work. But they can only hint at a reality which is far more important: the commitment and passion for souls that characterize Rev. Cabrera and *Vision of the Future*.

How has this been accomplished? And what is its contribution to the mission of the churches?

Distinctive Characteristics

Methodology

Vision of the Future has adapted its methodology as a result of the experience obtained throughout its years of activity. Before starting meetings in a city, a radio program will be broadcast for a year. Little by little the people become familiar with the ministry, and the quantity of letters sent to the central offices increases. A feeling of expectancy is created.

Some people who may in the past have travelled thousands of kilometers to attend the meetings now realize that the message has arrived in their own city, and visualize the possibility that a new extension center may be organized there. Dr. Cabrera considers that to be able to move in God's will it is necessary to know how to wait patiently for the appropriate time. The meetings do not begin until all the necessary conditions are met. Some of the underlying principles are:

a) *The meetings are not an "evangelistic crusade"*, in the sense of a passing evangelistic event. *Vision of the Future* arrives to stay and extend in each city the stake of the Kingdom of Heaven.

(b) *The support of the local churches is not sought* for the meetings. Rev. Cabrera explains this policy by the following argument:

In the first place, the churches are generally not prepared for serious evangelization. To obtain any cooperation, one has to invest up to two years in preparing churches. Secondly, churches tend to be interested and concerned that people be "evangelical" in cultural terms before they are saved. A series of "evangelical" rules and activities is transmitted to the new convert, which tend to confuse and end up distracting him from the center of salvation that is Christ. In the third place, many of the human and economic resources in the united crusades tend to be spent in evangelizing those already evangelized. Fourthly, no church is prepared to receive in two or three months a group of three to four thousand people. Neither the building, nor the ministers, nor the ecclesiastical structures are designed for fast growth. Generally, the churches are structured for their self-preservation and not to fulfill their mission. In the fifth place, the evangelical attitude can be one of condemnation. They turn people away because they hate sin and the sinner. Christians may believe themselves to be so just that they are not capable of looking at others as "sheep without a shepherd." And finally Rev. Cabrera affirms that it is harder to convince the pastors than the unbelievers that God can move a city.

c) Each preaching center is started by holding *monthly meetings, generally, for two or three consecutive days*. After that, meetings are held every two weeks. In the interim, the people are not left without help. Through the radio programs and the abundant literature they receive plenty of teaching which permits them to grow in their faith.

d) Generally, *preaching touches on very practical themes*: "How to Pray"; "How to win over Temptation"; and the like. After each meeting the congregation goes out having learned something useful for their daily lives.

e) The first part of each meeting is structured to share *testimonies of what God has done* in the lives of those present, and to pray for the needs of the people. There is a special sense of the presence of God and His will to bless men.

Salvation is not announced merely as a theological doctrine to be believed, but as something real which begins to be experienced in the present as a foretaste of a future event.

The faith of the participants is constantly being stimulated by what God does in their midst.

Theological Emphasis

There are some distinctive theological emphases in *Vision of the Future,* although of course it shares many others common to any Christian tradition.

a) Salvation is not eschatological only. We live in it now by the power of the resurrected Christ.

b) It is not the will of God that the believer be sick, worry, or live in misery.

c) The message of the Gospel, as good news from God, must emphasize forgiveness before condemnation. People who are under condemnation cannot believe, only fear.

d) The wonders and miracles of God are not merely "decorations" of the gospel, but the logical result of the action of a powerful God who is alive and wants to save us.

Ministerial Structure

Although it is true that the figure of Rev. Cabrera occupies a central place in the ministry of *Vision of the Future*, it must also be noticed that through 10 years of service he has been surrounded by a supporting team of 90 workers.

Once a month Rev. Cabrera sends a letter to "the fellow workers" with rules and instructions for the development of the work. Also, twice a year he meets with all the people who work with him to have a period of fellowship and mutual edification. The workers and the 450 volunteers are taken from the groups of new converts.

Many of the preaching centers are visited only once or twice a year by Rev. Cabrera while the rest of the meetings are tended by his workers.

We must outline here the emphasis that *Vision of the Future* gives to the ministry of women. The example given by Mrs. Marfa Cabrera, in her total commitment to the work with her husband, has served as real encouragement and a pattern to follow for the wives of the different workers, in giving themselves to the service of the Lord. Each couple constitutes a work team and shares responsibilities—in the pulpit, in the meeting of social needs, or in administration. Taking into consideration the predominant *machismo* in Latin America, this attitude is truly revolutionary.

Finances

In such a difficult economic situation as the one presently existing in Argentina, with a growing percentage of unemployed and a level of inflation that has broken world records, the financial prosperity of *Vision of the Future* is surprising, especially considering that all its resources come from people related to this ministry within the country. According to Rev. Cabrera, this is due to the following causes:

a) People are taught that prosperity comes from God and that there is blessing in the act of giving to the work of the Lord. And *Vision of the Future* practices the principle that it teaches. It contributes monthly to the support of several dozen pastors and missionaries of other denominations, including Roman Catholics. It gives to jails and poor children.

b) The believer proves in his own life that what is taught about prosperity is true.

c) People see that there is honesty in the management of funds. There is an accounting department, employing six people, where expenditures are strictly supervised. The annual balances are supervised by an audit.

d) People tithe and give offerings because they see that their money is employed in the work and the funds are used for the things for which they are designated.

Conclusion

Without a doubt the pattern of *Vision of the Future* is a challenging alternative to the traditional pattern of mission of the Church. It may be doubted whether all the elements involved in it are totally unique and new. But its structure, methodology and emphasis have undoubtedly produced significant results in the preaching of the Gospel.

The story of *Vision of the Future* prompts several questions for the church:

1. How can we assess here the growth and maturity that each Christian should reach? Are literature, radio programs and meetings every two and four weeks sufficient to produce it?
2. How can the seminaries provide able ministers to work with these multitudes?
3. How much should the churches change their structures and theological emphasis in order to accommodate a ministry such as this?
4. What is the type of relationship that can be expected between a formally established church and a ministry such as *Vision of the Future*?
5. What does *Vision of the Future* teach us about the mission of the church and the provision of God for everything needed to fulfill it?

Let us pray that He who has given us a mission will give us also the wisdom and humility to serve Him effectively.

Dr. J. Norberto Saracco is President of the Church of God Seminary, Capital Federal, Argentina.

23

Radio and TV: Church or Para-Church?

BEN ARMSTRONG

Introduction

Twisting the dial of a borrowed television set, a desperate young man was looking for a program that would distract him from his agony.

"I had already decided to end my life by driving my motorcycle into a wall. I had lost everything—my job, my wife, my kid—because of drinking and drugs," Brad Raymond recalls. "That day I had taken more drugs than ever. I wanted to get myself stoned so high that I wouldn't know what I was doing. Just to fill in time until the high started, I was turning the TV dial, hoping to find some rock music. Accidentally, I stumbled across a Chicago station that I had never come across before. What stopped me was a guy with a guitar singing a quiet song. He was Barry McGuire. His record, 'The Eve of Destruction', had been the theme song of the sixties. I could relate to him. Now he was singing about Jesus, saying that Jesus was waiting for me. For me? I had spent twenty-four years rebelling against my family, running away, dealing in drugs. It made me wonder. Could I have the hope he was singing about? I'd tried drugs, alcohol, women, money. But I'd never given Jesus a chance. Maybe He was the answer. I prayed, *Lord, if you can, change my life*. Right away there was a deep sense of peace. Instead of ending my life, that night was the start of a new life. The next morning I wanted to get out of the rooming house and away from the drug scene. I found myself drawn to a building with a big cross. It turned out to be Pacific Garden Mission, and one of their counselors helped me to understand what had happened the night before. As the counselor talked to me, I remembered that my dad had listened to the Pacific Garden Mission radio program *Unshackled*. In fact, he became a Christian through that program. And here, ten years later, I had just met Jesus Christ myself through a TV program on a Christian station!"

Brad Raymond, who now is a member of my staff at National Religious Broadcasters and has four years' experience as a volunteer prison chaplain, is one of thousands who owe their lives to religious broadcasts. One ministry alone, the nationwide *700 Club*, receives approximately 4,000 telephone calls a year from people who are on the verge of suicide. In 1979 the *700 Club* received 1.4 million telephone calls from people seeking all types of spiritual counsel. Almost 100,000 of these called to report that the program had led them to give their lives to Christ.[1]

These people are part of an exciting new fellowship, which started at an evening vesper service on January 2, 1921. That service, in a prestigious church in Pittsburgh, Pennsylvania, sowed the seeds for a tremendous transformation of American church life. Today, six decades after the historic evening when Calvary Episcopal Church made the first religious broadcast over pioneer radio station KDKA, virtually every church in the nation feels the effects of religious broadcasting.

Paralleling the pervasive influence of the broadcast media upon American life in general, religious radio and television are now part of the American scene. In an average week the number of people who hear a religious message by radio or television is far greater than the total attendance at all of the nation's churches. Church attendance averages 41 percent, while more than 47 percent of all adults hear or see at least one religious broadcast per week.[2]

With more than 8,000 radio stations in the United States, about 1000 stations—or one out of eight—offer at least 14 hours a week of religious material. Approximately 600 stations offer religious programs and music virtually full time. Religious television stations are operating in most major markets, and hundreds of secular television stations across the country are presenting a wide variety of religious programs. According to *Time* magazine, TV industry executives say that "there is no apparent saturation point in sight."[3] In addition to TV programs "popping up at an incredible rate" on secular stations, the religious media are multiplying with one new religious radio station going on the air every week and one new TV station every month.

Thanks to radio and television, almost 130 million Americans a week hear the gospel message. Special programs, such as a Billy Graham Crusade telecast, frequently gather audiences of more than 50 million people. In addition, millions throughout the world hear the gospel from powerful international radio stations operated by American believers. Never before in the history of the world has it been possible to take the message of Jesus Christ to so many people. Radio has the capacity to cut across man-made barriers of all kinds—including geographical boundaries, language differences, Iron Curtains, and double-bolted apartment doors. Even people who live beyond the reach of electrical mains supply and other technological amenities have a link to the world through low-cost transistor radios. Today millions who cannot read can hear the gospel in their own language via transistor radio. Communications satellites open the intriguing possibility that in the near future it will be possible for everyone on earth both to hear and to see an event instantaneously.

The Concept of the Electric Church

The unprecedented linking of twentieth-century technology with Christ's commandment to "Go . . . into all the world, and preach the gospel to every creature" (Mark 16:15) has created a dynamic new phenomenon that I call "the electric church". In New Testament times the members of the church gathered in homes, shared the Scriptures, prayed together, praised God for the gift of His Son Jesus Christ, and testified to His presence in their lives. They were on fire for the Lord, and their lives had been changed by Him. As a result they changed the world.

Radio and television have broken through the walls of tradition and have restored conditions remarkably similar to those of the early church. In the electric church, as in New Testament times, worship once again takes place in the home. The speaker is the guest, as was the apostle Paul who travelled to people's homes. As a guest the radio or television minister earns the right to be heard by the content of his message. Reversing the long-established roles between the person in the pulpit and the person in the pew, the leadership role in the electric church does not belong to the radio or television speaker—not even a Billy Graham or a Jerry Falwell. The real leader is the individual who has the power to turn the dial and thereby to wipe out the image or sound of the program in a second. Similarly, the first evangelists and teachers, and the people whom they visited, came together as equals. All were people who had personally found Christ. In New Testament times, visiting evangelists and teachers were expected to bring a message from the Scriptures, which listeners could then apply to the needs of their lives. The book of Acts tells us that Paul, Peter, Stephen, and others chosen by God spoke not in their own power but through the power of the Holy Spirit. That's what made their message dynamic, bringing as many as three thousand listeners into the community of Christ in a single day!

What is the essential ingredient, the power that links the messenger and the hearer? Isn't it the transforming power of the Holy Spirit transmitted through the spoken Word of God to the listener? That is the power that brings the electric church into being. The electric church is not a manifestation of modern technology but of the power of the Holy Spirit. Through the broadcast media the local assembly of believers is able to reach out, to transmit the good news to others. Far from supplanting the local church, the electric church enlarges, enhances, extends, and complements it. All believers who beam God's message over the broadcast media and all who hear that message are part of the electric church.

The Effect of Radio and TV on the Local Church

Ever since January 2, 1921, when the senior pastor of Calvary Episcopal Church decided that radio was not worth his time and assigned his junior assistant to lead the evening vesper service which became history's first religious broadcast, there have been church leaders who were uninterested in the potential of broadcasting and church leaders who wanted to explore it. Lack of interest later changed into strong negative feelings about the use of radio and television for the communication of the gospel. This negativism may stem largely from an emotional or psychological preference for the printed word versus the spoken or visual word of television. Such is the opinion of James A. Taylor, managing editor of *The Journal of the United Church of Canada*. In an article for *The Christian Century* (April 20, 1977), he draws a parallel between today's liberal churches and the church of Rome at the time of the Reformation. Pointing out that the entrenched theology of liberalism faces a technological revolution comparable to the "invention of printing, which put the Scriptures into the hands of the laity," he believes that just as "the Reformation was the child of printing," so today's born-again movement "is a child of television." Taylor concludes that the chasm between evangelicals and "the older liberal churches goes beyond differences" in theological interpretations of Scripture, sin, and salvation to "differences in perception rooted in their parent technologies."

Almost nobody is neutral about broadcasting, particularly television, and almost everybody has intense feelings about "the church". There are almost as many different definitions of the Church as there are churchgoers. It is not surprising then that the phrase "the electric church" should send shock waves through the leadership ranks of American religious institutions.

In the same vein William F. Fore of the Communications Commission of the National Council of Churches (NCC) insists, "What worries me is whether this electronic church is in fact pulling people away from the local church, whether it is substituting an anonymous and therefore undemanding commitment for the kind of person-to-person involvement and group commitment that is the essence of the local church." He maintains that "it is relatively easy to raise funds through radio and TV, but it is almost impossible to channel that kind of support and interest back into a local church."[4]

The power of radio and TV is indisputable. Around 1977, the American media suddenly discovered that evangelical Christians had grown in numbers to become a very large sector of American society. *Time* and *Newsweek*, devoting cover stories to the born-again movement, reported that it stretched from the White House and university campuses to factories and farms. To the secular media it was remarkable that spiritual concerns could matter to millions of men and women who came from the mainstream of American life. *Time* and *Newsweek* sought in their comprehensive articles for an explanation of how this could be happening in today's world. Their research pointed to religious radio and television as an active, forceful influence. Coming by an entirely different path, they too had discovered the electric church.

In radio alone, several programs have ministered to audiences in the United States and overseas for more than four decades. A partial list includes such favorites as *Haven of Rest, Thru the Bible* with J. Vernon McGee, *Morning Sunshine* with Ralph Neighbour, and *Lutheran Gospel Hour* with Pastor J. Norheim. The largest churches in California—Hollywood First Presbyterian, Calvary Chapel of Costa Mesa, Melodyland, and Garden Grove Community Church—all have broadcast ministries. Garden Grove's *Hour of Power* with Robert Schuller reaches four million viewers across the nation every week, making an impressive outreach for a local congregation of 8,000 members.[5]

The outstanding success of *Hour of Power* has brought Dr. Schuller a steady stream of criticism, not only from secular journalists but increasingly from other ministries. Critics from both the liberal and the conservative ranks have raised questions about his theology, his style, and the spread of his ministry. When Dr. Schuller spoke at the 1979 convention of National Religious Broadcasters, reiterating his evangelical beliefs and sharing his experience as a communicator of the gospel, some broadcasters hailed it as a high point of the convention and others deplored it as a concession to worldly success.

Billy Graham ends almost every crusade telecast by urging viewers, "Go to church this Sunday." Many prominent radio speakers, such as Theodore Epp, J. Vernon McGee, and John D. Jess devote a portion of their daily broadcasts to underscoring the importance of joining a local church and participating in its life. Robert Schuller claims that his favorite letters come from people who say that they are no longer able to watch his program because they now attend worship services at a church near home. Every reputable electric church practitioner agrees that his work is not over until the listener or viewer becomes part of a local church. Reaching the unchurched is an urgent priority for every organization holding membership in National Religious Broadcasters. Some nationally syndicated programs reach out to the unchurched through personal follow-up by local churches of various denominations.

The idea of local follow-ups originated with denominational broadcasts. At the community level Christian radio stations guide callers to neighbourhood churches where they will find a warm welcome and an opportunity to grow spiritually. The Moody stations in the Moody Radio Network and Family Radio Network are outstanding in this effort.

Most of the vast religious radio-TV audience seems to be heeding the broadcaster's advice. Church attendance in the United States is considerably higher than in Great Britain and Western Europe. Significantly these countries have relatively little gospel programming on their state-operated radio and television systems. Few of their programs are either evangelical or evangelistic, although there are encouraging signs of change. The correlation between Christian broadcasting and church attendance is obvious. During the past fifty years religious life in Great Britain and Europe has declined precipitously. By comparison religion in America has remained remarkably stable during this past half century of economic depression, war, and social upheaval.

Religious radio and television programming is the unique distinction which makes American Christianity different from its overseas counterparts.

Many of today's evangelical leaders grew up listening to the powerful messages of Walter Maier (on *The Lutheran Hour*), Charles Fuller (on *Old Fashioned Revival Hour*), Donald Grey Barnhouse and Paul Rader. Two examples of leaders who can testify to the impact of radio messages on their lives are D. James Kennedy of Coral Ridge Presbyterian Church (Fort Lauderdale, Florida) and Jerry Falwell of Thomas Road Baptist Church (Lynchburg, Virginia). Both now use the broadcast media to carry the gospel message beyond the confines of their church buildings.

Obviously the churches that have a stake in broadcasting, either through direct sponsorship of programs or through follow-up activities, have reaped the greatest and most direct benefits from evangelical radio and television. Naturally, people who have been moved by gospel broadcasts seem to have joined evangelical churches, where the sermons, Bible teaching, and basic theological approach are similar to what they have heard on the air. The growth of evangelical churches in recent years is one of the most significant developments in the nation's religious life. Concurrently, membership in mainline churches whose leadership espouses liberal theology has declined steadily.

For clergymen facing empty pews, shrinking membership rolls and dwindling budgets, the rising popularity of evangelical radio and television suggests that religious broadcasting is the enemy. Bolstering that point of view is a steady barrage from executives in major denominations, particularly from executives who are experts in communications. In the past decade they have competed with other denominational departments to capture a small portion of the reduced funds now coming to national headquarters. At the same time they have lost their hold on the nation's airwaves, obtaining less airtime for liberal presentations even as the evangelical share of airtime has multiplied.

Radio and TV Meet Felt Needs

Gospel broadcasts can give the undecided person spiritual support and psychological reinforcement. The experience of many evangelical denominations offers clear evidence that religious radio and television acts as a recruiting agency for the local church. Additionally Christian broadcasts help to strengthen the faith of the 130 million listeners and viewers of the electric church, thereby strengthening the local churches in which they participate. Some theorists criticize religious broadcasters, oddly enough, for beaming more programs to the person who is active in the church rather than the one who is still outside the church. The charge that religious radio and television fail to preach "the whole gospel" is echoed by some arch-conservative critics in the evangelical camp.

Nevertheless, the critics grudgingly admit that people participate in the electric church because religious radio and television programs are fulfilling their deepest needs. Edwin Diamond of MIT, who dislikes and distrusts Christian television, acknowledges that spiritual hunger "as well as materialistic and entertainment cravings" makes many religious TV viewers feel that going "to church on Sunday morning and to prayer meeting on Wednesday night . . . isn't enough." Reporting that these churchgoers "want the Christian message in between times as well," he adds that "they feel the need for God's television as surely as they need food or sleep."[6]

The craving for spiritual food prompts the typical religious radio listener to leave the radio dial permanently tuned to a religious station. In survey after survey, the favorite weekday offerings on religious stations are Bible-teaching programs in the style of *Back to the Bible* with Theodore Epp, *Chapel of the Air* with John D. Jess and David Mains, *Radio Bible Class* with Richard De Haan, and *Encounter* with Stephen Olford. Millions enroll in the Bible study correspondence courses that supplement the broadcasts of these teachers and other radio-TV speakers. Responding to this need for a deeper understanding of the Word of God, the Sunday School Board of the Southern Baptist Convention has developed a multi-media effort that utilizes broadcasts, print, and local church involvement. The television component, *At Home With the Bible*, proves that it is possible to present serious, challenging material on the home screen. Approximately 100,000 people a year write in for the intensive study course offered on the program. More and more teaching programs will appear on religious television in the years ahead, experts predict, with the growth of Christian TV stations fostering the development of a wide range of programs for specific audiences, as in Christian radio.

Is this emphasis on the broadcast media diverting dollars away from the local church and its work? The statistics indicate that in the audiences of the major religious broadcasters, somewhere between five and ten percent of the viewers and listeners send in some financial support during the course of a year. The average gift ranges from $5 to $10. For every $1 gift to a broadcast organization, the average donor gives $4 to the local church, according to a national study conducted by an independent research firm. Of the donors questioned in the study, 20 percent say they are more active in church affairs as a result of listening to religious programs, ten percent say they are less active, and the majority indicate no change.

Dr. Ben Armstrong is President of National Religious Broadcasters, Morristown, N.J., USA.

Footnotes

1. "CBN Counseling Center Receive Record 1.4 Million Telephone Calls," News release from CBN (Virginia Beach, Virginia), December 21, 1979.
2. Ben Armstrong, *The Electric Church* (Nashville, Tennessee: Thomas Nelson, Inc, 1979), p. 7.
3. "Stars of the Cathode Church," *Time* (February 4, 1980), p. 64.
4. "Back to That Oldtime Religion," *Time* (December 26, 1977), pp. 52–58; and "Born Again!" *Newsweek* (October 25, 1976), pp. 68–78.
5. Armstrong, *op. cit.*, pp. 111–115.
6. Edwin Diamond, "God's Television," *American Film* (March, 1980), p. 30.

Comments on the rightness of the term "Electric Church"

JOHN L. TEIBE

Is it really possible that the Electric Church as described by Dr Ben Armstrong in his paper can be in any sense related to a New Testament church? Does one or two people, or even an entire family, watching a Christian program on TV on Sunday constitute a New Testament Church in the home, or does the collective sum of all viewers constitute a scriptural church? I believe not. Are there not too many missing elements of the real Church? How many viewers are entering into worship, praise, giving, receiving, exercising spiritual gifts, doing the work of evangelism, ministering to the physical, social and spiritual needs of others, and being the salt and light God intends them to be because they have been watching Christian TV programs? How does the electric church effectively offer the ordinances and sacraments of the New Testament Church expected to be observed by believers?

It is important to ask why there are more people viewing Christian programs than attending church. Is it the result of genuine spiritual hunger and thirst, or something else? Might it not be an easy way of substituting the convenience of staying at home for church going? It can be appealing to the natural man; there is no need to dress up, bundle the family in the car, drive to church, sit through a controlled hour of worship, interact with people or try to fulfill the responsibilities of a church member. Observing people's bent for freedom we wonder if this hour or so of TV each week might not become many Christians' replacement for the local visible, active body of believers. If this is so, they will unfortunately miss receiving the person-to-person fellowship, encouragement, teaching, exhortation and involvement in service to others as well as forego the protection, care, authority and blessing of the local church. Does the Electric Church provide the environment and needful elements that even a small organised home church would have?

A home church as I understand it must have some specific plan of regular attendance and involvement. It should have some minimal leadership so that those present can realize and sense that they are a small visible and functioning part of Christ's great Church. Just how many TV viewers of Christian programs actually realize they are a church? Or are they just viewers and spectators feeling themselves at an even greater distance than that between the pastor and the pew in the local church?

Why not encourage the pattern and practice that TV and radio be used by the *local* church wherever and whenever possible? These tools in the hands of that local church can become an effective extension of its ministry, multiplied many times over in doing the work of evangelism and teaching. Is there not also a far greater probability of some definite follow-up taking place with possible channelling of viewer into active participation within the local body of believers? Would this not be more likely to happen than with independent, inter-denominational programs that have no local church affiliation?

We must seek to use the media more and more effectively for the building up of the body of the Christ both at home and abroad, universally and locally. It may well be one very significant way through which Christ will fulfill His promise that "I will build my church and the gates of hell shall not prevail against it."

Rev. John L. Teibe is pastor of the Bethel Baptist Church, Calgary, Canada.

SECTION VII

The Church Triumphs in Suffering

24

The Witness of the Suffering Church in China

JONATHAN CHAO

Introduction

It is thirty-six years since China fell into the hands of the Communists. During these years the Christian church in China has gone through a prolonged period of suffering and experienced various forms of persecution.

The history of the church in China raises several questions. Why did God allow such prolonged periods of suffering? What has God done through the suffering church? What can we learn from the sufferings of the church in China?

As an historian of the church in China, I have discovered, after four years of research, that the Protestant church in China has increased by nearly 500 percent in just over thirty years. In 1950 there were fewer than a million Protestant communicant members, 840,000 to be exact. Today, the Chinese Church Research Center estimates that there are about 50 million believers. The suffering church, tested by many trials, has been purged of its impurities and weakness and has become a missionary church that is trying very hard to reach the one billion nonbelievers in China.

In my opinion, the church in China is growing by leaps and bounds because it has suffered for Christ's sake and has learned that suffering is central to Christian maturity and to church growth. Let us, therefore, consider the place of suffering in the Christian life.

The Place of Suffering in Jesus' Life

Jesus brought salvation to us through suffering and paved the way for us to follow in His footsteps.

Luke 24:26 says that "*It was necessary that Christ should suffer* and enter into His glory." This was what Jesus told two of His disciples on the way to Emmaus on the day of the resurrection. The disciples saw Him as a prophet and expected Him to redeem Israel from foreign domination. They didn't understand a very central message in the Messianic prophecies—that it was necessary that Christ, the anointed one, should suffer to accomplish His redemptive task.

From Hebrews 2:10 we learn that Christ became our Savior and was entitled to become the pioneer of our salvation because of His suffering. He was the first man to enter into God's presence and be given honor and glory. He accomplished this through suffering. Thus we see that suffering is the gateway to glory.

The first man, Adam, failed God through disobedience because the garden of Eden was too good. There was no suffering. According to Hebrews 5:8–9, the second man, Christ, did God's will through obedience, and He learned obedience through suffering. It was through suffering and death that He was made perfect in obeying the will of God. Such a perfected Savior became the source of eternal salvation for all who follow Him in obedience.

There was a young preacher in Shanghai who was greatly used of God in the 1950s. Through one week's evangelistic meetings 500 came to know the Lord. In 1960 he was arrested and imprisoned for preaching the Gospel. He served for 10 years in a hard labor camp. In 1970 he was released. He began to preach the Gospel again, this time in Henan, his home province. After four years of secret itinerant preaching, in 1974 he was arrested and imprisoned again and was not released until late in 1979.

Five months after his release my wife interviewed him. In the course of conversation he reflected upon the meaning of his suffering. He said that the 16 years of imprisonment had taught him two lessons: (1) suffering enabled him to know God more profoundly; and (2) suffering helped him to learn obedience to God's will. This is the experience of our Savior. God also intends for us to experience suffering so that we may learn obedience and be perfected in it.

The Believer's Share in Christ's Suffering

Peter told the slaves to submit themselves to their masters, even to those who were harsh to them. To suffer for doing good is commendable. 1 Peter 2:21 says, "To this you were called because Christ also suffered for you, leaving you an example, that you should follow in His steps."

In Philippians 1:29 Paul says, "For it has been granted to you on behalf of Christ *not only to believe in Him, but also to suffer for Him.*" The Living Bible says, "It is given to us as a privilege to suffer for Him." In other words, there is a grace in suffering. Suffering is an endowment from Christ.

Recently 14 young preachers were arrested in central Henan for preaching the gospel without permission. They preached in a town where 5,000 came to hear them. The police forced them to stay in a kneeling position with their hands tied to the back of their necks and feet for three days and three nights. One of them, a girl, fainted and was released earlier, but the rest suffered nine days of imprisonment. After their release, the girl who was released earlier wept feeling ashamed because she suffered for only three days. She felt that she was underprivileged!

When Jesus calls us, He calls us to suffering and death. He did not call us just to believe. Faith alone without suffering is cheap grace.

During the Cultural Revolution a Christian high school teacher in Swatow, South China, the most educated man in his village, was publicly humiliated and abused simply because he was a Christian. After being "struggled" against in public meeting, he was tied to a telephone pole for several weeks, exposed to the sun and the rain. Even children could spit on his face. At night his ten-year-old son would bring food to him. Afterwards he felt so ashamed and depressed that he contemplated committing suicide. As he stood on a bridge overlooking the water, his eight-year-old daughter ran after him. Coming close to him, she said, "Dad, I know that you are disgraced because of Jesus." He burst into tears. Holding her in his arms, he confessed his weakness before the Lord.

For the believer suffering is not accidental, but comes to us as our share in the suffering of Christ and is given to us for our glorification. This is the message of 1 Peter 4:12–13.

The Chinese church was caught by surprise in the early 1950s when persecution and trials fell upon it. The Christians had not anticipated the tactics of the Communists, nor did they understand that it is our *share* to suffer for Christ. But they learned this truth during the 1960s, especially through the period of the Cultural Revolution. Now in the late 1970s and early 1980s, they even rejoice to be counted worthy to suffer for Christ. They rejoice in their suffering because they are being prepared for glory and will share Christ's glory in that day.

Philippians 3:8–10 says that Paul considered everything as loss compared to the surpassing greatness of knowing Christ. He forsook everything in order to know Christ; to know the power of His resurrection; to know the fellowship of sharing in His suffering; and to become like Him in His death.

This knowledge of Christ is not just a rational or theological knowledge of our minds alone, but entails knowing Him in the depths of our being—knowing Him experientially.

The Chinese preacher who suffered imprisonment for 16 years says that he did not really know Christ as fully as God intended until his second imprisonment. He told us that his knowledge of God and of

Christ and his style of ministry were all limited by tradition. Through suffering, he said, "My religious traditions, like a jade jar, were broken and the ointment of Christ came out. Now I have come to know the depth of the love of God, the mercies of God, and the faithfulness of God through suffering. I came to know what it means to be identified with the death of Christ and to enjoy the power of His resurrection." Suffering, for Christians in China, has become an avenue for knowing God. "You don't know the holiness of God," they say, "until you have suffered."

The Place of Suffering in the Believer's Life

If we understand that we are called to share Christ's suffering then we can appreciate the role of suffering in the believer's life. From the Christians in China we have learned four purposes for suffering in our Christian life:

Suffering Liberates the Christian from the Dominion of Sin

Chinese Christians have shown us the meaning of 1 Peter 4:1–2: "Therefore, since Christ suffered in His body, arm yourselves also with the same attitude, because he who has suffered in his body is done with sin." One house church leader in central China used to be bound by the sins of adultery and stealing. One day he was caught stealing a fellow farmer's savings and was imprisoned. This imprisonment led him to have a conviction of sin. After he became a Christian, he was still bothered by these two sins until he was imprisoned again for the Gospel's sake. Now he testifies that the second suffering released him from the lust for women and the desire for money. He is now pastoring a house church that is more than 400 strong in his village. He is completely preoccupied with preaching the Gospel. Recently he was the team leader on a mission trip to a nearby province.

Suffering Tests and Refines Faith

1 Peter 1:6–7 tells us that trials are sent our way in order to try our faith so that it may be proved genuine and may result in praise, glory, and honor at the appearance of Jesus Christ.

Before the Communist takeover there were many "rice Christians" in China who joined the church for material benefits such as free education, free medicine, and possibly church employment. Persecution separated the genuine believers from the false believers, who quickly denied that they were Christians. Persistent persecution has preserved the purity of the church in China because it has made it costly to confess Christ. A young high school boy was recently severely beaten by his party-member father for accepting Christ. The father's beating was done in love because by becoming a Christian his son had virtually forfeited his future prospects. So the suffering comes even from a believer's loved ones.

How does suffering refine faith? A believer in Peking was arrested in the early 1950s because a fellow Christian betrayed him to the government. After 20 years of imprisonment he was released and came to Hong Kong. I asked him, "How do you now feel about the man who betrayed you?" He replied, "I have learned to forgive him after hating him for the first ten years." Such is the reality of refined faith: it forgives and is displayed in a gentle spirit.

Suffering Produces Steadfastness which leads to Maturity

James 1:2–3 tells us that the testing of our faith produces perseverance and when perseverance finishes its work, it results in maturity.

Wang Ming-Dao was the best known evangelical Chinese pastor before the "Liberation". He was arrested twice, once in 1955 and then again in 1957, for not supporting the TSPM (Three-Self Patriotic Movement). Altogether he served 23 years in prison. He testifies to visitors that there was a time when he, too, was weak and even "denied" Christ. But he took courage from Peter's failure and is repentant now. After prolonged suffering he tells his fellow believers that there is now nothing in the whole world that would ever shake his faith or destroy his loyalty to Christ. Suffering has made him more steadfast in the Lord than ever before.

Suffering Trains the Believer in Christian Maturity

In Romans 5:3 Paul tells us that suffering produces perseverance, perseverance produces character, and character produces hope. In China, many faithful pastors and Christian leaders were imprisoned for 15 to 23 years. Many promising young people spent their most creative adult years in prison doing hard labour. During these years they were subjected to long hours of Marxist and Maoist political study and pressured to abandon their "idealistic world view" and "superstitions". They were promised early release or better treatment, such as having enough to eat, if they renounced their faith. Many opted for a shorter term by compromising. The test was one of endurance under pressure. Often Christians did not even have access to other believers for mutual encouragement. The challenge was to hold on to the end. The faith of those who persevered was literally stretched. But in the process of such prolonged deprivation, they learned to endure suffering and to persevere in Christ.

Strong Christian characters have emerged out of these trials of endurance. One man was exiled to northern Manchuria in 1958. At that time his son was only six years old. In 1978 his grown-up son went to visit him. "It is not really necessary that you spend all that money to come so far to see me. The important thing is that I see you there, before the Lord, in that day," he said to his son. His strength of spiritual character was sustained by his hope of the appearance of Jesus Christ.

Anyone who had fellowship with house church leaders in China would be impressed by their strength of character. They are marked by strong faith, boldness in preaching the Gospel, breadth of love for fellow co-workers, and a self-sacrificing attitude. One of the itinerant preachers told me that he is a target for arrest by the Public Security Bureau (the police) in the district where he ministers. He preaches every day in different villages. As soon as the local police learn of his arrival, they attempt to arrest him. One day as he was preaching in the courtyard at a house church meeting, a police chief arrived suddenly. The believers immediately encircled the police chief and meanwhile led the preacher away to a hiding place. Local believers, at first, didn't know where to take him for safety. But suddenly they got the idea of taking him to the home of the police chief, because the policeman's mother, wife and children were all believers. There he stayed with the policeman's son until he was escorted away at midnight to another village. "Repeated deliverances like this incident," he said, "have made me bold in the Lord because I believe that the Lord will protect me." Christian character is built in the heat of trials where we experience the power of God.

Conclusion

An American youth came to our Research Center in Hong Kong for a month's internship this summer. Before he left America, a Christian friend asked him: "If God loves the Chinese church so much, why did He allow so much suffering to come upon it?" The youth had no answers to this question. Then he travelled to China and had personal fellowship with those believers who had gone through much suffering and were zealously doing the work of evangelism. This experience completely changed his life. "I now have the answer to my friend's question," he said to me. "I am going back to America to ask him this question: If God loves the American churches so much, why hasn't He allowed us to suffer as He did the church in China so that our faith might be strengthened, our lives purged, and our relationship with Christ deepened to serve him wholeheartedly?"

As a student of modern Chinese history, I see that the Chinese people, particularly the young, are ready for ideological and institutional change. In fact, they desire greater toleration for the coexistence of a number of ideological views and for the quick establishment of an objective, and even of an independent, legal system. The Chinese people also want political machinery that will solve the problem of poverty, stagnation, and feudalistic traditions in their society. The 40,000 or so students who study abroad will become significant agents of ideological and social innovations in the next two decades. But most importantly, the Christian church, especially the house church movement, has become the most vital spiritual and ideological force in China among the young.

When these factors are viewed through the eyes of faith, they enable me to look forward to a great harvest in China by the end of this century. And China, be it noted, contains one third of the world's unreached people. It is my prayer that the Christian churches worldwide will be prepared for that day.

Dr. Jonathan Chao is Director of the Chinese Church Research Center, Hong Kong.

25

House Churches in China: A Report

THOMAS WANG

Introduction

When the Communists took over China in 1949, there were 110 Protestant mission groups at work there. The estimated baptized Christian community was 1.8 million, of which 834,000 were communicant members. Over 6,000 Protestant missionaries were at work, together with 13,000 Chinese Christian workers, ministering in some 19,500 churches and chapels. In addition, there were 270 Christian middle schools and 262 Christian hospitals. At that time, China was, perhaps, the largest Protestant mission field in the world.

But during the past three decades there has been a drastic change. It was in God's providence that all Western missionaries were removed from China (a process largely completed by 1951). God allowed the Church there to be severely tested. The authorities determined to break its ties with the West and make it subservient to the State. Many suffered for the faith and died in prison.

The Formation of House Churches

Historical factors

It was after the Republic Revolution (1911) that Chinese Christians, gradually influenced by the accelerated development of Chinese nationalism, began to contemplate loosening their Western moorings. This was especially so in the northern part of China. It was largely due to the emergence of a growing and vigorous Chinese leadership, which began to take over responsibility for the formerly mission-oriented churches and thus produced indigenous Christian movements. The most famous indigenous churches included the Church of Christ in

China, True Jesus Church, Jesus Family and Little Flock. These churches were the prototypes and forerunners of the house churches in China today.

Political factors

From 1949 to 1962 all Protestant churches in city or rural areas were unified and brought under the control of the State through the "Three-Self Patriotic Movement". Under its leadership, all denominational structures and organizations were destroyed in the name of unity. The number of churches was reduced drastically. In Shanghai, 200 churches were reduced to 15; and in Peking, 66 to 4. For all practical purposes, pastoral leadership over congregations was brought to an end. Christians were thus forced to meet privately for worship at their homes and were able to partake in community life only at irregular intervals.

During the Cultural Revolution (1966–1969), all types of professing Christians were driven further underground. Even the few state-controlled institutional churches were eliminated from society. It was thought at first that the rise of house churches was limited to the coastal provinces where Protestant missionary activity had a longer history and where the process of indigenization had been most successful. It is now clear that house churches were far more widespread than was realized. Reasonable estimates today put the number of house churches in China at around 50,000 and the number of Christians at between 30 and 50 million.

Factors related to China's religious policy

According to article 35 of the new constitution of 1982, "All religious organizations must accept the leadership of the party and the state. All religious activities must be conducted and managed by these religious organizations under the directives of the 'Religious Affairs Bureau'." The following eight types of activities fall outside of approved religious activities:

(a) Inculcating religious thinking in youths under 18 or leading children to participate in religious activities.
(b) Interference with politics, education or marriage.
(c) Disrupting the social order.
(d) Economic exploitation, financial deception or harming people's health.
(e) Using communal property for religious activities.
(f) Restoration of religious feudalism or oppressive systems which have been abolished.
(g) Asking for, or receiving, gifts from abroad, or propaganda materials from Hong Kong and Macau.
(h) Conducting free itinerant evangelism.

Characteristics of House Churches

House church leaders believe and hold on to the following essentials of Christian life and witness:

1. The Lordship of Christ over the individual believer and over the corporate Christian community—the church. This recognition of Lordship implies the organization and development of Christian witness according to the teachings of Scripture, even if the activities which result run counter to state policies.
2. Assembly for worship and the celebration of the ordinances of baptism and the Lord's Supper. Contrary to state prohibitions, Christians have been meeting for prayer, for worship, and even for evangelistic services on their own, clandestinely or openly, depending upon the current political atmosphere. Recent state regulations prohibit those who have not been approved by the Three-Self Patriotic Movement to administer baptism. Yet local house church leaders continue to baptize new converts.
3. Proclamation of the Gospel. State regulations also prohibit non-approved pastors from preaching the Gospel, or preaching to minors under 18 years of age, or any type of itinerant preaching. Yet house church leaders are busy training young preachers, and are doing itinerant preaching across counties and provinces.
4. Teaching and discipline. Proclamation in China is directed toward conversion and incorporation into local house churches, where biblical teaching and discipleship is conducted, gifts are developed and discipline administered.

Key Factors in Growth

Spiritual Purification

After thirty years of severe testing, Christians have become more spiritually mature. They have vividly experienced the love of God in times of distress and loneliness, and also the reality and power of their faith. With such a deepened experience of God and His power, they are deeply committed to witnessing to the living God through their transformed lives.

Total Mobilization

The house churches actually represent a genuine people-movement at the grass-root level. As a lay movement, house churches put greater emphasis on Christian experience than on theological formulation. When they come together, they share their experiences of God and His Word in their lives.

Prayer

Prayer and sharing are the two major functions in house church meetings. Twenty-four-hour prayer chains are organized for stifling the attacks of Satan in expectation of the Kingdom. Some churches list prayer items such as church revival, names of workers, church unity, other churches, fellowship, spiritual provision from God, the government, and so on.

Contextualization of the Christian Faith and Christian Life

The house church is diffused into existing Chinese social structures and lines of relationship such as the family, the "work unit", the neighbourhood block, and the commune structure. Without institutional leadership or structure the house churches have become relatively free from governmental administrative control. Furthermore, these social relationships and structures have become natural avenues for evangelism.

Methods of evangelism developed by house churches may be summarised as follows:

(a) Sharing their faith with their immediate and extended family members and trusted friends;
(b) Incarnating the gospel in their lives and letting them speak for Christ;
(c) Using public occasions, such as funerals, to witness for Christ;
(d) Testifying to God's power through the exercise of the gifts of healing and exorcism.

The patterns of church growth in mainland China, and the speed with which the Church is growing (from less than a million in 1950 to nearly 50 million today), under conditions of persistent suppression, suggest to us that there are more elements in church growth than anthropological and cultural factors. The Church under pressure has learned a great deal of spiritual truth about evangelism and church growth. There seems to be a closer relationship between the New Testament pattern of Church growth and that which is found in mainland China today.

Needs of House Churches

Literature, radio and cassettes

They are in need of Bibles, hymnals, and Christian literature as well as radios and cassettes to enhance their spiritual nurture and growth.

Theological training for the leadership

A great majority of the house churches do not have formal biblical training. This constitutes a crisis in general leadership and doctrinal instruction. Short-term training for the leaders is therefore much needed.

Financial support

Hundreds of laymen are engaged in full-time itinerant evangelism. They are in need of prayer and material support for their living, transportation (*i.e.* bicycles) and other working expenses.

Conclusion

Today the house churches are to be found in every province from north to south, as well as in the border areas and autonomous regions. It is estimated that there were 20,000 churches and evangelistic centers in 1949. As we have seen, this has risen to a figure of perhaps 50,000 today. We believe that the Chinese house church's model of existence and modes of evangelism could well become a pattern for the Church in closed societies everywhere.

Rev. Thomas Wang is Executive Secretary of the Chinese Co-ordination Center for World Evangelism, Hong Kong.

A Personal Testimony

GEORGE CHEN

Early in 1957, Mao Tse Tung instigated his "Two Hundreds" period, his "Let a hundred flowers bloom; let a hundred thoughts contend." The people were encouraged freely to voice their thoughts so that a healthy criticism of Mao's Communism would emerge. But in 1958, after intellectuals had declared themselves, those who held ideas contrary to those of the Party leadership were punished. In effect, they were condemned out of their own mouths. Many intellectuals were accused of being "rightists" and were treated as counter-revolutionary.

The Closure of the Churches

At the same time, some of the Christian workers who had joined the Three-Self Movement, and were already in leadership positions, were accused of being "rightists". A general order was given that all Christian workers and representatives of member-churches should gather at designated locations on appointed dates to discuss and study the problem and to conduct self-criticism. Church services stopped. Day after day there were mass meetings and discussion groups for self-criticism and discussion. The Christian workers had no idea of how long this disruption would last.

One or two in a group would suggest that it would be better to transfer to a secular calling than to remain a church worker. Notice was taken of such suggestions, and they were reported in public as wise decisions.

Later, everyone was forced to be transferred to secular work. The Three-Self Christian workers all went, willingly or unwillingly, to the factories. They had thought that by joining the Movement they were safeguarding their positions in the pulpit, so they could continue to serve the Lord and the saints. Many had joined the Movement for the Church's sake. But now the churches were shut and the ministers had to labour in the factories.

Formerly there were 66 churches in Beijing; by 1958 only four remained open. In Shanghai 200 churches were reduced to eight. This was the result of the policy of freedom of religious belief in China. Pastoral positions in these churches were delegated to those who served the purposes of the Three-Self, not because they were spiritual and regenerated, but because they were obedient to the highest authorities of the Three-Self and the Party.

Finally, during the Cultural Revolution, even the legal churches were closed, and the remaining Three-Self employees were put out of their positions. Bibles were searched out and burned. It seemed as if there were no more churches, no more Bibles or literature. It seemed as if Christianity had been wiped from the face of China.

Nevertheless, throughout this period, the house churches were taking their present shape. They were not a new thing. Even before the Communists took power there were many home services in the cities and the countryside. Most of these fellowships could not or would not meet in a church-shaped building, but met in homes. House churches preached and protected the true Gospel and came to be adopted by the great majority of believers. Very few professional ministers took part in the house churches, so the people at first came together only for fellowship, singing, and scripture-reading and praying. But as a leadership emerged, gradually the house churches began to function fully as churches.

Imprisoned as a Pastor

During all this time, I was in prison. I heard conflicting reports of what was happening. Had Christianity been wiped out? Or were there some of the faithful left? I was anxious to find out the truth.

In 1954 I had established a church in a salt district on the northern coast of Zhejiang province. The inhabitants there produced salt from seawater. Their life was poor and undeveloped, and still is. I was the only minister in that district. Because it is a large district there were three meeting places and I had to walk from place to place to preach and minister to the people.

At one time I was detained by the authorities for several weeks because I was leader of the church. When I was released the Three-Self officials held a regional Christian workers' meeting to criticize me publicly. But they did not frighten me out of my ministry. Finally, the government expelled me from the countryside, and I continued my ministry in the city until 1960 when they sent me to undergo "ideological reformation".

Before I was arrested in 1954 there were 300 believers in my church in the countryside. There were a few more by the time of my arrest in 1960.

Miracles of Church Growth

From 1960 to 1978, while I was in prison, the church suffered much tribulation and persecution. The Cultural Revolution shut church doors and burned Bibles. Christians were arrested, beaten, and imprisoned. The Gang of Four announced that the Four Olds (old traditions, old customs, old cultures, and old religions) had been eliminated from China. Those who held on to the old were branded "reactionary".

In prison, the only thing that caused me grief was to think of my believers. How were they faring? I assumed they had diminished or had turned away from their faith. How could the church flourish after this onslaught?

I was released in 1978, and allowed to go home. I had heard that Christianity had not died out. I was anxious to find out the truth. I hurried to the north coast, to the salt district, to see what had happened.

What I saw was that God had worked nothing less than a miracle in the nearly twenty years I was away. Many gathered to listen to my preaching—and most were unfamiliar to me. There were many young people. An elder of this church, who had been a young man when I was there, told me that there were now about 5,000 believers in about 20 meeting places.

I asked, "Who has done this?" They told me that no one other than Christ had accomplished it. Since the beginning I had been the only professional minister to work there. Jesus himself attracts and draws people to the Cross.

In October 1981, I visited a certain county in Henan province and preached there. I went to each of the 22 communes in that county. At each one I inquired about the numbers of believers there. The number of believers in each commune varied from 400 to 20,000; the total for the county was 92,500 believers. This is out of a population of 650,000 in that county—one in every seven is a believer!

I saw with my own eyes the prospering of the gospel. Crowds of believers met on hillsides, in graveyards, or in houses, to worship. They sang hymns, prayed together, read Scripture. They always hoped there would be someone to preach, but there were not enough trained leaders to go round; they were often disappointed. They were very glad when an itinerant preacher, such as myself, was able to share the Word.

Needs of the Church in China Today

Because of this rapid growth of the house churches, they also have great needs. When I chatted with those young believers in Zhejiang province, I found that many had accepted Christ after hearing Christian radio broadcast programs. Radios are common, even in the countryside, where they are sometimes the only evidence of modern technology. Church growth in China has been great, partly because of Christian broadcasting. But there are many churches which are without adequate leadership. There is a great need for training the young people by radio broadcast, among other means, as well as for further radio evangelization.

When I was in Henan in 1981, I learned that for all those 92,000 believers in that one county there were only 26 Bibles.

These are matters for prayer: that God will supply the need for scriptures and supply the means to train house church leaders in the scriptures so that they would be able to carry on their pastoral ministry.

Rev. George Chen is pastor of the Lutheran Ming Tao Church, Hong Kong.

26

Romanian Baptist Churches

A Case Study

JOSEF TON

Introduction

There are conflicting reports about the church in Communist lands. Some speak only of persecution, hardship and suffering, while others bring glowing reports of dynamic church activity and growth. Reporters from both sides tend to give the impression that only theirs is the true story.

Some are very fond of emphasizing the differences between registered and non-registered churches (the so-called "underground" churches), with the oversimplifying tendency of saying that the registered churches have compromised or have even betrayed their faith, and that only the non-registered or the "underground" churches are true and faithful. However this situation is confined almost exclusively to the Soviet Union and China.

A further misunderstanding is to think that all Communist countries are in the same situation with regard to religion. For example in Poland where there is a very strong Roman Catholic Church, with well over 90% of the population giving open allegiance to it, the Communist Party is having to come to grips with that powerful force. Another example is in East Germany, Czechoslavakia and Hungary, where there is a strong Protestant Lutheran and Reformed tradition, unfortunately weakened by liberal theology. Then there are places like Romania where there is a strong and dynamic evangelical movement (Baptist, Pentecostal and Brethren), which was heavily persecuted by the Eastern Orthodox Church before being persecuted by the Communist regime. People in the West are not aware that in Russia, where the persecution is generally much stronger than in any of the countries named above, the Communists have changed their policy towards religion several times. For instance, while the Russian Orthodox Church was being heavily hit in the twenties, the Protestants were relatively free from persecution. However in the thirties all of the churches were almost completely crushed with priests and pastors sent to labor camps and churches being desecrated and transformed into storehouses, theatres or clubs.

In the Great War, when Stalin needed all the support he could get, he restored some freedom to the churches, freedom which was extended for quite a long time after that. With Kruschev came the desire for de-Stalinization which included a new drive against religion; this took the form of closing thousands of churches and imposing restrictions and state interventions in the life of the churches that were allowed to stay registered.

With such a diverse historical background, it is indeed difficult to generalize about "the situation of the church in Communist lands." Communists are Communists, and while they have to consider their given situation, they still have the same declared aim of abolishing all religion and indoctrinating the whole of society with atheism. They say openly and loudly that their ultimate goal is a totally atheistic society. Only the methods used at particular times differ slightly because of the given situation in their respective countries.

To add a further dimension to the whole problem, Communists are very concerned about their image in the world. After all, they want to convince the whole world that their system is the ultimate of democracy and freedom! Knowing how sensitive this issue of religion is for many nations of the world, for propaganda's sake, the Communists do not want to be seen as brutally destroying churches and openly persecuting Christians. In order to convince the world that they are a democracy with freedom of religion, they generally write in their constitution that there is freedom of religion and the churches can function legally.

Now, here we have a conflict of interests: on one side, the desire to show democracy and freedom; on the other side, the desire to destroy all religion and create an atheistic society. Is it possible to satisfy both of them? That was what they deliberately tried to do in Romania, and—as one who followed and studied this development for 30 years there—I want to tell you the whole story.

Pressures on the Baptist Union in Romania

The Eastern European countries were acquired by Stalin in the Yalta Agreement, in 1945. Although the Russian armies were already in those countries, it took a few years until they organized a Communist leadership and structure. It was not until 1948 that the Communist Parties were really in control. In the meantime, there was complete freedom of religion, and in Romania the Evangelicals were experiencing a great revival.

In 1949, the new Communist regime brought in a new "Law of

Religions". One important change was that it abolished the status of "State Religion", held until then by the Romanian Orthodox Church, and it declared all the existing denominations (14 in all) as "equal before the law." This law gave the Ministry of Religions (known today as "The Department of Cults") many regulatory powers and control over the denominations, but they still felt safe under it. This law—still in force today—gave the Communist regime the opportunity to boast abroad that they had secured religious freedom in their country. This law satisfied their desire for propaganda.

However they did not forget the other goal of destroying all the denominations. To accomplish this they created in the Ministry of Religions a "department" known as "The Department of Studies". Its task was to study closely each denomination, its specific features, its weak and strong points, and then conceive of a plan to destroy it, taking advantage of this detailed knowledge.

The guidelines given to destroy all religions were that surface religious freedom must at all times be preserved, and that actions taken against the denominations should not be seen as breaking the law. We heard the Communist leaders say again and again, that they fight religion but "not by administrative actions," that is, not by closing the churches or by imprisoning the Christians.

That "Department of Studies" needed about five years to develop its plan. One has to keep in mind that one of the essential characteristics was its intention to deceive: it should not be seen that the State does anything to destroy a particular denomination.

I shall describe how that plan was applied to the Baptist denomination. Its deceptive nature will be immediately obvious. With minor variations, this sort of action was taken against all the other Christian denominations.

In 1954 the President of the Baptist Union, Rev. John Dan, was summoned to go to the Ministry of Religions. He was informed by them: "We have been studying your denomination for quite a while, and it struck us that you have meetings and activities in your churches every night of the week. We do not like that. We want people, and especially youth, to be free for social activity, for entertainment, for education. So you should release them for that. We came to the conclusion that you should have only two meetings for worship with the whole church, one on Saturday night and one on Sunday morning. The rest of the time your churches should be closed. No youth meetings and no other group meetings should take place in your church buildings. Now, it is not we who are going to tell this to your churches. It is you. You must write to them to this effect. Do not tell them that the State asked you to do it. You have to write to them that you came to see this need of education and social activity and entertainment, and you decided to release your people to do these things. To make your job

information there. These are very expensive projects. But we believe that they can be the tools to penetrate that dark world of Communism with the light of the Gospel of Jesus Christ.

Pastor Josef Ton of Romania is now President of the Romanian Missionary Society, Wheaton, USA.

27

Mekane Yesus Church, Ethiopia

A Case Study

TESFATSION DALELLEW

The Founding of the Evangelical Mekane Yesus Church

During the Italian war (1936–1941), Christians in Ethiopia who had come to faith as a result of the work of different missions were trying to maintain their faith by coming together and reading the Holy Scripture and praying; they decided to form the *Ethiopian Evangelical Council of Churches* (CEEC).

An annual conference continued after the Italians were expelled. But attempts to establish the Ethiopian Evangelical Church Council failed after the tenth conference in 1954 when the missionaries came back to the country after independence. Independent Bible schools, elementary schools and medical work were established by the missionaries, resulting in theological differences and a widening of the gap in relationships.

As a result of the work of several different missionary societies, many evangelical groups had been started. One of these groups had begun in Addis Ababa in 1920 and called itself the Mekane Yesus Church. This church had a Lutheran Confession as it was started by the Swedish Evangelical Mission.

The attempts of local evangelical believers to come together under one Evangelical Council, and the influence of the Lutheran World Federation on the different missionary societies, resulted in the establishment of one Evangelical Lutheran church, the Ethiopian Evangelical Church, Mekane Yesus (EECMY) in 1958.

The EECMY has contributed much to the healthy growth and mature fellowship of the churches in Ethiopia. Due to its openness to other churches, the Bethel Church (Presbyterian) joined the church in 1975 with 30,000 members.

GAFC-Q

The EECMY has greatly encouraged student mission and has been a sponsoring body for the Evangelical Student Movement in Ethiopia.

The Growth of the Church

The church is one of the fastest growing in the world. The membership is growing by ten percent every year. When the church was established, there were 20,000 members; now the church has over 500,000 members. The reasons for numerical growth, according to Oskar Nydal's study of church economy, are these:

1. Conversions because of healing from sickness and evil spirits' possession: 61 percent.
2. Conversion through attraction by the Christian way of life: 40 percent.
3. Conversion by accepting the Gospel as the way of life: 27 percent.
4. Conversion for material advantages: 11 percent.
5. The influence of the education given by church schools.

Another Church leader stated that the reasons for growth were:

1. High lay involvement.
2. The Charismatic movement's influence since 1966.
3. A radio program through the Radio Voice of the Gospel (RVOG).
4. The church's involvement in community development.

In the last ten years, there has been a great revival throughout the country and many young people have come to the church as a result of this revival. Through songs and personal witness, these young people won many people to the Lord.

As recorded in the 1980 statistical book, the church has 218 pastors, 472 evangelists, 1,952 congregations, 544 preaching places and 495,223 members. From these statistics we can see that each pastor has to serve at least nine congregations. However, the lay leaders in every congregation share these responsibilities and the pastor is left to baptize and conduct Holy Communion. Now the elders, although not ordained, are allowed after some training to minister baptism and Holy Communion to their congregations.

The church now has 30 Bible Schools, and 2 Theological Seminaries. In these Bible Schools and Seminaries, short-term and long-term courses are given for pastors, evangelists, lay youth and women leaders. Theological Education by Extension (TEE) is also organized by the Seminaries and many people who are not able to enrol full time are participating in that program. Sunday school for children, and special spiritual meetings for youth and women, are conducted in every congregation. Different devotional books are prepared by the Christian Education and Literature departments of the church.

The Ministry of the Church

The Church has called the Lutheran World Federation and other organizations to understand her philosophy of ministering to the whole man, stating:

(a) that there are values in life beyond those of modern technology and economic betterment, without which man's development will never be meaningful and lasting.
(b) that the suffering man who needs help is also the most important agent of development.

As a result of this policy, the church is engaged in many activities such as evangelism, community development, health, literacy, education, agriculture, aforestation, water drilling schemes, bridge and road construction and relief work.

The Mekane Yesus Church, although Lutheran, has many types of worship styles. As a church which came into being as a result of work by Swedish, German, Finnish, Danish, Norwegian and American missionaries, the worship style and other values inherited from the missionaries vary accordingly. The missionaries, varying widely in background, still play a major role in the church's ministry. They have extreme convictions from "liberalism" to "conservatism" in their approach to the gospel and development. Hence, the question of identity is still apparent in the church.

Today there are not many trained leaders in the church. Some of the very few trained leaders remained abroad at the end of the war. Moreover, some who came back, although trained, varied in their degree of Christian commitment. As a result, the church is facing leadership problems at the top.

However, the church is blessed in its lay leaders. As the numerical growth was due to the lay movement, its leadership is also strengthened by the participation of lay people. These people are mainly responsible for leading and nurturing the local congregations. Many of them today are participating in Theological Education by Extension courses.

The Church Under Government Pressure

The church was recognized and registered by the Government in 1958. Since the Orthodox Church was a state church during Haile Selassie's regime, every time the EECMY had a conflict with the Orthodox Church, the Government sided with the Orthodox. However, because there were some evangelical Christians in the leading ranks of the Government, the Government used to respond positively to appeals. The Government encouraged the church to work in areas where the Orthodox was not strong.

Today the church is facing new challenges from the Marxist-Leninist philosophy of the Government and the rapid economic, social and political rate of change in the country.

Because of the relationship the church has with the sister churches in the west, she is suspected of being an agent of the West—reactionary, revolutionary and anti-establishment. As a result, the leaders and the members are being restricted in their ministry.

Conclusion

The EECMY has always been a church under tremendous pressure. Life has never been straightforward. Yet amid the difficulties God has blessed, and continues to bless, the growth of His Church in Ethiopia.

Mr. Tesfatsion Dalellew is on the staff of World Vision, Ethiopia.

SECTION VIII

God Renews his Church for Change

28

Renewal and the Doctrine of the Church: Issues in Modern European Church History

KLAAS RUNIA

Introduction

There are several reasons why it is very necessary for us as Evangelicals to give serious attention to this topic.

1. The main churches of Europe generally find themselves in a *situation of crisis*. Nothing has really changed since Alfred Kuen wrote in his book *I Will Build My Church* (E.T. in 1971): "Everything that bears the name church is at present passing through one of the most serious crises in history, at least in Europe."[1]

2. The *solutions* offered so far are not really hopeful and helpful. I mention a few. There is the *ecumenical* solution offered by the Ecumenical Movement as embodied in the WCC. Here all emphasis is put upon the organic unity of the Church. But is this really *the* solution? Will the lame and the blind, when they go together, really be able to help one another in reaching the goal?[2] Others including many in the ecumenical movement believe that the churches should concentrate on their social task. In this way they might become relevant again. But does the world really need a Church that basically has no other message than the progressive political and social parties of our own day? Others again feel that the churches' problem can be solved by a more sociological approach to the institutional side of the Church. Being a human organization, the Church should listen to the advice of the sociologist, whose job it is to study human organizations, and who can offer remedies for organizations that have lost their touch with reality. Usually the solution offered is a pluralist Church that should try to cater for the needs and problems of today's people.

3. Now I am sure that these solutions do not have a strong appeal for

most Evangelicals. But do we have a better solution? Here I come to the third reason why it is necessary for us to give serious attention to the question of ecclesiology. I am afraid that it is *one of the most neglected parts of our doctrine*. In my preparation for this paper I glanced through and at times also carefully studied many books on Evangelicalism. What struck me time and again was the fact that little or nothing was said about the evangelical doctrine of the Church. When for example Donald G. Bloesch enumerates the doctrinal hallmarks of Evangelicalism,[3] he mentions many important matters, but there is no separate item on the doctrine of the Church. The Church is mentioned only under the heading "The spiritual mission of the church". The same is true of Millard Erickson's *The New Evangelical Theology*[4] and Fritz Laubach's *Aufbruch der Evangelikalen*.[5]

For all these reasons it is high time for us as Evangelicals to give serious thought to the doctrine of the Church. At the same time we must realize from the outset that it is a very difficult topic. For can one really speak of *the* evangelical doctrine of the church? Are Evangelicals not hopelessly divided, not only as to their doctrine of the Church, but also as to their actual place within the Church? Some belong to established or national churches. Others belong to free churches. Others again belong to assemblies of Brethren or charismatic groups. How can we ever find a common doctrine of the Church in such a situation?

I have been asked to approach the matter primarily from a European-historical perspective. When I studied my subject, I found it to be increasingly fascinating, but I also discovered that the pattern is so intricate that after a while one has the feeling of wandering in a labyrinth without an exit!

The Renewal of the Church in Historical Perspective

Evangelicalism has a very *intricate and complicated pedigree*. Historically it has its origin in the Reformation of the 16th century. But there is not a direct and straight line from the Reformation to today's Evangelicals. In the intervening centuries all kinds of developments took place and in each case one can discern a specific ecclesiology. At times there were even several ecclesiologies side by side. In this main part of my paper I shall briefly outline the various developments, each time concentrating on the concomitant doctrine(s) of the Church.

The Reformers

a) Luther and Calvin

I shall start with the *16th century Reformation* itself. It is a well-known fact that the doctrine of the church had a central place in the theology of the Reformers. One can even defend the thesis that for the first time in history a fundamental and full-orbed ecclesiology was developed. Medieval theology had no doctrine of the Church. No council had ever formulated such a doctrine. The Church was simply there! Yet there was an underlying conception which was generally accepted. The Church was the Church of the sacrament and of the priest, it could dispose of God's grace and therefore was an institution of immense power. Consequently all emphasis was placed upon the visible institution. God's Church, the Body of Christ, was simply identical with the visible organization of the Roman Catholic Church.

Following Luther's rediscovery of the Gospel of justification by pure grace and by faith alone, the Reformers arrived at an altogether different conception of the Church. For them the Church was fundamentally an object of faith. It is the people of God, called into being by the preaching of the Word of God. The first of the *Theses of Berne* of 1528, one of the oldest official documents of the Reformation, puts it thus: "The holy Christian Church, whose only Head is Christ, is born of the Word of God, abides in the same, and does not listen to the voice of a stranger."[7] The first Lutheran confession, the Confession of Augsburg of 1530, says basically the same in part. VII: "It is . . . taught among us that one holy Christian church will be and remain for ever. This is the assembly of all believers among whom the Gospel is preached in its purity and the holy sacraments are administered according to the Gospel."[8]

The same idea we also find in all the Reformed confessions of the 16th century. The Church is essentially spiritual in nature. It is a spiritual reality which can be seen and recognized only by the eyes of faith. Yet this emphasis on the spiritual nature of the church did not mean a flight into spiritualism, as if the true Church were a kind of Platonic reality, floating somewhere above the historical reality of the institutional Church. On the contrary, the Church which is invisible as to its spiritual nature, at the same time is visible in the earthly community of believers, in whose midst the Gospel is being preached and the sacraments are being administered. Calvin in particular always placed much emphasis upon the visible aspect of the Church. In his *Institutes*: "Wherever we see the Word of God purely preached and heard and the sacraments administered according to Christ's institution, there, it is not to be doubted, a church of God exists (*cf.* Eph. 2:20). For his promise cannot fail: 'Wherever two or three are gathered in my name, there I am in the midst of them' (Matt. 18:20)."[9] He liked to call this Church "the common mother of all the godly, which bears, nourishes, and brings up children to God, kings and peasants alike; and this is done by the ministry".[10] Similar ideas we find in Luther's writings.

At this very point, however, of the unity of the visible and invisible aspects of the Church the Reformers were facing a very difficult problem. The medieval Church, which they tried to reform, had always been a *Volkskirche*, a national or multitudinist church. Every citizen of the land was automatically a member of the Church. In the Reformation this pattern continued. Entire cities and villages joined the Reformation movement. Entire parishes turned wholesale from Roman-Catholic into Lutheran or Reformed. But could one really call such parishes 'true' churches of Jesus Christ? Luther became very vexed by this problem. Around 1522 or 1523 he began to wonder whether it was correct to offer the Lord's Supper indiscriminately to the crowds who asked for it, not out of spiritual hunger, but for the simple reason that it had always been like that. In a sermon on Good Friday, 1523, he suggested: "One could gather separately those who believe correctly . . . I have been wanting for a long time to do it, but it has not been possible; for there has not yet been sufficient preaching and writing".[11] A few years later, in his book *The German Mass*,[12] Luther actually advocated the idea of the *ecclesiola in ecclesia* (the little church within the Church), *i.e.* a nucleus of true believers existing within the territorial church as a leaven. To be true, this was not his ideal. The ideal was the reformation of the entire Church. But since the latter was unattainable, the idea of gathering the true believers into an inner church seemed "second best".[13] However, as far as we know, Luther never practised it. Already in *The German Mass* he wrote: "As yet I neither can nor desire to begin, or to make rules for such a congregation or assembly. I have not yet the persons necessary to accomplish it; nor do I observe many who strongly urge it."[14] I think there were several reasons why Luther never came around to putting the *ecclesiolae* into practice. First, he leaned too much on the civil authorities for the execution of the reformation of the Church. In fact, he allowed them to organize the Church and to govern it by law.[15] Second, he retained the idea of the Constantinian *corpus Christianum*, that is, of a Christian nation, which in its totality is regarded as Christian and in which 'throne and altar' are so closely related that the State also has a say in the affairs of the Church. Third, he was frightened by the impact of the spiritualist movement, in particular of the Anabaptists.

b) The Radical Reformers—Anabaptists

This leads me to the views of the *Radical Reformers*. They had a much more radical conception of the reformation of the Church. In their opinion the Church had "fallen" in the era of Constantine, when the illicit union of Church and state came about, a union which ever after was perpetuated by the rite of infant baptism which caused numberless nominal Christians to be added continually to the Church. The radical Reformers believed that it was impossible to revive and/or to reform the existing Church. The only solution was to restore it to its prime virginity. Not reformation but restitution, was their slogan. This meant:[16] (1) rejection of infant baptism—one could enter the Church only through baptism following a personal confession of faith; (2) strict discipline among those who had entered the Church; (2) evangelistic witness to those outside the Church; and (4) abolition of all hierarchical distinctions between believers.

The main Reformers were strongly opposed to this view of the Church. As a matter of fact, the Anabaptists and others belonging to the Radical Reformation were persecuted by the new Protestants no less than by the Roman Catholics. Yet the ideas of the radical Reformers continued to have their impact on many people in the following centuries. In a way, one could say that the varous strands of thought present in the 16th century have influenced all the following movements. All the main ideas were already present in that formative century and they all return in subsequent developments: the idea of the esentially spiritual nature of the Church, the idea of the national Church, of the *ecclesiola in ecclesia*, of the free Church, of the gathered Church, and so on. They do not always return in simple purity. Sometimes the lines cross each other; at other times they repel each other. But whatever may be the case, they are all basic ideas of the 16th century, recurring in ever new patterns.

Movements after the Reformation

a) The Puritans of England

In the period after the Reformation we see various developments. The first one we must mention is the *Puritan Movement* in England, in the 16th and 17th centuries. One can distinguish three concentric circles of concern within the Movement: (1) It sought the inward reformation of people through conversion and sanctification. (2) It sought the outward reformation of the church by a closer adherence to the biblical structures of the Church. (3) It sought the renewal of society as a whole by promoting more respect for the things of God and the laws of England.

Most Puritans had a high view of the Church, basically similar to that of the main Reformers. For this reason they were very wary of all separatism. They did not want to break away from the Church of England, but sought to reform it from within or, as J. I. Packer put it, they wanted to eliminate "Popery from its worship, prelacy from its government, and pagan irreligion from its membership."[17] The primary object of its leaders was to influence the whole of the Church of England and to carry on the reform, which they felt had stopped instead of going on and completing itself. Unfortunately, political developments did not allow them to reach their goal of reforming the Church from within, and consequently in the second half of the 17th century they were forced to establish their own Presbyterian and Congregationalist Churches.

b) The Reformed Pietists of Holland

A second development which is of interest for our subject took place in the Netherlands. It was the so-called *Second Reformation Movement*, later on issuing in *Reformed Pietism*. This movement was deeply influenced by the theology of the Reformers, on the one hand, and by English Puritanism, on the other. With the latter it shared the concern to complete the reformation of doctrine by a reformation of life. Hence its emphasis on personal piety and holiness of life. This naturally implied a critical attitude towards the situation in the national Church. To be fair, they were not separatists. Usually they did not break away from the established Church, but preferred to meet in so-called "conventicles", small gatherings of converted people, usually held on Sunday evening, for the purpose of discussing the sermons of the day or a portion of Scripture. Yet it cannot be denied that this practice did introduce an anti-institutional element into their view of the church, expressing itself in depreciation of the established Church with its preaching and sacraments. In this way separatist tendencies were encouraged, at times leading to actual separation.

c) The German Pietists

The third development is that of *German Pietism*. This was a movement for spiritual renewal, arising in the Lutheran Churches of continental Europe in the 17th and 18th centuries. In many ways it was a reaction against Lutheran Orthodoxy with its emphasis on pure doctrine and the objective aspects of the Christian faith as found in the Word, the sacraments and the confessions, tending to neglect the "inward" accompaniments of faith (such as regeneration, the indwelling of the Spirit, and so on). Over against this Orthodoxy the Pietists stressed the necessity of the Spirit's work in the believer. Likewise it is not surprising that in Pietism the idea of holding private gatherings of the converted came up again. Philip Spener, the father of German Pietism, started them in his own house in 1670. The object was to bring converted people together for Bible reading, prayer, discussion of the sermons, and so on, in order to deepen their spiritual life. Soon these circles were called *collegia pietatis* (hence the name "Pietism"). In his *Pia Desideria*, published in 1675, Spener developed the idea in greater detail. Over against the evils of the time, as found in both Church and society, he proposed the establishment of *ecclesiolae in ecclesia* not only for Bible reading but also for mutual watch and helpfulness. In support of these ideas he made a direct appeal to Luther, in particular to his doctrine of the priesthood of all believers. It should be noted that Spener and his followers did not reject, or separate themselves from, the institutional Church. In fact, Spener was very much against all separatism. Yet it is evident that their emphasis on the small groups of true believers could easily lead to indifference to the Church as an institution. The real Christian fellowship was experienced in the small circles.

One more thing must be mentioned at this point. There was a real ecumenical thrust in Pietism. The Pietists were quick to seek spiritual unity with other Christians. Denominational ties were far less important than the spiritual unity we have in Christ and through the Holy Spirit. This attitude has deeply influenced subsequent evangelical movements, such as the missionary movements and the student movement.

d) The Methodists

For the fourth development we move again to 18th century England, where *Methodism* came into existence. In many ways it was analogous to what had happened and was happening on the continent. Again we observe the emphasis on the small circles of converted people and on the priesthood of all believers, to which now is added the idea of lay-officers. As we all know, John Wesley did not deliberately seek a separation from the Church of England (as a matter of fact, he himself died a member of that Church), yet from the beginning it was virtually inevitable that Methodism should become a separate body. In particular when Wesley started an annual conference, he went beyond Luther's idea of the *ecclesiolae in ecclesia* and set himself and the whole movement on the road that led to separation.

Many Evangelicals in the Church of England did not go along with Wesley, but preferred to do their work within the established church. Even though critical of many aspects of Church life, they nevertheless believed that, as long as they were free to preach and/or believe the Gospel, they should try to reform the Church from within.

e) Revival movements

The fifth development we have to mention is that of the *revival movements* of the 18th and 19th centuries. Although they originated in the churches of North America, they have deeply influenced various sections of European Christianity, both on the continent and in the United Kingdom. Their emphasis on conversion and personal holiness, to a large extent derived from Puritan writings and Methodist preaching, changed the face of many congregations. One of their richest fruits was the rise of the modern missionary movement. Yet we must also add that revivalist thinking has strongly contributed to a further neglect of the doctrine of the Church. Due to its emphasis on personal faith, it strongly promoted the idea that the spiritual unity of true believers is the main and real thing and that, compared with this, the institutional Church is of secondary importance.

Movements in the 19th Century

All these various movements of the 16th, 17th and 18th centuries continued to exert their influences on the *19th century* and often provided impulses for new developments. Quite often there was a cross-fertilization between the various movements. Time permits me to mention only a few important aspects.

a) In the United Kingdom

For the *United Kingdom* I must mention two developments in particular.

(i) In 1846 the *Evangelical Alliance* was established. In a time of increasing secularization, on the one hand, and a growing strength of ecumenism, on the other, leading people from various Protestant churches and groups came together with the object of enabling Christians "to realize in themselves and to exhibit to others that a living and everlasting union binds all true believers together in the fellowship of the Church of Christ."[18] These last words are taken from the tail-end of the first resolution, unanimously adopted by the Inaugural Conference. What did the brethren mean by the word "Church"? What did they mean by the term "unity"? Let us listen to the first part of the same resolution. It starts as follows: "That the church of the living God, while it admits of growth, is one church, never having lost, and being incapable of losing its essential unity. Not, therefore, to create this unity, but to confess it, is the design of their assembling together." Dr. J. B. A. Kessler has pointed out that these words have played a vital role in the whole development of the Evangelical Alliance.[19] According to these words essential unity can never be lost. So whatever is lost by all our divisions is virtually non-essential. Or to put it in another way, visible, organizational unity is not directly related to the essence. "From here it is only a small step to say that our divisions are not so important after all."

(ii) The second development to be mentioned for the United Kingdom in the 19th century is the rise of the *holiness movement* in the second half of the century. Here the great object was the deepening of spiritual life and the promotion of practical sanctification. The movement found its main platform in the Keswick Conferences, which were inter-confessional and inter-denominational in structure. It cannot be denied that these conferences have been a great blessing for many Christians, but it must also be admitted that by their one-sided emphasis on the spiritual nature of Christian unity they have fostered the idea that the institutional Church is virtually of secondary importance. Many people, belonging to "mixed" local congregations experienced their real spiritual fellowship at the conferences, rather than in the local congregation itself.

b) *On the Continent*

For the *Continent* we first of all mention the so-called *Reveil Movement*, which became very influential in certain parts of Switzerland, France, Germany and Holland. Having its origin in the awakening of the early 19th century, it strongly emphasized the need for a personal relationship with Christ. In some sections of the movement the style was very confessional, this fact at times leading to separation from the national Church. Others stayed within the national Church and tried to reform it from within. Others again were forced out of the national Church and thus compelled to establish their own free churches. On the whole, they were convinced of the importance of the institutional Church. But since the leadership of the Church, both locally and nationally, usually was in the hands of liberal churchmen, the people of the Reveil Movement often sought an interim solution in bringing the faithful together in small groups for Bible study, prayer, etc. In other words, the ideal of the *ecclesiolae in ecclesia* again played an important role.

As for 19th century *Germany,* we must mention the fact that there were several movements of awakening. Some of them were more pietistic, others more confessional, others again a combination of both. One of the most important movements, arising in the third quarter of the century, was the *Gemeinschaftsbewegung* (the Community Movement). According to the recent *Gemeindelexikon*[20] it had several roots: the Reformation of the 16th century; Pietism in the form of Neo-Pietism; the Revival Movement; and the Holiness Movement. Various organizations and conferences belonged (and still belong) to it. As regards its relationship with the institutional churches, we observe two different attitudes. Some tried to work within the institutional Church; others exhibited more separatist tendencies and had their own fellowship meetings. Yet even they generally did not break with the institutional Church.[21] Nowadays there is a general tendency to be active within the Church.

In the 19th century we find similar patterns in the *Scandinavian countries*. Many evangelical Christians worked within the establishment Church. Others were led to the establishment of Free Churches, either on the ground of their own ecclesiology or by compulsion on the part of the State and the State Church.[22]

Looking back for a moment we may conclude that there were some traits common to nearly all these 19th century movements:

(1) They placed much emphasis on personal piety and holiness.
(2) They all believed that there is a spiritual unity of all true believers.
(3) They often exhibited an ecumenical spirit. Believers, belonging to different confessions and denominations, worked together in the area of missions, social and philanthropic work, education, and so on.
(4) In many cases there was little interest in the reformation of the institutional church. The real fellowship was often experienced in small groups which met for personal devotions. Consequently, the doctrine of the church remained underdeveloped.

Movements in the 20th Century

All these lines continued in our *20th century*. Especially in the second half of this century, Evangelism appears to be a growing force everywhere. Yet the doctrine of the Church remains a very problematic area. In terms of their ecclesiastical allegiance, Evangelicals are sorely divided. Many of them belong to the national Church in their country. Many others belong to various Free Churches, but by now the older and larger of these have also obtained a *Volkskirche* character. There are some Evangelical Free Churches, but usually they are rather small. I am inclined to think that by far the greater number of Evangelicals still experience their real spiritual fellowship in inter-denominational organizations rather than in their local parish or congregation.

As I said, the doctrine of the Church is still a problem. This became quite manifest in the *Covenant of Lausanne* (1974). After an introductory article on the Purpose of God, there are two articles on Scripture and Christ. Next, Articles 4 and 5 immediately speak of the evangelistic and social responsibilities of evangelical Christians. The Church is mentioned only at the end of Article 5, where "incorporation into his church" is mentioned as one of the results of evangelism. It is only in Article 6 that the church is explicitly mentioned, but this very same article closes with the statement: "The church is the community of God's people rather than an institution." Although I fully agree with the first part of this statement (the Church in its deepest essence is the community of God's people), I must object to the implicit suggestion of a contrast between the Church as the community of believers and the Church as an institution. It is always both at the same time, and exactly here we find our real problem; Article 7 of the Covenant contains a call to co-operation and unity, but it is all expressed in individual rather than in ecclesiastical terms, even though the article starts with the beautiful statement: "We affirm that the church's visible unity in truth is God's purpose." I believe that the ecclesiological ambiguity of Lausanne is characteristic of the evangelical movement as a whole in our day.

Theological Issues in the Doctrine of the Church

I would like to start this part of our subject with some general comments on Evangelicalism made by W. Stanford Reid. Some twenty years ago he wrote a rather sharply worded article in *Christianity Today* on "Evangelical Defeat by Default."[23] In it he mentioned four significant shortcomings of evangelicals in general: (1) They have failed to come to grips with the contemporary situation. (2) They have not shown sufficient churchmanship. (3) They have often failed to support fellow-evangelicals when they tried to rectify the situation by action. (4) They have failed in the realm of thought. A little further in the same article he also mentions some of the causes, such as "sheer worldliness" (he means that we are scared of what liberals may say about us); laziness, both spiritual and intellectual; a false spirituality, manifesting itself in a refusal to take action; and, finally, the *erroneous doctrine of the Church* which is so often found among Evangelicals. He describes this error by commenting that many Evangelicals "tend to regard the visible, organized church as relatively unimportant, primarily because in it one finds many who have little faith, if any at all."

Is this charge of Stanford Reid borne out by the facts discovered in our historical survey? Let us see what we have found so far. I mention the following points.

1. There often was (and is) a *one-sided emphasis on the spiritual nature of the church*. I do not deny, of course, that the deepest secret of the church is that it is the people of God, the body of Christ, the temple of the Holy Spirit. It is not by chance that I mention Father, Son and Holy Spirit. The real nature of the church can be seen only within a trinitarian framework, and this real nature can be recognized only by faith. Luther was well aware of this, as appears from his famous dictum: *sub cruce tecta est ecclesia, latent sancti*—hidden under the cross is the Church, hidden are the saints. But where do we find this spiritual reality? Nowhere else than in all those congregations, parishes, assemblies (or whatever other name may be used), in which people come together to worship God, to hear the word preached and to partake of the sacraments. It is unfortunate indeed that in our evangelical tradition we have often overstressed the distinction between the visible and the invisible aspects of the Church. We have even used this distinction as a means of escaping from the troubles in our own local church or denomination. Although we are still members of the visible church, have our children baptized in it and celebrate the Lord's Supper with the local congregation, yet we find our real fellowship outside it. We experience our real fellowship in the many undenomin-

ational organizations which have come into existence in the last century and a half. When we go to our undenominational conferences and conventions, we even have communion services!

2. My second point is closely related to the foregoing: there was (and still is) a *one-sided emphasis on the spiritual unity of the believers.* At Lausanne Henri Blocher put it thus: Most evangelical Christians "believe unity is given, and they stress it; it is *invisible* and 'spiritual'. No one can destroy the link which joins all the true believers, the answer to Jesus' request which the Father could do nothing but fulfil, because He always grants his Son's request. The existence of varied denominations has nothing to do with this certain unity, definitely obtained 'in the Spirit'."[24] Again I must immediately add that the unity of God's children is essentially of a spiritual nature. But again we may not fall into the dichotomy of invisible versus visible. I am afraid that we often do fall into this trap and that this is largely due to the fact that we have too individualistic a concept of faith. We put all emphasis on the personal relationship with Jesus Christ, in and through the Holy Spirit. Wherever one recognizes this in another person, there is unity. This is true, of course, but it is not the whole truth! When Jesus in the high priestly prayer in John 17 prayed for the unity of his followers, this was not just a matter of spiritual unity only, but he also spoke of its visibility. As a matter of fact he mentioned it twice and in both instances it had a bearing on the missionary task of his followers. Twice our Lord prayed "that they may be one . . . so that the world may believe that Thou has sent Me" (17:21, 23). Are we, with our emphasis on spiritual unity across denominational barriers, really obedient to this prayer of our Lord?

3. My third point is a question: To what extent are we moving along *Anabaptist* lines rather than along the path shown by the *main Reformers*? I do not ask this in judgmental spirit. I do not want to glorify the main Reformers, nor do I want to condemn the radical Reformers. It may well be that we have to learn from both parties. At any rate, I am inclined to think that both parties have left us with an unsolved problem. I mean the problem indicated by the terms, "national" or "gathered" Church, or if you wish, "multitudinist" and "voluntarist" Church. In the former case people belong to the Church by birth and therefore are baptized as infants. As long as they do not intentionally withdraw, they are regarded and treated as rightful members of the church. In the case of the gathered or voluntarist church, only converted or born-again people can be members of the church. Usually admission takes place by means of adult or believers' baptism.

These two views are often identified with the main position of the time of the Reformation. The great Reformers would have opted for the national Church idea, the Anabaptist for the gathered Church idea. In a very general sense this is not incorrect, yet it is not fully correct either. As far as the main Reformers are concerned, the situation was more complicated than that indicated above. Calvin, for instance, did not simply accept every citizen of Geneva as a rightful member of the Church, but tried to purify the Church by a strict discipline. Luther, as we have seen, was not happy about the existing situation either, as appears from his suggestion to establish *ecclesiolae in ecclesia*. On the other hand, there is no reason to idealize the Anabaptist position either. It may solve certain problems for a certain period of time, but usually after one or two generations the old problems recur. Moreover, may we exclude the children of believers from the membership of the Church?

I often have the feeling that as Evangelicals we are not at all clear about the matter. At any rate, there is not a great deal of unanimity at this point. Some Evangelicals emphasize the continuity of the Church and believe that they should try to reform the church to which they belong from within. Others also stay within their historic denomination, but "only just", almost *contre coeur*. Their real allegiance is somewhere else. In actual fact, with Luther and the Pietists, they are opting for the idea of the *ecclesiola in ecclesia*, although in their case it is an undenominational rather than a denominational *ecclesiola*. Others again opt for the gathered Church idea. In 1944 the (German) Union of Evangelical Free Church Congregations even put into its confession: "The congregation of the Lord belongs to God's new creation and is not yet there, where God's Word is preached and heard, but only there, where people come to the new life and join the fellowship of God's children."[25] There is much confusion indeed. What G. E. Duffield says about the Evangelicals in the Church of England about the middle of last century seems to apply still to many Evangelicals of our day. He writes, "Many Evangelicals began to abandon their Reformed heritage and become Anabaptist. They neglected their doctrine of the church, they treated the sacraments rather lightly, they formed little interdenominational groups which sought to win individuals for Christ but neglected the wider needs of society, the nation and the state." When in about 1930 the Anglo-Catholics tried to recapture the Church of England, Evangelicals could do hardly anything at all. "Just because they were interdenominational, they could not tackle the doctrines of the church, of society, of church and state, of baptism, etc., for on all these they were divided."[26] I am glad to notice that today Evangelicals generally are more aware of the problem than their counterparts in the 19th century and the first half of this century. Yet we still have a long way to go.

4. In the same way we also have to give serious consideration to the question of *separation*. It cannot be denied that in our historical survey we often noticed separatist tendencies. Admittedly, it would be wrong to equate the ideas of *ecclesiolae in ecclesia*, of conventicles, of *collegia*

pietatis, of societies, etc., with separation. In fact, most advocates of this kind of informal gathering of true believers were bitterly and violently opposed to the very idea of separation. Yet history also shows us that their efforts often ended either in frustration or in separation (followed by the formation of a new church, as for instance the Methodists). There are also Evangelicals who follow the Anabaptist line of thought and consciously defend the idea of separation. Alfred F. Kuen, for example, in his book *I Will Build My Church*, categorically states that all attempts to revive the multitudinist churches and to transform them gradually into churches of professing believers have failed.[27] He, therefore, calls for "regrouping the true believers."[28] But will not this course of action lead to an endless proliferation of new churches and denominations? I believe we have to make a serious study of both separation and separatism.[29]

5. Likewise we have to make a serious study of *church discipline*. There can be no doubt that the New Testament requires such a discipline. There can no doubt either that all Reformers, both the main and the radical Reformers, advocated it. Of the Anabaptists this is well known. Menno Simons wrote: "A Church without the practice of genuine apostolic excommunication would be like a town without ramparts, or barriers, a field without enclosure, a house without doors or walls."[30] Calvin also was a strong advocate of ecclesiastical discipline. In some Reformed confessions it was even mentioned as the third mark of the true Church.[31] But Luther also strongly advocated it. In two works published in 1539 and 1540 he included it among the seven marks of the visible Church! In all Reformation churches it was actually practised in both the 16th and 17th centuries. From the 18th century onwards the larger churches became very lax about it. Today it is virtually non-existent in the mainline denominations. Evangelicals belonging to these churches often acquiesce in this situation. Admittedly, it is a very difficult point. It may be true that it is almost impossible to revive it in today's amorphous churches. Still we should at least reflect upon it and ask ourselves what ought to be done and what can be done. And it may be good for us to remember that, as Dean M. Kelly has pointed out, discipline or "strictness" has always been characteristic of virtually all significant and society-transforming religious movements.[32]

Towards Revival and Reformation

Allow me to make a few personal remarks. I realize that what I have said may at times have sounded rather negative. But I am afraid that this could not be avoided. Yet I also realize that what I have said is not the whole story by far. There are other aspects which also must be mentioned. Not everything is negative. One could also defend the thesis that the evangelical movement was and is a movement of protest against the decline of the historical churches. One could see it, for example, as a protest against the spiritual and missionary indolence of the churches, against the rigid structures of the churches, against the clericalism of many church leaders, and so on. But all this does not alter the fact that as Evangelicals we are often woefully weak in our ecclesiology and that it is high time for us to start asking ourselves what our own attitude ought to be and what we can do to bring the Church back to a new openness and a new submission to the Word of God.

I am convinced that it is *not enough* for us to pray for a *revival*. Of course, we should do that too. Revival is necessary indeed. It points to the divine dimension, the mighty work of God the Holy Spirit. It shows us that in the final analysis the healing of the Church is God's work. It also reminds us of our own utter dependence upon God, since we cannot revive and renew the Church. Only God can do it. And yet revival is not the only word to be said here. We also need the word *reformation*. The Holy Spirit in his reviving activity does not exclude human activity, but rather takes it into his service. What we need are men and women who are willing to be used by the Spirit and who are willing to transform their own lives and the life of their Church. Yes, we need both revival and reformation.

It will be clear that in using the word "reformation" I do not mean a simple return to the 16th century. Apart from the fact that such a return is impossible, it would also be wrong. It would not be reformation, but restoration and repristination. I mean "reformation" in the sense of the famous phrase: *Ecclesia reformata semper reformanda*, a re-formed Church must continually be re-formed. What I mean, therefore, is a renewal of the Church of *today*, taking into full account the situation and problems of this day and trying to find new ways to make the Church again what it ought to be according to the New Testament: "the household of God, which is the church of the living God, the pillar and bulwark of the truth" (1 Tim. 3:15). This can be done only when we are really willing to listen to what the Lord in his Word has to say to us in our day. At this point I would like to recall the well-known words which John Robinson said to the Pilgrim Fathers in 1690: "I am absolutely convinced that the Lord has other truths to impart to us through his Holy Word." He then went on to warn against pure traditionalism. "The Lutherans can see only what Luther saw; they would die rather than accept a certain aspect of the truth revealed to Calvin. As for the Calvinists, they cling to the heritage left them by that great man of God, who, nevertheless, did not know everything."[33] As Evangelicals too we are often inclined to cling to our own traditions and to judge others by them. Likewise we often judge the churches to which we belong by the same standards. And in the meantime we go our own individualistic ways, ignoring our calling to work towards the reformation of the Church.

I am very happy indeed that Evangelicals are waking up to this calling. Perhaps we do not yet know what we ought to do. But the main thing for the moment is the realization that we have to act. Some people believe that we have to wait for a crisis before we can act. I beg to disagree with this. If we are waiting for a crisis before we act, the crisis may never come, because crises come only when the trends of the day are opposed by action.[34] We must not sit down and wait in an attitude of mere passivity. Let us be active in obedience, having a strong confidence in the Lord. We are not alone. He will guide us by his Spirit. We have his promises which are sure. If only we on our side obey his word and do what He tells us in his Word! May the Lord give us the grace to be obedient without question, to be confident without doubt, to go forward without hesitation!

Dr. Klaas Runia is Professor of Pastoral Theology at the Theologische Hogeschool, Kampen, Netherlands.

Footnotes

1. Alfred F. Kuen, *I Will Build My Church*, 1971, 283. He mentions the following 'manifestations' of this crisis: the dechristianization of Europe, depopulation of the churches, the dwindling of the Church into a ceremonial institution, internal secularization of the church, multitudinism, social Christianity, the weakening of the message, clericalism and institutionalism, and the scattering of the Christians. He also mentions some causes, such as liberal theology, intellectualism of faith, the Constantinian system (299–304).
2. *Cf.* Alan Cole, *The Body of Christ*, 1964, 86.
3. Donald G. Bloesch, *The Evangelical Renaissance* 1974, 48–79.
4. Published in 1968.
5. Published in 1972.
6. *Cf.* K. Runia, (ed.), *Reformation Today*, 1968, 34f.
7. Arthur Cochrane (ed.), *Reformed Confessions of the Sixteenth Century*, 1956, 49.
8. Theodore G. Tappert (ed.), *The Book of Concord*, 1959, 32.
9. John Calvin, *Institutes*, IV, i, 9.
10. John Calvin, *Commentary on Eph.* 4:13.
11. *Cf.* Kuen, *op. cit.*, 204.
12. Bard Thompson (ed.), *Liturgies of the Western Church*, 1961, 124f.
13. Thompson, *op. cit.*, 126.
14. M. Lloyd-Jones, 'Ecclesiola in Ecclesia', in *Approaches to Reformation of the Church*, 1965, 61.
15. *Cf.* E. Brunner, *The Misunderstanding of the Church*, 1953, 97.
16. *Cf.* D. P. Kingdom, 'The Anabaptists', in *Approaches to Reformation of the Church*, 1965, 21.
17. J. I. Packer, 'Puritanism as a Movement of Revival', in *The Evangelical Quarterly*, Vol. LII, 1980, 3.
18. *Cf.* J. B. A. Kessler Jr., *A Study of the Evangelical Alliance in Great Britain*, 1968, 36.

19. Kessler, *op. cit.*, 36–37.
20. Erich Gedlbach *et al.* (eds.), *Evangelisches Gemeindelexikon*. 1978, 201.
21. *ibid.*, 212.
22. *Cf.* Philip E. Hughes (ed.), *The Encyclopaedia of Christianity*, Vol. IV (1972), 118.
23. *Christianity Today*, Vol. VI, no. 7.
24. Henri Blocher, 'The Nature of Biblical Unity', *Let the Earth Hear His Voice*, 1975, 381.
25. J. F. Gerhard Goetters *et al.* (eds.), *Bekenntnisse der Kirche*, 1970, 282.
26. Gervase E. Duffield, 'New Evangelical Impetus in England', *International Reformed Bulletin*, No. 19 (October 1964), 13f.
27. Kuen, *op. cit.*, 330.
28. *ibid.*, 332.
29. For an initial attempt, see my *Reformation Today*, 109–124.
30. See J. Leclerc, *Toleration and Reformation*, 1960, 1, 212.
31. *Cf.* Belgic confession, art. 29—"The marks by which the true Church is known are these: If the pure doctrine of the gospel is preached therein; if she maintains the pure administration of the sacraments as instituted by Christ, if church discipline is exercised in punishing sin; in short, if all things are managed according to the pure Word of God, all things contrary thereto rejected, and Jesus Christ acknowledged as the only Head of the Church." See Cochrane, *op. cit.*, 210.
32. *Cf.* Dean M. Kelly, *Why Conservative Churches are Growing*, 1972.
33. *Cf.* Kuen, *op. cit.*, 314.
34. Taken from a statement of one of the Leicester Conferences in the sixties. *Cf.* my *Reformation Today*, 143.

29

St Michael's Church, York, England

A Case Study

GRAHAM CRAY

Comments

HELEN HARRISON

Introduction

St. Michael-le-Belfrey is an Anglican church in the historic heart of York within the shadow of York Minster. Today Sunday services attract a total attendance of over 1,100, yet at the beginning of 1973 the congregation numbered only 30. What happened? It is the purpose of this report to examine the growth of the church, the style of leadership that it has adopted and the message that it has proclaimed.

The story begins with another church in the centre of York: St. Cuthbert's. By 1965 the congregation of this church had been declining for several years and numbered only a handful; the church appeared to be dying. 11th July 1965 was the first Sunday in St. Cuthbert's of the newly appointed curate-in-charge, David Watson. On the very next day he had to attend a meeting with the Redundancy Commission to consider the future of the church. But by 1972 over 750 were attending services on a Sunday and the church had become physically overcrowded. Discussions were held with a view to "moving" to the much larger church, St. Michael-le-Belfrey, which would otherwise itself have been declared redundant. On 11th January 1973 David Watson was licensed as priest-in-charge, and the congregation of St. Cuthbert's moved to St. Michael's.

What caused the growth at St. Cuthbert's and what has happened since then?

Key factors in the growth of the church

The Archbishops' Council on Evangelism has undertaken two reports on the church; first in 1972 and then in 1977. Much of the history of the church in this paper is based on their reports. The 1972 report stated that there were four keynotes in the development of St. Cuthbert's: prayer, evangelism, fellowship and the ministry of the Holy Spirit. To understand the growth of St. Cuthbert's it is necessary to examine each of these.

(a) *The importance of prayer*

On his arrival, David Watson instituted a weekly meeting for prayer and Bible study held in the Rectory; by 1969 attendance at these meetings had increased to such an extent (to about 70) that four rooms in the Rectory were being used, linked by sound relay. By 1971 the number had reached about 175 and meetings were held in the church. In the early days David and Anne Watson often used to set aside a day for prayer and fasting. There were monthly half-nights of prayer and a number of smaller prayer groups meeting in homes throughout the week. There was also a telephone prayer chain, by which a large number of people could be quickly linked in prayer, should there be any specially urgent need. Above all, people prayed, really believing God would answer.

(b) *Evangelism*

Shortly after his appointment to St. Cuthbert's was announced David wrote in the church newsletter: "What do we aim to do? Quite simply: to proclaim Christ. We never cease to wonder at His mercy and compassion, His forgiveness and peace. How perfectly He understands us! How faithfully He meets all our needs! Our greatest desire is that others, too, may increasingly experience the 'unsearchable riches of Christ'." Guest services were held from the earliest days, and by 1969 were being held about once a month. David Watson almost invariably preached on these occasions which were used by members of St. Cuthbert's (including students) to bring along their non-Christian friends, and also attracted a large number of people from towns and villages around York. There is no doubt that David's considerable gifts as an evangelist contributed greatly to the growth of the church. Occasional series of evangelistic mid-week lunch hour services were also held. Tape recordings were available of all the main sermons and mid-week Bible readings and were used not only in York but throughout Britain and abroad. By invitation teams were sent out to take services in other churches in the villages around York. The church was closely involved in, and financially supported, a coffee bar in the centre of York and detached youth work in the city. From the beginning, David Watson continued his wider evangelistic ministry which had begun during his days as a curate in Cambridge. He led missions to universities and elsewhere; this work was to expand considerably after the move to St. Michael's. The church supported this ministry both financially and in prayer.

Helen Harrison adds,

> The model for evangelism has been "come and see" rather than "go and tell". Over the years there has been an increasing sense in which the worshipping community has been seen to be evangelistic in itself rather than being merely the context in which David exercises his gift. Since David's departure the onus for evangelism has rested much more with every individual in the congregation with the two models "come and see" and "go and tell" complementing each other.

(c) *Fellowship*

There is no doubt that one of the main features of St. Cuthbert's was the atmosphere of love and warmth in the fellowship. As we shall note later a key element was the emphasis on the value of each member as part of the body of Christ, with a valuable role to play. Everyone had something to do—whether it was to visit the sick or elderly, help prepare visual aids for the Family Services, offer hospitality, or provide transport. In many cases people were attracted by the Family Service as they wanted to be able to worship together as a family. Above all, people were encouraged to get to know each other, and serve each other as brothers and sisters in Christ.

(d) *The ministry of the Holy Spirit*

The necessity for the Holy Spirit's power to be manifest in individual Christians, and in the life of the whole church, was frequently stressed by David Watson. His experience at his previous curacy at Cambridge had convinced him that the gifts of the Holy Spirit were for today. In 1966 David wrote: "By far the greatest need for us all at St. Cuthbert's is this: to know the fulness and power of the Spirit of God in our lives." In 1967 he wrote in the newsletter, "I long for revival, that God should come down upon us with the power of the Holy Spirit, to purge away complacency and unbelief, to make us into people whose lives are centred on Jesus Christ, to give us a new concern and love for those around us, and new power to meet their needs." During times of prayer at mid-week meetings particular "gifts of the Spirit" (notably prophecy but occasionally tongues and interpretation) were sometimes manifest. The author of the 1972 ACE report commented: "I found no evidence at all of any divisions within the church caused by the 'charismatic' element. There has not been any stress on the necessity for a dramatic post-conversion once-for-all 'Baptism of the Spirit', but David Watson has taught clearly that there is a divine command to Christians to 'Be filled with the Spirit', (and to go on being filled with the Spirit) and that when the Holy Spirit takes control of a human life we should *expect* God's power and His gifts to be manifest. The gifts are for all and not for a select few, and because of the prevailing atmosphere of love and the recognition that the gifts are for the good of the *whole* church, there seems to have been no tension whatsoever between those who possess certain gifts and those who do not. This atmosphere of love is, perhaps, the most obvious manifestation of the work of the Spirit."

Says Helen Harrison:

> God graciously visited us as a Church sharing with us the vision of the Body of Christ and enabling us in rich measure to enter into the reality of it. Something happened before our eyes. Notwithstanding many battles and opposition, God brought us into an experience of a corporate life together which simply was not there before.

The Life of the Congregation

(a) Members

The four aspects outlined above show the foundations for growth both at St. Cuthbert's and subsequently, at St. Michael's; fundamentally the work has not changed. To understand more about the growth of the church, it is necessary to examine the composition of the congregation. The combined parish of St. Michael's and St. Cuthbert's is not predominantly residential. The last estimate for its size (600) is based on 1971 figures and we believe the population is now far smaller than that. Figures from the 1977 ACE study indicated that only eight members of the congregation were drawn from the parish itself; approximately three-quarters of the members of St. Michael's lived within the city of York (population 100,000) and the remainder come from surrounding villages; about 65 percent of the congregation are women. It is probable that these figures have not changed much. The congregation at St. Michael's has always contained a sizeable number of students and visitors, and can be described as middle-class. In May 1982 when accurate figures were last recorded the average *total* attendance on a Sunday was 1,272. Allowing for people who attended more than one service, the average number of people attending the church was 1,137. Of the 1,272, 281 (22 percent) were children, 176 (14 percent) were students and 209 (16 percent) were visitors, (as two of the five Sundays in May occurred as part of Bank Holiday weekends, the number of visitors and therefore the total attendance is higher than normal). The move to St. Michael's, with its position opposite the Minster, increased the number of visitors and Christian tourists attending the church. In recent years the percentage of wage-earners among members has fallen. The number of families with young children has increased. There is a significant number of single-parent families attending church; there are also a number of separated and divorced people who have come into the family of St. Michael's and rebuilt their lives. The church has also acted as a refuge for some mentally-ill members. It is interesting to note that the growth in the congregation in St. Cuthbert's and at St. Michael's has been partly determined by the physical size of the respective churches. In both cases the congregation reached a plateau point at which growth stopped. This does not mean that evangelism ceased as quite a number of members of the church, including students, are in York only for a short while, and therefore the church is always welcoming new members while remaining the same size.

(b) Neighborhood Group

So far we have examined growth in terms of numbers added to the church congregation, but life *within* the church body has also grown. Initially, as we have seen, the church operated with services on Sunday and one mid-week fellowship—the latter being attended by the "core" members of the church. In 1973 it was decided to start neighborhood-based area groups, each with about twenty members, for the pastoral care of the congregation. These groups provided fellowship on a more personal and deeper level than the large fellowship meeting allowed. When Graham Cray was appointed vicar in the Spring of 1978 (David Watson remaining as rector) he took particular responsibility for developing these groups which had, by this stage, grown rather large. Now the groups are much smaller (about a dozen members each) and more attention is paid to developing the skills of the leaders of these groups so that members can really share with each other and learn together. The groups now meet fortnightly, and the church-wide fellowship has been replaced by area fellowships (a gathering of neighboring area groups meeting together) which also meet fortnightly. Area groups and fellowships have not in the past been seen as opportunities for evangelism but rather as a means of the members of the congregation getting to know each other better and to worship, pray and be taught in smaller numbers. It is perhaps worth noting that excluding students, visitors and children (none of whom are included as potential members) approximately 70 percent of the congregation is active in area group membership. Over the years various groups have been formed to cater for the needs of children and young people. These are composed of: Children's Workshop (5–11 years old), Pathfinders (age range 12–15) and Eureka (15–20 years old). The emphasis in all these is to supplement attendance at church rather than to replace it, emphasising that children and young people are part of God's family *now* and they need to *share* with their peers what this means.

(c) Worship

Worship has played an increasingly important part in the life of the church. The emphasis has been on sensitivity to each other, allowing all members to worship God freely together and an attempt to make each service a coherent whole in its own right. Through the years dance, drama and music have gradually played a greater part in worship. The dance group contributes to liturgical worship in the services, interpreting hymns and choruses. The church offers some financial support to a professional Christian theatre group, "Riding Lights", which started in 1977 and is based in the fellowship. Since then they have regularly performed during services in St. Michael's, illustrating talks and sermons. The music in the church is the responsibility of a full-time musical director and has developed to include a choir (which has produced three records) and a children's orchestra. The music includes both modern arrangements of songs (many written by members of the congregation) and older-style choral settings, in an attempt to provide both variety and balance. In these different aspects there has been an emphasis that living worship discloses God as much as preaching. Today the media bombards people with information in a variety of ways other than the spoken word, and it is right that the church should use these various forms to communicate the gospel. Some of the energies of the church have gradually been directed away from the expansion of numbers into developing the internal life of St. Michael's. As the ACE report of 1977 commented: "The growth period over, the organism begins to flower, creating in the medium of art, music, dance, drama and liturgy something quite breathtakingly beautiful."

(d) Extended Households

An emphasis on the need for close, loving relationships and the practical advantages of sharing material resources led to the establishment in the early and mid-Seventies of extended households. They were able to support a large number of full-time Christian workers extending very considerably the forms and quantity of ministry to, and by, the whole congregation. The ACE report of 1977 commented that these households were acting as the areas in which the church allowed the more difficult, negative emotional facets of fellowship and maturation to happen. Most of the extended households have now disbanded. It is now accepted that *all* members of the church should attempt to share their lives fully with others rather than leaving it to a few pioneers. Pain, conflict and suffering are now much more openly accepted within the fellowship as people have learnt that sharing in such difficulties leads to deepening relationships and greater maturity.

Changing Patterns of Leadership

The Appointment and Role of Elders

The question of what kind of leadership is operational within the church is both crucial and complex; the style and method of leadership has developed dramatically over the years and is continuing to change. In the first years at St. Cuthbert's David Watson was, undoubtedly, very much the dominant leader although St. Cuthbert's was part of a team ministry under the care of the vicar of Holy Trinity, Heworth. By 1970 David felt that he could no longer adequately deal with all the pastoral needs of the church and recommended the institution of elders to meet some of these needs. The Parochial Church Council (the body, elected by the congregation, which is legally responsible for the administration of an Anglican church's affairs) approved this and seven elders (all men) were appointed for a year. The method of appointment has remained the same since then, with members of the congregation suggesting the names of possible elders and David (subsequently Graham Cray) himself prayerfully considering who should be appointed. In every case the two lists have matched. It is important to note that elders have never been elected. In recommending the institution of elders, David emphasised that in the Early Church leadership was always shared, and that spiritual leadership, as opposed to practical administration, was in the hands of elders; in the New Testament the role of elders was to lead, to teach, to work hard, to set an example, to tend the flock of God, to encourage and to pray for the sick. David placed before the elders all his invitations to speak and the sermon series were planned together. Decisions at elders' meetings were, and are, unanimous; if there is a disagreement no decision is made until agreement is reached. The size of the eldership (now appointed for three year periods) has gradually increased; currently there are 16 elders who meet weekly. An area which long exercised the minds of the leaders of the church was the role of women in leadership. Gradually, women became area group leaders. A woman was appointed as full-time parish worker in 1975 and she occasionally preached and led services. David Watson's own ideas concerned with the role of women in leadership changed to the point where he believed it could be right to have women elders. His book *I Believe in the Church* (Hodder and Stoughton, 1978) covers much of his thinking on church leadership at this stage. Graham Cray was appointed vicar in the spring of 1978, with David Watson becoming rector and concentrating almost exclusively on his mission work outside York. Graham first appointed elders in 1980 and immediately prior to this taught the congregation by a series of sermons on leadership in the New Testament churches; Graham stressed that while he believed women could be elders, and that this was desirable, he would not force this view on the congregation, unless the recommendations to him included much support for particular women to be appointed. The elders subsequently appointed included three women.

(b) *The Pastors*

In considering the developing style of leadership within the church it is necessary to examine the transition from David Watson to Graham Cray. Graham became a member of the congregation when he moved to York in 1975 to work for the Church Pastoral Aid Society, travelling throughout the north of England. He was appointed an elder in 1977 and, as we have noted, became vicar in the spring of 1978. David remained as rector until July 1982. Thus, Graham knew the church intimately before becoming vicar and David remained afterwards; although the change in day-to-day responsibility happened immediately, the transition was, because of these factors, a smooth one. It is important to remember this when considering their differing personalities and gifts. David was very much a pioneer, with a particular gift of evangelism, who exercised strong, directive leadership and was very much involved in most decisions. Graham's gifts lie as a pastor and establisher, as a supportive leader who is inclined to proceed more cautiously. It is probably fair to comment that the gifts of each man have complemented the stage the church has reached. Originally the need was for dynamic, strong leadership to expand church membership; subsequently there was a need to consolidate this growth. Gradually, the eldership has developed into a more truly shared leadership; agendas are no longer dominated by the vicar and currently the business part of the meetings is not chaired by him.

As the vicar has the sole right of appointing (and dismissing) elders, he has, at least in theory, the ultimate authority; but as a *caveat* to this, there has been an increasing emphasis on servant leadership. As Jesus said to his disciples: "You know that the rulers of the Gentiles lord it over them—it shall not be so among you. Instead, the greatest among you should be like the youngest, and the one who rules like the one who serves" (Luke 22:25–26).

Helen Harrison comments:

> I am sure it is right to say that the management styles of David and Graham have both been appropriate to the different stages in the life of the Church. The style David adopted and his very diverse range of functional skills (as ACE pointed out) played a determinative role. One of his gifts was the gift of teaching which beautifully complemented his gift of evangelism in building

up the fellowship. These twin gifts are seldom seen in such a rich way in the same man.

It is interesting to note how under David, then Graham, the church has been grappling to come to terms with the principle of "every member ministry". David, it has been noted, began to share the leadership and the exclusively male eldership took an increasingly important role. This has been further developed under Graham with the inclusion of some women yet there is still a long way to go.

The Parochial Church Council

With the institution of the eldership, the Parochial Church Council (which includes many elders and some staff) tended, for a long period, to become a much more routine administrative group. However, gradually the role of the PCC has been reinstated: recently the church faced a financial crisis (caused largely by the Diocesan quota being increased from £9,000 to £25,000 in successive years) and joint meetings were held between the PCC and elders to consider all the implications of this. In addition, the PCC has undertaken particular responsibility for the employment of staff, defining their responsibilities and examining their performance.

(d) Staff and volunteers

Apart from David Watson, the first full-time member of staff appointed was a lay pastor in 1972. Since that date the number of staff has undergone dramatic fluctuations. Currently, there are ten members of staff; not all of these are salaried, some being supported by households within the church. In considering the staff's role it may be helpful to view the elders, PCC and staff as compromising three interlocking circles (the membership of each group overlaps considerably) with Graham in the centre in a co-ordinating role, and the staff as the executive arm. In addition, the church has always made use of a large number of volunteers in tasks ranging from cleaning the church to manning the office switchboard. In 1981 St. Cuthbert's church was converted to a pastoral and administrative centre at which most of the staff are now based. This has enabled the administration to work more efficiently, although the definition of precise roles and managerial responsibility is still being worked through.

Helen Harrison comments:

> Ever since the early days under David there have been several people working for the church full-time, having given up professional status and salaries, and some of them have lived in households. Out of love for God and the fellowship these sacrifices were made to the enrichment of their lives and that of the fellowship. Yet these people become very vulnerable to those possessing power in the church. It has been good to see several of these individuals moving on, either back into secular professions or into the

professional structures of the wider church rather than sticking at the level of dependence.

The message of the church

In many ways the message proclaimed in the church has remained constant. There has always been an emphasis on the centrality of the work of Jesus Christ in offering salvation to all who repent, the reviving power and gifts of the Holy Spirit and the inspired nature of the Bible. For long periods there has been an emphasis on evangelism taking place at church services. The work of the Holy Spirit has been stressed, with a clear teaching that a full Christian life depends upon the indwelling "fullness of the Holy Spirit." This is demonstrated in the love within the fellowship and the other gifts that the Spirit imparts. The recognition that the gifts of the Spirit are available to all and that individual gifts have to be exercised within the body of Christ led to the development of eldership, area groups, the choir, the young people's work, and so on. It also led to the teaching becoming a shared activity, with licensed lay readers preaching on Sundays in addition to the clergy, and members of the congretation leading area groups and fellowships. It is important to note that while there has always been an emphasis on charismatic gifts, there have been many in the fellowship who were not charismatics, including some elders, and they have always been fully accepted within the church. The teaching has tended to be thematic rather than an expounding of Bible passages but has always been based on, and supported by, reference to the Bible. Evangelism and teaching have been concentrated on meeting people where their needs are and demonstrating how the risen Christ can meet and answer problems. The ACE report of 1977 commented that there was little emphasis on the doctrine of creation, little preaching on social righteousness as found in the prophets of the Old Testament, and little stress on Christian political action; and that there was a need for the congregation at St. Michael's to be less immersed in church affairs and more dedicated to serving in society in places where they could influence decisions. Since that time there has been far greater emphasis on the need for social righteousness and on the fact that sin undermines not only the lives of individuals but also is endemic in institutions. In the past two years courses have been held attempting to relate Christianity to many contemporary issues in society.

Outreach of the Church

What of the relationships between St. Michael's, the rest of York and the wider world? We have already noted David Watson's ministry outside York. This changed in emphasis from university missions to missions in major centres taken by teams led by David, stressing evangelism, renewal and reconciliation. This work (and his publications) has led to St. Michael's becoming internationally known, through coverage in the media, and has attracted many visitors. To cope with the increasing number of visitors, Renewal Weeks were instituted in 1977. These were opportunities for people to stay with members of the fellowship for a week and to share the things God has been doing in the church, by attending seminars and teaching sessions. By invitation, lay teams have been sent out to other churches, increasingly to help in depth with the problems of a particular church situation. The church has helped support a number of missionaries sent out from the fellowship, both financially and in prayer. St. Michael's has, in these ways, given a considerable amount to the wider church body. It is, therefore, appropriate to report the visit of a team from Calvary Chapel, Yorba Linda, California in June 1981 when the church was greatly blessed. Many experienced new gifts of the Holy Spirit and there was healing in the physical, emotional and spiritual realms. The pains of divisions were healed and the church's vision was renewed; it was also a time when those who felt exhausted or left out by the speed of past changes were refreshed and the church entered a more settled period.

As David spent much time away he never had the opportunity to get involved in the wider church life of York. With Graham's arrival this involvement has developed and Graham is currently chairman of the York Council of Churches. The Diocese has always fully supported the work of the church and this is, perhaps, best illustrated by its rapid approval of the appointment of Graham as vicar.

Within the life of York, St. Michael's has a particularly large number of members working in all aspects of the medical and teaching professions. The different full-time workers in detached youth work have always been members of the congregation and the current Drop-In Centre for unemployed youth is mainly staffed by volunteers from St. Michael's.

What of the Future?

It is right to note that along with the successes and development of the church there have been difficulties and failures. As we have alredy seen, the relationship between men and women in leadership has been a problematic area and the church has still a great deal to learn in this sphere. The church has suffered one division, when in 1980 about twenty members left the church to form another fellowship. This group emphasised the need for strong, directive leadership and were unhappy with the developing role of women in St. Michael's. For about three years the church ran a restaurant and gift shop, The Mustard Seed, which acted both as a meeting place for Christians in York and a place for low-key evangelism. This closed down because relationships between those working there could not be maintained. It is also true to say that many of the extended households ended because of the failure to cope with relationships of such proximity and perhaps because members failed to foresee potential difficulties and to maintain a united vision.

What of the future? The church is still committed to the vision of evangelism and the addition of new members. Because of the physical size of St. Michael's church, this may mean different area fellowships holding services at different times. With the departure of David Watson it will certainly mean more emphasis on evangelism at the individual and area group levels. With the considerable throughput of members the church has to be committed to finding new members to remain the same size. There is a particular need for many members of the congregation to commit themselves to remaining for a long period so that the body of Christ in St. Michael's can be built up.

Further growth will continue the pressure on remaining united as one body, while having varied interests. Can the church maintain its unity amidst its diversity? Can central leadership be upheld while encouraging "devolution" and consultation? Perhaps these are too often seen as polar opposites; with clear, central leadership "devolution" can occur. In the past there has been a tendency to move too fast and there is a need to ensure that changes are made only with the understanding and support of the congregation. Perhaps one of the key future needs is to work through the social and political connotations of being Christians today in York and to face the conflicts and difficulties that this involves. In particular we have come to examine closely the Biblical concept of the Kingdom of God. The coming of God's Kingdom, through the work of Christ, establishes the possibility of a restored relationship with Him and restored relationships with others beginning *now*. Such restoration means challenging not only the sin active in individuals but also the sin endemic in institutions. Becoming a Christian means turning from all sin (including social sin), serving the poor and oppressed and becoming part of a local church community which clearly demonstrates the lifestyle of the Kingdom. The challenge facing us is how to live as a community, in radical obedience to Jesus, demonstrating the Kingdom of God to the people of York.

Rev. Graham Cray is Rector of the Church of St. Michael-le-Belfrey, York, England.

Helen Harrison is Deaconess of St. Stephen's Church, South Lambeth, London.

30

The Javanese Churches, Indonesia

A Case Study

S. Y. SUTJIONO

Introduction to Java

This case history focuses on Javanese churches, which are worthy of study because of their deep experience of renewal—quantitatively as well as qualitatively.

"Javanese churches" here does not mean churches belonging to the Javanese tribe, but those churches located on the island of Java.

The case history is based on observations, personal experiences, direct interviews with church leaders, reports, notes and statistics.

The Island of Java is one of the main islands of the archipelago belonging to the Republic of Indonesia. It is situated between the Java Sea to the North and the Indonesian Ocean to the South.

Although the land area of the Island of Java is only 7 percent of Indonesia, the population rate is the highest, *i.e.* 91 million or 60 percent of the population of Indonesia. Its population density is 690 persons per square kilometer.

In accordance with its development plan, Java's priority is social welfare. This fact is reflected by its increasing budget for health, education, religion, residential areas, and the like.

The 91 million people of the Island of Java consist of numerous tribes. The dominant one is the Javanese tribe, and the second largest tribe is the Sundanese. Then there are the Madurese, immigrants from regions outside Java, and Chinese descendants, scattered all over the island.

Although the Indonesian language has become the national tongue, the Javanese vernacular is still spoken in East Java, Central Java and Yogyakarta while the Sundanese vernacular in West Java still holds an important place.

Javanese culture has a great influence on the daily life of the people, in their way of thinking and acting and their philosophy of life.

The Javanese sees human life in relation to the cosmos. Accordingly it is impossible to separate the sacred from the profane, the natural from the supernatural, things rooted in the world and those rooted in the eternal.

Existence in the cosmos is viewed as something orderly and hierarchical. The duty of every existing thing is to be in agreement with the universal order. Going against this agreement is sinful because it disturbs the true order of things. That is why every community is required to organize its members in accordance with the universal order so that it will be well-balanced.

Restlessness and chaos are confusing and evil. The sources of chaos are competitive and egotistic individuals.

The experience and philosophy of life of the Javanese people is inseparable from that of their community. Individuals cannot be separated from their environments or their groups. It is also impossible to isolate the worldly realm from the spiritual realm. The Javanese people are inclined to mix ideas and symbols with physical objects.

Because the life of the Javanese people is so bound up with their community, to be cast out from one's community can bring serious psychological problems to a person.

That is why the Javanese people are afraid to depart from collectivism. The saying "better starve than not live together" well describes their concept.

This creates great resistance to receiving outside influences, even though such influences might bring progress.

Though the Sundanese people are more advanced and flexible in their way of thinking, in areas touching their philosophy of life they are not different from the Javanese.

The Moslem Religion is embraced by the majority of the Javanese, especially the Javanese and Sundanese tribes. There are two Moslem groups, of equal size: the "Abangan" group who are only nominal Moslems and still practise animism, and the "Santri", who are very devout.

The Development of the Churches in Java

There has been a steady rise in the numbers of Christians. In 1971 the number of Christians was 603,997. In 9 years there was a 256 percent increase. The average was 15.14 percent a year. This increase can be seen taking place in two stages. The first stage, up to 1965, was a slow increase due to the fact that it was very difficult for the Javanese to accept outside influences, including the Gospel. Further, Christianity was identified as the religion of the colonialist past. And the political situation of that time prohibited open preaching of the Gospel.

But during the second stage (from 1965 to the present), the churches in Java have experienced tremendous increase.

Some reasons for this rapid growth are:

1. The "September 30 Movement", which was an insurrection staged by the PKI (The Communist Party of Indonesia) in 1965. After the event, the government of Indonesia decreed that every citizen had to have a religion. Thus churches were flooded by many people. Those new members chose the churches for their protection. They saw the love and kindness shown by the Christians who offered help during the bloodbath caused by the insurrection.

2. The development of thought. The Javanese entered a transitional period, starting to move from the old conservative thought pattern to the more modern values. The Gospel is seen as a new, attractive and good way of looking at life.

3. The help of the Government, who opened doors to religious missions to allow them to spread their religion.

4. The establishment of many new Bible Schools, growth centers, and so on, that are active in evangelism.

5. The increase in Christian publications, and the printing of Christian books and tracts.

6. The birth of many Pentecostal churches with their fervent evangelism. They increased rapidly because they did not place daunting requirements on their ministers and on those who wanted to be members. This is still true today.

Case Study of Gereja Kristus Rahmani (The Evangelical Church of Indonesia)—GKRI

One of the churches in Java that experienced tremendous growth was the GKRI. While other churches in Java increased by 15.14 percent a year for the last 9 years, during the same period GKRI has increased its membership by 667 percent during 9 years or 56.91 percent a year.

The development of GKRI is a fascinating accomplishment by a relatively young church of about nine years of age. GKRI is now a large congregation, self-supporting in its operation and evangelizing efforts, not only in its immediate area but also to far flung provinces and areas.

What is GKRI?

GKRI consists of congregations which comprise the fellowship of believers who have been baptized and who live according to the Word of God, and who participate in the sacraments.

The GKRIs goals and ministries are:

1. Evangelization in its widest meaning.
2. Developing fellowship among church members.
3. Ministering love to church members and to other members of society.

4. Training, teaching and building up church members.

GKRI's Confession of Faith is in line with the historic evangelical faith.

Pattern of Work in the Church

The pattern of work of the GKRI is based on the Lord Jesus' commission to preach His good news and glorify His name in evangelization, in the ministry of love, in secular education ministry, and in interchurch ministry, through discipleship and prayer meetings.

The history of GKRI started with its first service, attended by 21 people, held in a borrowed classroom of Rukun Sejati Elementary School on December 12, 1971.

From that one classroom, the attendance grew to occupy three rooms. But even these classrooms became so small that an additional tent had to used.

By 1972 the need to look for a suitable and permanent building to worship in was felt. One was purchased and worship began in it the next year.

Baptisms are held at the end of every year at Bina Rai Beach. Within the time-span of 9 years, the membership of the GKRI has grown from 21 to 1211. There are in Jakarta 14 Home Churches, and 19 prayer meetings. Branch churches have been opened in other cities.

The Secret Of The Rapid Development of GKRI

What is the secret of GKRI's astonishingly rapid progress? There are many reasons that lie behind it.

The Pastor and his Role in Pastoring the Church

The Pastor pays great attention to the life of his church members. There is unity and mutual responsibility between the pastor and the church members.

In some Indonesian churches church members are not giving support to their pastor, so that the pastor seeks to meet his economic needs through side-activities, such as trading and cattle breeding. The time in which he should be performing his pastoring duties is wholly consumed.

This situation was prevented in the GKRI. There is an intimate relationship between the pastor and church members. The pastor's problem is the members' problem, and *vice versa*, so that an ideal and harmonious relationship is created.

Responsibility of the Church Members in Financial Problems

The high participation and responsibility of church members in respect to their church is the key to the GKRI's success. Regular providing of information on the necessity of church membership is stressed. Church members are taught the principles of giving and the need for proper reporting of the use of funds. Church members are assured that the management of the administration of funds has been performed honestly, and in an orderly manner.

The Training of Lay Leaders

Talented church members, both adults and youth, are given ample opportunity to participate in giving service jointly with the pastor. This causes the members to have a feeling of possessing the church and a secure sense of being needed, so that they increasingly love their church, with the result that the church becomes active and alive.

Church members who are called to serve God are given the opportunity to join Leadership Training programmes.

The teaching on any subject is given systematically for 3 months in about 12 sessions. While being trained and equipped, the people are also given a practical field task to complete. They report the results during the sessions and all the problems they have encountered are jointly discussed. Through this way the effectiveness of the church members can be increased.

Pastoring the Church

The ministry of pastoring the church is given priority. The pastor regularly visits his church members, assisted by some others, twice a week. Every church member is also given the opportunity to meet with the pastor at home by appointment. Church counselling is also given to sick members, for marriage preparation, distress cases, backsliders, and the like.

The Lord's Supper is given once a month, and is also served at the homes of church members who could not come to the church due to sickness or some other cause.

Home Church and House Meetings

The Home Church plays an important role in increasing the number of church members and giving them guidance. Every Home Church, besides having a responsible person in charge, has a Board of Members including a Chairman, Secretary, and Treasurer. The person responsible for the Home Church is granted the status of deacon. He is responsible for guiding and organizing the services. He is not given a salary, nor does he receive a transportation allowance. Any expenses of the Home Church, especially for any outside preacher, are arranged by the Principal Church itself.

In addition to the Home Church another important link in the church's development is house meetings. For these house meetings church members offer their homes as a place of worship.

The activity of such house meetings gives the opportunity to the surrounding community to get acquainted with Christianity.

Rev. S. Y. Sutjiono is President of the Independent Baptist Church & GKRI, Jakarta Barat, Indonesia.

31

An Inner City Church in the Middle East

A Report

RAMEZ ATALLAH

S. is an impoverished, neglected, and run-down district in a large Middle East city. It is close to the center of the city, but does not benefit from many of the modern services now available there. At present most of the streets are flooded with sewage and often impassable. The area gives the distinct feeling of having been forgotten by city planners.

At the turn of the century missionaries began a school and a church in the district. The work developed rapidly and was soon taken over by nationals. As the area became more and more run-down, however, many of the church members "emigrated" to other parts of the city.

In 1971, a recent seminary graduate came to pastor the church. The number of members on the church roll was 107, but only five actually attended the services! The church building was unfinished and in a very primitive condition. The task facing Rev. N. seemed formidable. Was there hope for reviving the ministry in this forsaken place?

His first task was to visit those on the membership rolls, many of whom had moved out of the area. Through these visits, attendance began to increase gradually. Many of those who began to attend were new believers who had come to know the Lord through the pastor's visits. Thus the first aspect of the pastor's strategy was *evangelism*.

As these new believers increased in numbers it became apparent that there was a need for *discipling* them. This was done initially by the pastor, but very shortly thereafter by responsible laymen who were trained for this task.

As the number of people attending church increased, many other needs appeared. There were no people in the congregation who could play musical instruments. So the church paid to have people with potential take music lessons, so as to be able to lead the congregation in singing. Sunday School teachers were trained and classes begun. This provided an additional outreach to families in the neighbourhood.

With many very poor families attending, it soon became obvious that the church had to be involved in *social and economic problems* in a deliberate way. A child care program was developed to meet the nutritional, clothing, and medical needs of many families through their children. This program also had a tremendous evangelistic impact on these families and helped rapidly to enlarge the Sunday School attendance.

People with potential were helped to learn a trade, attend university, or train for a particular job. A special program was developed to subsidise the expenses of several university students each year. Poor families were identified and linked up with those who could give them personal help on a continuing basis.

The church gradually developed a *missionary vision* for unreached areas of the city or nearby villages. Some members became involved in beginning house meetings.

Thus, by the time Rev. N. completed ten years as pastor of the church, the actual membership had grown to 133 active members, in addition to dozens of other participants. The Sunday School had grown to over 200 children. High school and university students' meetings were held weekly. A ministry to young couples and families was begun. Evangelistic and social outreach into the community was going on in an organized fashion. The church had several active committees, and tasks were effectively delegated to responsible people. Thus building was completed.

The following factors had certainly been both directed and used by the Holy Spirit:

—Rev. N's own dependence on the Lord and patience in prayer
—The systematic and consistent exposition of God's word on a weekly basis
—Perseverance in a well-planned evangelistic visitation program
—The evident expression of Christian compassion in ministering to the needy in all areas of need
—The deliberate training of leaders in areas of ministry needed by the church, and the concern to equip future leaders by giving them an opportunity to develop their gifts.